Praise for *Abraham Lincoln, Philosopher Statesman*

"An exceptional scholarly treatment. Highly recommended for Lincoln scholars, both professional and avocational."
—**David J. Kent**, author of *Lincoln: The Man who Saved America*

"Fornieri has written an excellent book explaining what made Lincoln great." —**Rodolfo Hernandez**, *VogelinView*

"In this relatively short and highly readable book, Fornieri argues that Abraham Lincoln was not only a great statesman who combined political effectiveness with moral goodness but also a political philosopher in his own right."
—**James Fetter**, *American Political Thought*

"In this wonderfully concise work on the politics of Lincoln, Joseph R. Fornieri performs to perfection the task of laying out the lines of Lincoln's politics, not only for his time but also in terms of the seven classical characteristics that make for 'greatness of soul.' Put away the treacly little handbooks that promise to deliver Lincoln's 'leadership secrets'—here is the real stuff of Lincoln's statesmanship."
—**Allen C. Guelzo**, author of *Fateful Lightning: A New History of the Civil War and Reconstruction*

"Viewing Lincoln through the lens of political philosophy, Fornieri convincingly shows how the sixteenth president piloted the ship of state prudently between the Scylla of utopian perfectionism and the Charybdis of mere cynical shrewdness."
—**Michael Burlingame**, editor of *Sixteenth President-in-Waiting: Abraham Lincoln and the Springfield Dispatches of Henry Villard, 1860–1861*

"Fornieri has gone beyond his brethren in successfully synthesizing a portrait of President Lincoln as embodying characteristics grounded in an impressive understanding of Aristotle and Thomas Aquinas, and constituting a level of virtue only truly great servants of a people could achieve." —**Bruce Frohen,** *The Imaginative Conservative*

Abraham Lincoln
PHILOSOPHER STATESMAN

Abraham Lincoln, May 16, 1861, at the beginning of the war—bearing the awful weight of responsibility. Library of Congress.

Abraham Lincoln

PHILOSOPHER
STATESMAN

JOSEPH R. FORNIERI

Southern Illinois University Press • Carbondale

Southern Illinois University Press
www.siupress.com

Cover illustration: *Lincoln-186*, oil on canvas, by Wendy Allen.

Chapter 4 is adapted, with permission, from Joseph R. Fornieri, "Lincoln
and Biblical Magnanimity," pp. 171–96, in *Magnanimity and Statesmanship*, edited by Carson Holloway (New York: Lexington, 2008). Chapter 6
is adapted from Joseph R. Fornieri, "Lincoln's Reflective Patriotism," pp.
108–17, in *Perspectives on Political Science* 39, no 2 (April 2010); reprinted
by permission of Taylor & Francis (http://www.tandfonline.com).

ISBN 978-0-8093-3059-1

The Library of Congress has cataloged the hardcover edition as follows:
Fornieri, Joseph R.
Abraham Lincoln, philosopher statesman / Joseph R. Fornieri
   pages   cm
Includes bibliographical references and index.
ISBN-13: 978-0-8093-3329-5 (hardback)
ISBN-10: 0-8093-3329-5 (cloth)
ISBN-13: 978-0-8093-3330-1 (ebook)
1. Lincoln, Abraham, 1809–1865—Philosophy. 2. Lincoln, Abraham,
1809–1865—Political and social views. 3. Lincoln, Abraham, 1809–1865—
Ethics. 4. Political leadership—United States—History—19th century.
5. Political science—Philosophy. 6. Aristotle—Influence. 7. Thomas,
Aquinas, Saint, 1225?–1274—Influence. 8. Presidents—United States—
Biography. I. Title.
E457.2F729 2014
973.7092—dc23
[B]   2013035557

Printed on recycled paper. ∞

To my wife, Pam Benetti Anderson Fornieri—
my earth, my gift, my joy

Jesus called them together and said, "You know that the rulers of the Gentiles lord it over them, and their high officials exercise authority over them. Not so with you. Instead, whoever wants to become great among you must be your servant, and whoever wants to be first must be your slave—just as the Son of Man did not come to be served, but to serve, and to give his life as a ransom for many."

—Matthew 20:25–28

CONTENTS

PREFACE

What makes Lincoln great? The answer to this question inevitably depends on the Nature or character of greatness and the corresponding standard used to judge it. What typifies political greatness as such, and, to what extent does a particular leader embody this standard? Does greatness include goodness?

In her award-winning book *Team of Rivals*, Doris Kearns Goodwin attributes Lincoln's "political genius" to his "success in dealing with the strong egos of the men in his cabinet." His example reveals "that in the hands of a truly great politician the qualities we generally associate with decency and morality—kindness, sensitivity, compassion, honesty, and empathy—can also be impressive political resources."[1] Granted that interpersonal skills and managerial abilities were part of Lincoln's greatness, his "political genius" cannot be explained in terms of these qualities alone. While Goodwin richly and eloquently details the story of how Lincoln managed his cabinet, her historical narrative does not provide (nor intend to provide) a conceptual framework to identify and evaluate statesmanship as such. This more theoretical aim requires a philosophical account of the Nature or the essence of statesmanship as the marriage of wisdom and power. It necessarily involves a comprehensive inquiry about the function, purpose, and ends of the political art. Such an account of political greatness provides a reliable means of comparison between a true statesman and a mere politician or even a tyrant.

What *kind* of political leadership best characterizes Lincoln then? Was he a *pragmatist,* like Franklin Delano Roosevelt, who shunned theoretical inquiry and pursued policies in an experimental trial-and-error manner while evading questions of ultimate meaning? Was he a *realist,* like Germany's Bismarck, who believed that the issues of the day were decided by "blood and iron?" Was he an *idealist,* like some of the abolitionists and social reformers of the time, whose dedication to abstract moral claims overrode all other political considerations, including the limits of public opinion and the rule of law? Was he a *revolutionary* who supplanted the founding through a "Second American Revolution," or was he strictly a *conservative* leader who preserved the status quo ante?

The purpose of this work is to reveal Lincoln's "political genius" in terms of the traditional moral vision of statesmanship or statecraft as understood by the epic political philosophers Aristotle and St. Thomas Aquinas, and to do so in an accessible manner. It is my contention that the sixteenth president was a *philosopher statesman* in whom political thought and action were united. His political greatness combined both theoretical and practical wisdom as those virtues were so clearly and profoundly understood by Aristotle and Aquinas. His speeches contain perennial wisdom about human nature, politics, and democracy. He saved the Union, presided over the end of slavery, and helped give birth to an interracial democracy. I further contend that Lincoln's character is best understood in terms of Aquinas's view of magnanimity or greatness of soul, the crowning virtue of statesmanship. True political greatness, according to Aquinas, involves both humility and sacrifice for the common good.

The more theoretical aim of this work does not require proof that Lincoln had read either Aristotle or Aquinas. It does, however, require one's openness to the possibility of timeless truths about human nature and politics. Indeed, Lincoln himself took for granted the belief in an unchanging human nature that served as the basis of philosophical wisdom about politics. After winning a hard fought election in 1864, he declared: "Human-nature will not change. In any future great national trial, compared with the men of this, we shall have as weak, and as strong; as silly and as wise; as bad and good. Let us, therefore, study the incidents of this, *as philosophy to learn wisdom from*, and none of them as wrongs to be revenged" (emphasis added).[2] If human nature does not change, as Lincoln believed, then it behooves us to investigate the enduring wisdom of those great minds throughout history who understood it so clearly and profoundly.

By relying on the epic thinkers and books of Western civilization as my guide, I also seek to show the important contribution of normative political philosophy to an understanding of our sixteenth president. This contribution can be summarized in terms of its textual method, its Socratic approach, and its normative evaluation of politics.

The method or modus operandi of the political philosopher involves a close textual analysis of primary sources. This is done in an effort to understand authors as they understand themselves rather than interpreting them through the ideological lens of race, class, or gender. While I rely primarily on Lincoln's speeches and writings in support of my interpretation, my thinking on the subject has also benefited and built on the outstanding contributions of many fine Lincoln scholars in the various fields of history, literature, and political science. I recognize and engage this secondary literature where it both corroborates and challenges my own interpretation.

In addition to the original sources and secondary literature, my approach as a political philosopher further consults the great books and thinkers in Western political thought for the enduring wisdom about politics and human nature. Throughout I make reference to great minds like Plato, Aristotle, Aquinas, Kant, and Nietzsche. In so doing, I have attempted to explain in an accessible manner to both experts and nonexperts alike how their teachings relate to Lincoln.

Whereas the primary method of the historian is to present a faithful chronology of the past, the political philosopher investigates norms or standards for judging and evaluating politics. In assessing statesmanship, political philosophy takes seriously claims about the reasonableness, universality, and validity of norms like wisdom, prudence, and magnanimity. It is my hope that this work may further in some small way the revival of statesmanship in both theory and practice in our time.

ACKNOWLEDGMENTS

Thanks to the following people for their support and friendship: my loving parents, Bea and Joe Fornieri; brother, Pete Fornieri; sister, Kathy Fornieri; Carl Silvio; Carol Silvio; my loving in-laws, Bruce and Jean "the Machine" Anderson; my children, Isabella and Natalie Fornieri; my stepchildren, John Joseph and Helena Morgano; Vivian, Mike, and Steven Iaculli; "Coombody" Kevin "Cat" Catalfamo and his wife, Key; Ronnie and Mike Numetko; Maryann Hinz; Tim "Starman" and Brenda Garman; Dusan and Mira Kolundzic; Craig "mind" DeLancey; Nina Baum Walker; Bruce Frohnen; Lee Cheek; Tommy Kirk; Robbie and Rick Mortillaro—guitar craftsmen; Stephen Sfekas and Dean Mesologites—"The Greeks"; Amy Beu Hughes and the Hughes family; Dick, Dana, and Lisa Kieffer; Nicky Lueck Hastings; Ann and Dan Turner; Lynn and Neal Bommele; Jeanine Boyd Edwards; Tracy Kane Pederson; Steve Wrinn; the Cristofori family; Jim and Pat Vazzana; Andy Gleasman; Jim Harrigan; Lucas Morel; Allen Guelzo; Michael Burlingame; John Waugh; Michael Green; Sara Vaughn Gabbard; Sean Sutton—the Mate; Dean James Winebrake; Kraig Kayser; Bob Paquette; Harlan Calkins; Todd and Susan Forke; Matt Kawiak; Fran Glover; Provost Haefner; Al and Carolie Simone; James S. Fleming; Bill Daniels; Jim Troisi; Barry Culhane; Dr. William J. Brorein; Frank Trotta; Lew Lehrman; Kelly Hanlon; John "The Captain" Murley; Monty Brown; Wendy Allen; Elaine Henderson; Frank J. Williams; Harold Holzer; Betty Anselmo; Jerry Desko; Ron Keller; Stan Domcek; my editor, Sylvia Frank Rodrigue, for her professionalism and patience; Barb Martin; and Steve Trembley, my student assistant.

Thanks to the Earhart Foundation for their generous support in providing a grant to research and write this book.

A special thanks, as always, to friend and mentor Ken Deutsch, whose soul combines that of a Jewish prophet, a New Yorker, a Thomist, and the Italian opera.

Abraham Lincoln
PHILOSOPHER STATESMAN

INTRODUCTION

$\mathcal{T}$his work explores Lincoln as a philosopher statesman in whom political thought and action were united. It understands the sixteenth president as a man of both ideas and action. Guided by a noble vision of the Union, imbued by a patriotic love of liberty, and bound by the dual covenants of the Declaration and the Constitution, Lincoln's statesmanship combined greatness of thought, speech, and deed. As a great thinker, he provides enduring wisdom about human equality, democracy, free labor, personal liberty, and free society. These insights were communicated in great speeches that have since defined us as a nation. As a great leader, he saved the Union, presided over the end of slavery, and helped to pave the way for an interracial democracy. Though rare, this combination of theory and practice in politics is not unprecedented in Western history. One can point to the examples of Cicero, Thomas More, Edmund Burke, and the American Founders, particularly Adams, Jefferson, Madison, and Hamilton. Speaking of how theory informed practice in 1776, John Adams marveled that he had "been sent into life at a time when the greatest lawgivers of antiquity would have wished to live."[1]

Four score and two years later, on the eve of the Civil War, Lincoln made explicit the connection between philosophy and statesmanship when he denounced the moral relativism of popular sovereignty in his seventh and last debate with Douglas, at Alton, Illinois, on October 15, 1858: "But where is the philosophy or statesmanship which assumes that you can quiet that disturbing element in our society [slavery] which has disturbed us for more than half a century . . . based on the assumption that we are to quit talking about it, and that the public mind is all at once to cease being agitated by it?"[2] Lincoln's plea for a philosophical statesmanship revealed the folly and futility of evading ultimate moral judgments about slavery's inherent goodness or evil. A large part of Lincoln's political leadership consisted in the task of civic education of his party and the public.[3] He sought to awaken and ennoble the public mind. Indeed, Lincoln's query above is highly reminiscent of the Greek philosopher Socrates' self-described role as a gadfly appointed by "the god" to sting the sluggish horse of Athenian democracy out of intellectual and

1

moral complacency.[4] His profound insights about self-government earn him a place as a teacher of democracy to be included in the ranks of great political thinkers like Plato, Aristotle, and Tocqueville.

In his rise to gain the Republican nomination, two years later, at New Haven in 1860, Lincoln would further underscore the extent to which public opinion must be anchored on an ultimate philosophical foundation for its permanence and legitimacy. "Whenever this question of slavery shall be settled," he declared, "it must be settled on some philosophical basis. No policy that does not rest upon some philosophical public opinion can be permanently maintained."[5] As John Burt recognizes in a recent work, *Lincoln's Tragic Pragmatism, Lincoln, Douglas, and Moral Conflict*, the issues debated by Lincoln and Douglas "were philosophical problems, not merely partisan ones, and the issues debated by Lincoln and Douglas continued to inform the speeches and policies of Lincoln's presidency."[6] In essence, the sixteenth president's philosophical statesmanship combined both theoretical and practical wisdom with a magnanimous, humble, and sacrificial service for the common good.

Because my approach is informed by normative political philosophy, what follows is not a historical narrative but a philosophical inquiry that provides a conceptual framework for exploring and evaluating Lincoln's political greatness. As will be seen, Lincoln's philosophical statesmanship may be understood in terms of six related dimensions that correspond to each chapter of this book: (1) wisdom, (2) prudence, (3) duty, (4) biblical magnanimity, (5) rhetoric, and (6) patriotism.[7]

Chapter 1 presents theoretical wisdom as a defining element of Lincoln's philosophical statesmanship. This theoretical wisdom was based on his profound vision of political life and his corresponding insights about human nature, equality, democracy, free labor, personal liberty, and politics. Chapter 2 demonstrates Lincoln's practical wisdom or prudence as the ability to realize as much of this noble vision as possible under the circumstances. Chapter 3 explains the importance of duty in an overall account of statesmanship and the extent to which it both constrained and empowered the sixteenth president. Chapter 4 displays Lincoln's biblical magnanimity as a crucial aspect of his character as a great statesman. Remarkably, Lincoln combined seemingly opposite traits of greatness and humility held in balance. He was righteous without being self-righteous, firm while being flexible, and great while remaining humble before God. Chapter 5 considers the role of rhetoric or public persuasion in Lincoln's statesmanship. Lincoln's mastery of the English language enabled him to communicate his vision effectively. As a civic educator, he employed a philosophical rhetoric that ennobled his audience and inspired them to sacrifice for a greater good. To be sure, this philosophical rhetoric was concerned with both the content of the message and the mode or style of its communication. Notably, the sixteenth president consistently distinguished this philosophical rhetoric from sophistry, the clever manipulation of truth for selfish ends. Chapter 6 reveals Lincoln's patriotism, the love of country, as a vital but overlooked dimension of his philosophical statesmanship. It shows how his honorable ambition was inspired by service and sacrifice for the country. In contrast to other disordered forms of allegiance like ethnic or racial nationalism, Lincoln's philosophical patriotism reconciled the love of one's own with the observance of universal principles of justice under God's Providence.

While recognizing the contributions of other fields to the study of the sixteenth president, I hope to show the unique and vital contribution of political philosophy. In particular, I am indebted to the brilliant, groundbreaking, and transformative work of political philosopher Harry V. Jaffa, who may truly be credited with the "discovery of a Socratic Lincoln who had been invisible to mainstream historians."[8] According to Jaffa, Lincoln "combined the perspective of citizen and statesman, but shared the dispensation that combined them with the perspective of a political philosopher."[9] It is my modest hope to revive in some small way statesmanship as a standard for judging political greatness.

Since a fuller appreciation of Lincoln's philosophical statesmanship depends on the recovery of the traditional understanding of statesmanship as such, the remainder of this extended introduction will first consider some of the causes that have obscured political greatness in our time. Subsequently, it will offer a clear definition of statesmanship in contrast to other types of leadership. Finally, it will engage alternative interpretations of Lincoln's political leadership.

The term "statesmanship" has become increasingly passé. It seems a quaint remnant of a bygone era. Statesmen, if they ever existed, belonged to a mythological age of heroes who have since been debunked as frauds and hypocrites. Today we are governed by professional politicians, experts, technocrats, administrators, and specialists. We no longer have statesmen. Over time, a potent combination of intellectual, political, and cultural forces have obscured the meaning and practice of statesmanship. If uncritical veneration of the past was once the trend in academia, the current vogue is to diminish, debunk, and ridicule greatness as a form of "false consciousness." The very notion of statesmanship, it is argued, overshadows the contributions of those considered less than great, who, through no fault of their own, were marginalized and excluded from national politics. Statesmanship, then, is nothing more than an ideological façade used to prop up the dominant race, class, or gender in power at any given time.

The twin doctrines of relativism and historicism have contributed further to the eclipse of statesmanship in our time. Moral relativism is the widespread belief, particularly among students today, that nothing is inherently good or evil, but relative to the changing preferences, interests and/or conventions of time, culture, and place. Denying a natural hierarchy of human goods, relativism asserts that all "values" are arbitrary and therefore equal. In effect, relativism denies the validity of any objective norms to evaluate or judge the actions of political leaders. There are no timeless truths, only different perspectives. The goal of education is to appreciate these relative perspectives on their own terms.

The doctrine of relativism appears in different guises including historicism, which may be defined as "the belief that historical circumstances determined thought no less than action and that we are all prisoners in thought no less than in action, of our particular time and place."[10] Historicism denies the existence of any universal or transhistorical principles for judging human actions and politics. It thus replaces the classical and Christian view of an unchanging Nature with historical change as the ground of morality.[11] Instead of looking to a fixed human nature or timeless truths to understand politics, the historicist looks to the varying conditions of time and place to grasp the dynamics of human thought and affairs.

Historicists are particularly suspicious of "great man" theories implicit to the study of statesmanship. The focus on individual greatness, they claim, abstracts from historical forces and contextual factors that serve as the "true" underlying springs of human motivation and action. The relative character of all so-called "truths" and "values" are to be understood strictly within their proper historical milieu. The political teachings of Aristotle in the fourth century B.C., they would argue, do not have much relevance for us today in the twenty-first century.

The rejection of historicism does not mean that context is irrelevant or unimportant in the study of statesmanship. On the contrary, the horizon of statesmanship is necessarily constrained and bound by particular circumstances, customs, mores, and traditions. While it is one thing to recognize the influence of these historical variables in a leader's practical decision making, it is quite another to *reduce* the same leader's thought and action to time and place or to claim that thought and action are *determined* by historical circumstances. For example, one may readily admit that Lincoln's statesmanship was constrained by the racial views of his time without saying that he was imprisoned by them and was therefore incapable of thinking or even acting prudently beyond the narrow limits of time and place.[12] Rather than being imprisoned by time and place, it is the mark of a great leader to consider actions *sub species aeternitatis* (under the aspect of eternity).

The contemporary historicist reduction of statesmanship in terms of the contextual forces of economic interest and class struggle is vividly displayed in Howard Zinn's *A People's History of the United States*, widely used at the secondary and college level:

> It was Abraham Lincoln who combined perfectly the needs of business, the political ambition of the new Republican Party, and the rhetoric of humanitarianism. He would keep the abolition of slavery not at the top of his list of priorities, but close enough to the top so it could be pushed there temporarily by abolitionist pressures and by practical political advantage.
>
> Lincoln could skillfully blend the interests of the very rich and the interests of the black at a moment in history when these interests met. And he could link these two with a growing section of Americans, the white, up-and-coming, economically ambitious, politically active middle class.[13]

In this Marxist narrative, the individual greatness of the statesman recedes into the background of historical context. History is driven primarily by economic interest rather than the "reflection and choice" of human agency.[14] Lincoln, the middle-class pragmatist, was adept at managing these interests until he was "forced into glory" by the more principled radicals and abolitionists who represented the vanguard of class consciousness.[15] While the proletarian revolution was incomplete, the destruction of slavery was nonetheless commendable because it led to a higher level of class consciousness and solidarity among the working class. Not surprisingly, Zinn repeats Richard Hofstadter's disparaging verdict that the Emancipation Proclamation had all "the moral grandeur of a bill of lading."[16]

Philosophically, historicism and relativism are both problematic since they undermine their own claim to authoritativeness. Their wholesale denial of absolutes is itself absolute. While rejecting transhistorical principles of judgment, the historicist nonetheless presumes the fixed vantage point of a professional historian who can interpret history "appropriately" by placing events in their "proper context." If historicism is true, then all interpretations of history are relative, including the valuations of the professional historian. Nietzsche forthrightly revealed and embraced the logic of historicism when he proclaimed, "There are no moral phenomena at all, but only moral interpretations of phenomena."[17] If all moral judgments about the past are relative, why prefer one set of "values" over another? Let us simply choose from the veritable smorgasbord of equally "true" values provided by history. After all, "one person's freedom fighter is another person's terrorist." Ultimately, the doctrines of relativism and historicism can provide no objective criteria for distinguishing between a statesman and a tyrant.

The study and practice of statesmanship has also been obscured by the widespread acceptance of a behaviorist and positivist methodology that seeks to measure and predict political decision making with the same mathematical rigor as the "hard sciences." This narrow approach to the social sciences rejects political norms such as "magnanimity," "prudence," and "wisdom" as vague or meaningless because they cannot be expressed in precise, quantitative terms. This demand for certainty is nothing new. Over two thousand years ago, Aristotle cautioned his students not to expect the same degree of exactitude in the study of human affairs as in mathematics.[18] Following Aristotle's advice, the contemporary political scientist James W. Ceaser likewise explains: "No one can quarrel with the pursuit of rigor. But a science ultimately can only be as precise as its subject matter allows. Excluding traditional concepts does more harm than good if the effect is to limit consideration of important issues, even when the meanings of these concepts are difficult to pin down."[19] While admittedly less precise than math and science, standards still exist in ethics and politics. Such standards inevitably provide a basis of comparison between things that are great, good, bad, and worse.

The positivist effort to make social science as rigorous as the "hard sciences" led to the invention of the fact-value distinction in the post–World War I era as the criterion for judging moral and political truth. In an attempt to avoid conflict over insoluble questions about religion and morality, well-intentioned positivists maintained that the task of the social scientist (whether that of a political scientist or a historian) was to describe "objective facts," and not to prescribe or evaluate "subjective values." According to the political philosopher Leo Strauss, the "rejection of political philosophy as unscientific is characterized by present-day positivism. . . . Positivistic social science is 'value-free' or 'ethically neutral': it is neutral in the conflict between good and evil, however good and evil may be understood."[20] Though itself a historical product of the post–World War I era, the fact-value distinction endures today.

As Strauss shows, however, the pretense of complete scientific neutrality in the evaluation of social and political phenomena is both illusory and self-contradictory.[21] The fact-value distinction is itself based on a normative imperative that we *"ought"* to prefer facts over values in the presentation of history. Thus, one's adherence to the fact-value distinction is itself a subjective "value" judgment rendered invalid by its own criteria. Indeed, the very act of choosing to write on one topic instead of another (say, the contribution of an underappreciated or a marginalized figure of the Civil War era) presumes an implicit "value" judgment about that figure's importance and significance in history. Furthermore, because all narratives necessarily involve a selective inclusion of facts and context (it is impossible to include everything), the inclusion of some facts and the focus on one context over another also presumes an implicit "value" judgment about the importance of the facts and context that are preferred and those that are excluded. Despite the claim to complete objectivity, then, moral judgments are surreptitiously "bootlegged" into social science as uncontested assumptions.

To reject the positivist dichotomy between facts and values, however, is neither to deny the existence of facts in history and politics nor to claim that they are merely relative to "the eye of the beholder." Social science must be true to the empirical record. However, the deeds and documents of the past do not simply interpret themselves. They call for interpretation, which necessarily involves underlying normative assumptions and judgments about what is worse, bad, good, better, and best. Rather than evading these normative judgments under a false pretense of neutrality, political philosophy seeks to make them explicit and to judge them based on rational standards.

Within the academy, the positivist diminution of statesmanship is reinforced further by widespread acceptance of the vocational model that regards education primarily as job training. This vocational model diminishes liberal arts as a poor investment. The liberal arts, it is claimed, fail to prepare students for the "real world." While most universities and colleges include leadership and management skills to a well-rounded education, few highlight the unique and indispensable role that statesmanship plays in founding, saving, and enhancing a nation.[22]

Once a staple of political science and history, leadership classes are now increasingly housed in business departments. Accordingly, the study of statesmanship as a distinct political art has been replaced by courses that emphasize managerial expertise and common skill sets that prepare students for careers in business. While recognizing the extent to which business leaders can genuinely learn from Lincoln's example, there are nonetheless important differences between a statesman and a CEO.[23]

Though business and industry are vital to the state's well-being, the CEO's responsibility to a particular corporation is qualitatively different from the statesman's duty to serve the common good. Unlike a CEO, a statesman wields governmental authority as a publicly elected official who is both constrained and empowered by a duty-bound oath to protect the Constitution of the United States. The public benefits of wealth creation, including philanthropy, depend on a successful business climate fostered by the actions of politicians and statesmen alike. As a good economic steward, the true statesman will follow the two-thousand-year-old advice of Aristotle in promoting policies that support a strong middle class. This means steering a course between the greedy interests of the oligarchic few without regard to the many, and the envious demands of the many to redistribute wealth without regard to merit.[24] It also means respecting the proper boundary between the public and private sphere, between goods and resources that are best shared in common and those best left to private initiative and care. As Aristotle well recognized, the attempt to make everything in the state common is just as misguided as the effort to make everything private.

The theory and practice of statesmanship is also suspect in a democratic culture that prizes equality of conditions above merit and excellence. Because statesmanship implies an aristocratic notion of greatness, it is in tension with the leveling impulses of a populist democracy. It necessarily involves discriminating between the superior and the mediocre. As Tocqueville warned in *Democracy in America* over 150 years ago, radical egalitarianism can undermine liberty in a democratic republic through the majority's tyranny over the mind.[25] To be sure, the Founders sought to reconcile greatness and equality in our democratic republic. Washington, Adams, Hamilton, and Jefferson all recognized the indispensable role of a natural aristocracy of talent in ennobling and tempering the excesses of democracy. For example, in his mature correspondence with Jefferson toward the end of their lives, Adams explained, "Few men will deny that there is a natural aristocracy of virtues and talents in every nation and in every party, in every city and village."[26]

Finally, political cynicism and apathy have likewise contributed to the demise of statesmanship in both theory and practice. Conditioned by perpetual scandal, spin, and corruption, content with a bland mediocrity, we seem to doubt even the possibility of human excellence. Accordingly, we no longer strive to attain it. As we continue to "define deviancy down" and to relax standards of decency and excellence in all areas of life, we expect even less from ourselves and from our leaders. In view of these trends, is it any wonder why today we no longer have statesmen?

Despite these trends, however, intimations of greatness linger. Comparatively speaking, we still recognize the difference between true greatness found in the likes of a Washington, Lincoln, and Mandela, and the mediocrity or venality of a mere politician of limited vision and dubious character.[27] We still distinguish, however vaguely, between the politician who thinks only of tomorrow's election and the statesman who stands for something higher. At bottom, the distinction between a statesman and a politician is inescapably a moral distinction between "great and mediocre," between "noble and base," between "high and low"; but is it justified?

In sum the revival of statesmanship requires an appreciation of its moral core: a rare combination of greatness and goodness. While managerial skill and technical expertise may be necessary to statesmanship, character is indispensable, as the ancients well understood. Technical know-how can be used to build a just society or to coordinate the efficiency of death camps.[28] As St. Augustine so profoundly noted at the twilight of the Roman Empire, one's political vision is inevitably affected by the character and orientation of one's love. "In order to discover the character of any people [or person], we have only to observe what they love."[29] That is to say, the nobility or baseness of the heart inevitably governs the head. Wicked visions proceed from wicked hearts. Noble visions proceed from noble hearts. During the Civil War era, William Tecumseh Sherman captured the essence of Lincoln's character as a statesman when he explained: "Of all the men I ever met, he seemed to possess more of the elements of greatness, combined with goodness, than any other."[30] Indeed, this rare combination of goodness and greatness springs from old-fashioned virtues (qualities of intellect and character) that have defined statesmen throughout history: wisdom, magnanimity, prudence, humility, and sacrificial service to the common good.

Given present day confusion, the revival of statesmanship further requires a clear definition of the term in contrast to other types of business, transactional, and reform leadership. The statesman wields government authority from inside the citadels of power. By definition, then, statesmanship is necessarily tied to legitimate political authority and governance. In a democratic republic, this includes not only those who are elected to office, but also high-level appointees sworn to serve them in this official capacity. Thus, although they were not elected but rather appointed, William Seward and George C. Marshall, two great secretaries of state, may nonetheless be eligible for inclusion in the ranks of American statesman. By contrast, lobbyists who are involved in the legislative process cannot be considered statesmen in the proper sense of the term. They are neither elected nor appointed to official positions of power in government. Nor are they duty-bound by a public trust to serve the common good. Rather, they are paid to represent the particular interest of their group.

Statesmanship seems to manifest itself most fully in times of momentous crisis. Great deeds of statesmen often occur in response to grave national threats. Traditionally, the momentous acts of founding and saving a state have been regarded as the pinnacle of statesmanship.

The potential use of state-sanctioned coercion also defines statesmanship as a distinct kind of political leadership. Though the ability to persuade is a common characteristic of all good leaders, the governing authority of a statesman pertains to the enactment and enforcement of far reaching national policies. The Civil War could not have been won without the Union's arms and Lincoln's use of extraordinary measures to suppress the rebellion, including the suspension of habeas corpus, a blockade of the South, conscription, and the Emancipation Proclamation. Undoubtedly then, part of the greatness of a statesman consists in the ability not only to persuade but also to use force within constitutional boundaries when necessary.

To recognize that statesmanship involves the wielding of state power is not to embrace the doctrine of realpolitik—the belief that considerations of success and power are all that really matter in politics, a view that owes much to Machiavelli's legacy. While realpolitik certainly describes the leadership of an Otto Von Bismarck, who unified Germany through a policy of "blood and iron," it does not capture fully the statesmanship of Abraham Lincoln, who was guided by immutable principles and just moral ends in his effort to preserve a Union that was "forever worthy of the saving."[31] Indeed, ancient political philosophers like Plato and Aristotle and the medieval theologian St. Thomas Aquinas envisioned statesmanship as a moral enterprise concerned with the *common good* of the regime. So understood, the common good was more than the summation of selfish interests; it corresponded to an overarching moral end or purpose based on an objective standard of human flourishing. Power and persuasion were to be used for noble and legitimate ends, not for the sake of personal or national aggrandizement.

Statesmanship is often confused with radical/reform leadership. In advocating a social, political or economic cause, an activist may be in the vanguard of public opinion. However, such leaders are not duty-bound by an oath of office. Neither are they constrained by the rule of law nor accountable to the nation as a whole. Unless enacted by public officials, the reformist's social and political agenda lacks state sanction. In a word, a statesman must ultimately answer to voters. While the radical/reformer's effectiveness often depends on concentrating the public mind on a singular injustice like racism, segregation, or sexism, the statesman's success further depends on maintaining a broad coalition within the party and government in support of realistic policy goals. In a democratic republic, successful policies require popular consent of the entire regime, not just a portion of it. Under our Constitution, the enactment of reforms into law necessarily requires the actions of public officials.

The true statesman educates and ennobles the public within the limits of public opinion and constitutional boundaries. Because human beings are imperfect, politics remains the "art of the possible." The securing of the common good necessarily involves compromise. Radical/reformers may forget this lesson in their immoderate and zealous pursuit of perfection.[32] As Jaffa well notes, "there is a danger of tyranny in the attempt to treat the desirable as if it were always possible, when in fact it is not. This teaching against political utopianism is certainly one of the great lessons of classical political philosophy. It is manifest in the Lyceum speech when Lincoln warns against freeing the slaves by enslaving the free."[33] The successful statesman must therefore possess a healthy dose of political moderation. Assuredly guided by principle, he or she strives to prudently achieve as much of the good as possible without being corrupted by power or blinded by radical schemes of utopian perfection. Put another way, the statesman is neither a pragmatist who pursues power without principle nor an idealist who pursues perfection apart from reality. In sum, his or her ultimate success depends on the rare ability to navigate the ship of state within moral, constitutional, and electoral boundaries. These parameters both empower and limit the statesman in achieving what is politically possible under the particular circumstances of time and place.

Though he shared antislavery convictions ("I have always hated slavery, I think as much as any Abolitionist"), Lincoln parted company with those radicals who would have dissolved the Union in order to end slavery.[34] Notably, he maintained that the Union's preservation was a precondition, the sine qua non, for preserving freedom and ending slavery in the long term. Lincoln's ability to achieve this aim was complicated by the need to knit together a broad war coalition that included (a) conservative republicans who fought to preserve the Union, but who distrusted radical policies that would transform the conflict into a war of liberation; (b) radical republicans or abolitionists who saw the destruction of slavery as the highest priority and overriding concern; and (c) war Democrats and border state men who supported the Union, but vehemently opposed abolitionism and the administration's broad measures to suppress the rebellion, including the Emancipation Proclamation and the suspension of habeas corpus.

In his "Oration in Memory of Abraham Lincoln" delivered at the Unveiling of the Freedmen's Monument in Lincoln Park, Washington, D.C., on April 14, 1876, Frederick Douglass perceptively distinguished between the competing demands and responsibilities of a statesman with the more singular agenda of radicals who "put the abolition of slavery before the salvation of the Union." While certainly not without his criticisms of the sixteenth president, Douglass correctly described Lincoln's statesmanship in terms of a "great mission to accomplish two things":

> first, to save his country from dismemberment and ruin; and, second, to free his country from the great crime of slavery. To do one or the other, or both, he must have the earnest sympathy and the powerful cooperation of his loyal fellow-countrymen. Without this primary and essential condition to success his efforts must have been vain and utterly fruitless. Had he put the abolition of slavery before the salvation of the Union, he would have inevitably driven from him a powerful class of the American people and rendered resistance to rebellion impossible. Viewed from the genuine abolition ground, Mr. Lincoln seemed tardy, cold, dull, and indifferent; *but measuring him by the sentiment of his country, a sentiment he was bound as a statesman to consult*, he was swift, zealous, radical, and determined.[35] (emphasis added)

These words from a great radical/reformer should be kept in mind to help us appreciate more clearly the particular duty and character of statesmanship in contrast to other kinds of political leadership. In a word, Frederick Douglass, Elizabeth Cady Stanton, and Martin Luther King Jr. were all great radical/reform leaders who challenged the status quo from outside of government; but they were not statesmen. This is not to diminish their greatness or their outstanding contribution to our democratic republic. Rather, it is to note that statesmanship is a different in kind of leadership that should be judged on its own terms.

To be sure, a statesman and a radical/reformer may work together in common cause. This combination was particularly potent in the case of antislavery politics of the nineteenth century and civil rights in the twentieth century. In his marvelous work comparing and contrasting Lincoln and Frederick Douglass from the respective standpoints of a politician and a radical/reformer, James Oakes tells the story of how these two men "converged at the most dramatic moment in American history."[36] As Oakes well recognizes, the convergence of these two leaders in the common cause of antislavery politics, however, should not obscure the differences between them and the type of leadership each represented.

Finally, a clearer understanding of Lincoln's philosophical statesmanship may be gained in contrast to alternative interpretations of him as a pragmatic leader, a progressive leader, and a revolutionary leader who refounded America. The elusive term "pragmatic," which dates to the progressive era, has often been applied to Lincoln's skill as a political leader. Sometimes the term is used to describe the virtue of practical wisdom in a way that resembles the classical and medieval understanding of prudence as presented in chapter 3 of this work.[37] However, other times (and more often than not) the term carries the philosophical baggage of the progressive era and the New Deal. This version of pragmatism shuns political theory and philosophical speculation in politics. It seeks to solve problems through an ad hoc, experimental, trial–and-error method. The pragmatic leader, in this sense, is a consummate bargainer who maintains a flexible style of leadership. Evading deeper questions about philosophical coherence, moral absolutes, and abstract principles in politics, the pragmatist focuses on more concrete matters like success, expediency, and compromise.

In his Pulitzer Prize–winning book *Leadership*, James MacGregor Burns describes Lincoln as a pragmatist in this less principled sense of acting without recourse to a noble vision and first principles. Oddly enough, Burns mentions Lincoln only in passing, claiming that he "acted in a wholly 'pragmatic' and operational manner in overriding his old Whig anti-presidential power views in order to fight the war. . . . [He] was also opportunistic and expedient in his attitude toward slavery during the early part of the war."[38]

The mark of a pragmatic leader, according to Burns, is to evade questions of ultimate value and purpose. Indeed, Burns goes so far as to compare the sixteenth president's putative pragmatism during the Civil War to Nixon's handling of Watergate and Vietnam:

The question of ultimate purpose remained. *What was one saving in saving the nation?* It was the Supreme Court that most aptly answered Lincoln, in a post–Civil War decision rebuking the late President for his theory of presidential war power: "A country preserved at the sacrifice of all the cardinal principles of liberty, is not worth the cost of preserving it." Wars, depressions, domestic unrest, great moral issues like Vietnam and Watergate have posed the most urgent questions of value and purpose for pragmatic politicians, however much they have sought to evade them.[39]

In sum, Burns fails to understand Lincoln's statesmanship because he fails to understand the difference between pragmatism and prudence, the difference between sailing without a moral compass and navigating rocky shoals with one. While Lincoln was certainly flexible and adept at bargaining, he was more than an opportunist and horse trader. Burns's description of unprincipled pragmatism applies more accurately to Lincoln's nemesis, Stephen Douglas, than the sixteenth president.

The characterization of Lincoln as pragmatic in this sense fails to do justice to the budding statesman who wrote in 1856, "Moral principle is all, or nearly all, that unites us of the North."[40] It omits the magnanimity of the president elect, who said in 1861, "I will suffer death before I will consent or will advise friends to any concession or compromise."[41] As used by Burns and the progressives, the term "pragmatism" has more in common with *astuzia* or cunning than with the virtue of prudence or practical wisdom as actually practiced by Lincoln as a statesman.[42]

By contrast, what distinguishes Lincoln as a *philosopher* statesman as opposed to a pragmatic politician was his profound insight about human nature and politics, and his ability to provide a comprehensive vision of political life. Notwithstanding recourse to controversial means at times to attain the right ends, the sixteenth president was nonetheless a visionary statesman who was unyielding in the defense of core beliefs.

As noted, the Declaration is central to Lincoln's noble vision as a philosopher statesman. The sixteenth president regarded it as the moral touchstone and the foundation of the American experiment.[43] He thus invoked the "laws of nature and nature's God" as the normative standard to judge the politics of his time. Its "self-evident" truths were not mere suggestions or arbitrary preferences, but moral imperatives that were binding on the nation. He measured the ultimate legitimacy of government policies in terms of their conformity to the norms of life, liberty, and the pursuit of happiness. Thus, at Springfield Illinois, in 1854, Lincoln proclaimed the philosophical foundation of the American regime in these terms: "The theory of our government is Universal Freedom. 'All men are created free and equal,' says the Declaration of Independence. The word 'Slavery' is not found in the Constitution."[44]

As "the central idea" of the regime, the principle of equality was axiomatic to popular government. "Our government rests in public opinion," Lincoln explained. "Whoever can change public opinion, can change the government, practically just so much. Public opinion, or [on?] any subject, always has a '*central idea*,' from which all its minor thoughts radiate. That 'central idea' in our political public opinion, at the beginning was, and until recently has continued to be, 'the equality of men.'"[45] Lincoln sought to educate public opinion in accordance with this great truth. Indeed, the norm of equality was the moral compass whereby he navigated the ship of state.

Pursuing inquiry in Socratic terms, Lincoln the philosopher statesman probed the underlying "philosophical cause" of the Union's success in maintaining ordered liberty. He attributed this success to the perpetuation of the principles of the Declaration as safeguarded by the Constitution. On the eve of the Civil War, the sixteenth president summed up his philosophical vision of the Union in a letter to Alexander Stephens, a former Whig colleague who had initially opposed Georgia's session. He used a biblical metaphor from Proverbs 25:1. "A word fitly spoken is like apples of gold in pictures of silver" to convey the complementary relationship between the Declaration and the Constitution in securing a "more perfect" Union; a full quotation is warranted:

All this is not the result of accident. It has a philosophical cause. Without the *Constitution* and the *Union*, we could not have attained the result; but even these, are not the primary cause of our great prosperity. There is something back of these, entwining itself more closely about the human heart. That something, is the principle of "Liberty to all"—the principle that clears the *path* for all—gives *hope* to all—and, by consequence, *enterprize*, and *industry* to all.

The *expression* of that principle, in our Declaration of Independence, was most happy and fortunate. *Without* this, as well as *with* it, we could have declared our independence of Great Britain; but *without* it, we could not, I think, have secured our free government, and consequent prosperity. No oppressed, people will *fight*, and *endure*, as our fathers did, without the promise of something better than a mere change of masters.

The assertion of that *principle*, at *that time*, was *the* word, *"fitly spoken"* which has proved an "apple of gold" to us. The *Union*, and the *Constitution*, are the *picture* of *silver*, subsequently framed around it. The picture was made, not to *conceal*, or *destroy* the apple; but to *adorn*, and *preserve* it. The *picture* was made *for* the apple—*not* the apple for the picture.

So let us act, that neither *picture*, or *apple* shall ever be blurred, or bruised or broken.[46]

In view of this metaphor, Allen Guelzo correctly explains that for Lincoln, the "Constitution did not exist merely for its own sake, as though it were only a set of procedural rules with not better goal than letting people do what they pleased with what they pleased; it was intended to serve the interests of "the principle of Liberty to all," which meant that the Declaration was the word fitly spoken which has proved an apple of gold."[47] Thus, according to Lincoln, the Constitution was animated by the spirit of the Declaration and should be read through the lens of its first principles. He saw the Declaration and Constitution as complementary charters of liberty that sustained one another. For Lincoln then, preserving the Union always meant preserving the principles for which it stood and the rule of law in the Constitution that best safeguarded these principles.[48]

As recognized by Frederick Douglass, Lincoln's statesmanship was guided by two overarching and interrelated goals: ending slavery and saving the Union. These twin goals were implicitly linked and integral parts of his noble vision. Because Lincoln viewed universal equality as latent to the principles of the Declaration, his statesmanship was not revolutionary in the sense of constituting a radical break or rejection of the founding. Nor is it proper to describe his statesmanship as merely pragmatic, as an experimental, ad hoc, trial-and-error approach to problem solving that evaded questions of ultimate meaning. The pragmatic view of Lincoln's leadership claims that the Civil War took on moral meaning only with the Emancipation Proclamation in 1863. On the contrary, in his outstanding work *President Lincoln: The Duty of a Statesman*, William Lee Miller describes "two deep errors in this view. In the first place, vindicating the Union was for Lincoln no mere power-political struggle but an undertaking with vast universal and moral significance—showing that free, popular constitutional government could maintain itself. . . . In the second place, the moral principles that Lincoln understood to define the Union placed slavery under condemnation from the start."[49] It bears repeating then that preserving the Union for Lincoln meant preserving the principles for which the Union stood—namely, the principles of popular government and equal opportunity for all. This connection was explicitly made in the Republican Party platform of 1860, which affirmed the Declaration of Independence as the foundation of the American republic: "That the maintenance of the principles promulgated in the declaration of independence and embodied in the federal constitution, 'That all men are created equal . . .' is essential to the preservation of our republican institutions; and that the federal constitution, the rights of the states, and the Union of the states, must and shall be preserved."

Lincoln's legacy has also been claimed by the progressive era.[50] As a philosophical movement, progressivism embraced the historicist thesis described above by combining Hegel's dialectical view of history with Darwin's evolutionary theory.[51] The progressive idea is based on an evolutionary model of organic growth that involves successive stages of inevitable improvement over time. Progressives thus see rights not as fixed principles, but as malleable aims to be redefined by the state. Indeed, the notion of a "living constitution" that is adapted by judges to changing conditions is also a legacy of the progressive era.[52]

As used by progressives like Woodrow Wilson, John Dewey, Oliver Wendell Holmes, Charles Beard, and Herbert Croly, the word "progress" meant much more than the realization of fixed, inalienable rights. While Lincoln certainly spoke of progress when he said, "I had thought the Declaration contemplated the progressive improvement in the condition of all men everywhere," he measured this progress in terms of the nation fulfilling its moral obligations to the universal norms of the Declaration.[53] On the contrary, the progressive notion of progress rejects transhistorical truth as static and instead maintains that human social and political relations *inevitably* improve over time. Surveying progressive interpretations of Lincoln before his landmark work *Crisis of the House Divided*, Jaffa notes that most mainstream historians "believed that, while Lincoln was praiseworthy for being on the side of Progress, it was Progress, understood as historical necessity, not Lincoln, or any abstract truth, that was destined to bring about the end of slavery."[54]

As mentioned, the term "pragmatism" was also used by the progressives to denote an experimental style of leadership that shuns abstract principles and theoretical inquiry in politics, focusing rather on what works at any given moment. The pragmatist, in this sense, is short on vision, but big on success. This lack of vision is not necessarily blameworthy since progress is inevitably driven by underlying historical forces beyond the control of human agency. Woodrow Wilson epitomizes the progressive distrust of theory in his speech *Abraham Lincoln: A Man of the People*: "What commends Mr. Lincoln's studiousness to me is that the result of it was he did not have any theories at all. . . . Lincoln was one of those delightful students who did not seek to tie you up in the meshes of any theory."[55] Jason Jividen, who critiques the progressive effort to claim Lincoln, states that "Wilson's purpose in this speech is to divorce Lincoln from abstract, natural rights thinking and to employ him as an example of progress."[56]

To be sure, FDR took his bearing from the progressive movement when he maintained that "the task of statesmanship has always been the re-definition of these rights [of the Declaration] in terms of a growing and changing social order. New conditions impose new requirements upon Government and those who conduct government."[57] Progressivism thus endorses a much larger and active role for government in creating and guaranteeing new entitlements than envisioned by either the Founders or Lincoln. The goals of the progressive movement could be realized only through an expansive administrative state committed to the redistribution of wealth. In the words of one of its most famous spokesmen, Herbert Croly, the progressive movement embraced "Hamiltonian means for Jeffersonian ends."[58] That is to say, the instrumentality of an activist federal government to provide social welfare. In their notable work *Presidential Greatness*, Marc Landy and Sidney M. Milkis clearly explain the differences between Lincoln and the progressive understanding of equality. "Lincoln's understanding of the equality that was guaranteed by the Declaration," they note, "was modest compared with the collective aspirations of twentieth century reform presidents such as Theodore Roosevelt, Franklin Roosevelt, and Lyndon Johnson. The Republican Party program was tightly bounded by the nation's long-standing commitment to private property, limited government, and administrative decentralization. Allied to local self-government, Republicans could not sanction the constant presence of the national government in the society and economy. Their contribution was to free local democracy from the taint of slavery and thereby establish the moral obligation of the federal government to ensure equal opportunity."[59]

Progressives mistakenly view Lincoln as the precursor to the modern, plebiscitarian presidency, which seeks a more direct link between the people and the president, the only nationally elected public official who carries a mandate to channel and translate the people's will into reform policies. Wilson believed that the success of this more direct link between the people and the president required abandoning the Founders' obsession with checks and balances and institutional limitations on power. He famously argued that checks and balances were the product of a Newtonian model of politics in the eighteenth century that had since been superseded by a Darwinian model of organic and evolutionary growth in the nineteenth and twentieth centuries. Just as it does not make sense to turn the limbs of a body against itself, so also the archaic reliance of checks and balances frustrate the will of the people, the body politic. The solution, according to Wilson, is to enable a closer connection between the people and the president who represents them and to remove barriers in the way of this direct link. It is no surprise then that the progressives introduced the direct primary and the direct election of U.S. senators.

While progressives applaud Lincoln for playing a leading role during the Civil War in transforming the Founders' limited notion of government into the modern administrative state, libertarian critics like Thomas DiLorenzo blame him for betraying the Founders' limited notion of equality of opportunity into an equality of results and an open-ended egalitarianism. Accepting the progressive interpretation of Lincoln's leadership, DiLorenzo refers to the sixteenth president as "the great centralizer"![60] However, as Allen C. Guelzo has shown through "a detailed historical scrutiny" of the "size and reach of government," the progressives, not Lincoln, were the *real* fathers of big government.[61] Notably, after the Civil War, the budget, size, and reach of the federal government shrunk close to its prewar levels. Furthermore, the postwar era was characterized by weak executives and strong legislatures.

Contrary to the progressive interpretation, Lincoln's task as a statesman was not simply to channel or reflect popular opinion, but to refine, enlarge, educate, and ennoble it. As early as 1838 in the Lyceum address, he warned against the furious passions of the mob. In defiance of popular opinion in Illinois, he opposed the Mexican war and stood firm on the principle that slavery was a social, moral, and political evil that should be restricted in the territories. And he refused to embrace a dishonorable peace that would have imperiled the Union's moral ideals by returning to the status quo ante and reinstituting slavery.

Finally, the progressive interpretation of Lincoln's leadership also fails to distinguish between the temporary exercise of broad power during extreme circumstances like the Civil War and the routine or permanent exercise of such power for purposes of economic redistribution and social reform without a principled limit. As will be seen, Lincoln justified his extraordinary use of executive power by distinguishing between the Constitution in times of war and in times of peace. This crucial distinction narrows the precedent of the broad exercise of executive power to times of actual crisis.

If Lincoln was not a progressive, was he then a revolutionary leader who refounded the American regime on a new basis? Indeed, much of the controversy over Lincoln's leadership stems from a related debate over his relationship to the founding and whether or not he acted consistently with its principles. The description of the American Civil War as a "Second American Revolution" has lent credence to the refounding thesis.[62] The debate centers over the meaning of the term "revolution" as either a radical departure from the founding or a fulfillment of the founding principles. For example, in describing Lincoln's act of refounding, George P. Fletcher explains that "the principles of this new legal regime are so radically different from our original Constitution, drafted in 1787, that they deserve to be recognized as a second American constitution."[63]

In his Pulitzer Prize–winning work, *Lincoln at Gettysburg: The Words that Remade America*, Gary Wills claims that Lincoln "remade" America by elevating the Declaration and its equality clause over the Constitution as "the central idea" of the American regime, an interpretation that was contrary to historical fact and precedent. While Wills praises Lincoln's "refounding" because it ushered in a more egalitarian America, conservative critics like Willmoore Kendall condemn it as a "derailment" that placed the American regime on a progressive course toward equality of results.[64] As will be seen, both Wills and Kendall are mistaken in their assumption that Lincoln overturned the principles of the founding.

Though it may seem far-fetched to those unfamiliar with Nietzsche's thought, Wills's description of Lincoln's refounding at Gettysburg is highly reminiscent of the German philosopher's understanding of the creative will to power. Notwithstanding Nietzsche's contempt for democracy, Wills similarly describes Lincoln's feat at Gettysburg as an expression of the will to power. Lincoln is comparable to a benign Super-man or *ubermensch* who undertakes a transvaluation of values, an overcoming of the Founders' old moral order in exchange for a new egalitarian one. In an effort to overcome the past and redefine the future, the sixteenth president posited a new set of values. Disguised as an elucidation of history, this "transvaluation of values" was instead a radically creative act that transcended old ways of thinking and introduced a new horizon of meaning and purpose. Just as Christians transvalued Roman martial values by using the same Latin vocabulary but investing it with a spiritual, otherworldly meaning, so Lincoln used the same language of equality during the founding but invested it with a radically new egalitarian meaning that was alien to the Founders.

The novelty of Wills's interpretation requires some familiarity with Nietzsche's thought. The latter asserts that all wisdom and knowledge are creative expressions of the will to power. Seeking to expose the relativity of all values, Nietzsche is a historicist *par excellence* who rejects immutable principles and transhistorical standards. All claims about discerning and acting in conformity to an objective "truth" or "good" are actually impositions of the creative will on to reality. Human action does not consist in knowing and acting in conformity with an objective good, but in the positing of new values. History, then, according to Nietzsche, is the story of how the will to power destroys old values and creates new ones. The pretense to discover universal norms is itself an illusion that masks the will to power. Because all standards are arbitrary creations, nobility for Nietzsche does not consist in attuning oneself to a universal standard of goodness or honor. On the contrary, says Nietzsche, "the noble type of man experiences *itself* as determining values; it does not need approval; it judges, 'what is harmful to me is harmful in itself'; it is *value creating*. Everything it knows as part of itself it honors: such a morality is self-glorification."[65]

Through verbal manipulation and the selective use of the past, Lincoln, much like Nietzsche's "noble type of man," was not elucidating history, but creating new values. Using the same language, he redefined American history and posited a new set of egalitarian values that continues to shape our national self-understanding. With remarkable candor, Wills praises Lincoln for benignly swindling America:

> Lincoln performed one of the most daring acts of open-air sleight-of-hand ever witnessed by the unsuspecting. Everyone in that vast throng of thousands was having his or her intellectual pocket picked. The crowd departed with a new thing in its ideological luggage, that new constitution Lincoln had substituted for the one they brought there with them. They walked off, from those curving graves on the hillside, under changed sky, into a different America. Lincoln had revolutionized the Revolution, giving people a new past to live with that would change their future indefinitely.[66]

Lincoln's refounding was superbly masked by the claim that he was merely "preserving" old ways of thinking, rather than innovating something radically new. Moved by the creative will to power rather than rational discernment of an unchangeable Nature, Wills contends that, "Lincoln does not argue law or history, as Daniel Webster did. He makes history. He does not come to present a theory, but to impose a symbol, one tested in experience and appealing to national values, with an emotional urgency entirely expressed in calm abstractions (fire in ice). He came to change the world, to effect an intellectual revolution."[67] Wills's description of Lincoln's rhetorical feat at Gettysburg bears comparison to Nietzsche's description in *Beyond Good and Evil* of how the will to power is likewise disguised as an act of elucidation or preservation:

> Those philosophical laborers after the noble model of Kant and Hegel have to determine and press into formulas, whether in the realm of *logic* or *political* (moral) thought or *art*, some great data of valuations—that is, former *positings* of values, creations of value which have become dominant are for a time called "truths." It is for these investigators to make everything that has happened and been esteemed so far easy to look over, easy to think over, intelligible and manageable, to abbreviate everything long, even "time," and to *overcome* the entire past—an enormous and wonderful task in whose service every subtle pride, every tough will can certainly find satisfaction. *Genuine philosophers, however, are commanders and legislators*: they say, "*thus it shall* be!" They first determine the Whither and For What of man, and in so doing have at their disposal the preliminary labor of all philosophical laborers, all who have overcome the past. With a creative hand they reach for the future, and all that is and has been becomes a means for them, an instrument, a hammer. Their "knowing" is *creating*, their creation is a legislation, their will to truth is—*will to power*.[68]

Is not Wills's account of how Lincoln came to Gettysburg to "impose a symbol" eerily reminiscent of Nietzsche's description of the positing of new values? In both cases, a "creative hand," "reache[s] for the future" and wields "a hammer" to "overcome the past." In sum, Wills's story of Lincoln at Gettysburg extols a creative superman who used rhetoric in the service of a benign will to power to redefine the meaning of America. Rhetoric defines reality. While Wills praises this particular transvaluation of values because it helped to create a more egalitarian America, libertarian critics understandably view it as a radical betrayal of the founding and the Constitution. Should we really embrace a model of leadership that seeks to create new values under the pretext of preserving old ones? What of the "dark side" of creative supermen and their will to power?

Wills's thesis nonetheless raises important questions about Lincoln's relationship to the founding and the meaning of the Civil War as the

"Second American Revolution." If the "Second American Revolution" means that Lincoln completed the unfinished work of 1776, then the description is accurate. However, if it means that Lincoln overturned the principles of 1776 and refounded the nation through a transvaluation of values, as Wills suggests, then it profoundly distorts Lincoln's self-understanding of his statesmanship during the Civil War era.

As will be seen, contrary to both defenders and critics of the refounding thesis, Lincoln's statesmanship is best understood in terms of affirming, defending, and extending the principles of the founding. Lincoln certainly saw himself as preserving the Founders' legacy, as when he proclaimed at Cooper Union in 1860: "This chief and real purpose of the Republican party is eminently conservative. It proposes nothing save and except to restore this government to its original tone in regard to this element of slavery, and there to maintain it, looking for no further change, in reference to it, than that which the original framers of the government themselves expected and looked forward to."[69]

Lincoln was not insincere in saying this. Before the war, he had consistently pledged that he had no authority to touch slavery where it existed in the southern states. The territories, of course, were a different matter since they fell under federal control. However, the circumstances of war led him as president to undertake transformative measures, which were not heretofore possible in peacetime. In sum, the sixteenth president's statesmanship was neither *simply conservative* (in the sense of merely preserving the status quo of the founding era) nor was it *completely revolutionary* (in the sense of radically overturning the founding). The "either/or" conservative/revolutionary dichotomy does not fit the character of Lincoln's statesmanship. Lincoln did not supplant the principles of the founding. Instead, his philosophical statesmanship is best understood in terms *of affirming, defending, and extending* them.[70] Understanding his statesmanship in these terms helps to avoid the either/or dichotomy while still recognizing the validity, to some extent, of each claim. It is useful insofar as it recognizes that changes wrought during the Civil War, such as the destruction of slavery, were transformational while still consistent with the regime's founding principles.

Since Lincoln was himself fond of using the Bible to illustrate a point, his relationship to the founding can be explained in comparable terms to what Christians believe about the New Testament's relationship to the Old Testament or the Torah. This relationship is best conveyed by Jesus himself in Matthew 5:17: "Do not think that I have come to abolish the Law or the Prophets; I have not come to abolish them but to fulfill them."

In recurring to the principles of the Torah, Jesus did not abolish the law and prophets, but renewed, clarified, and extended the latent universalism of the Jews to the Gentiles. He challenged the status quo insofar as it deviated from the true teaching of Israel, which he both illuminated and fulfilled in the biblical roles of priest, prophet, and king. Jesus was the culmination of something old while representing something new in the sense of extending and more fully realizing that which preceded him.

By analogy, Lincoln did not abolish or supplant the principles of the founding. His recurrence clarified and extended them to all human beings in a manner that was consistent with their inner logic and universalism. Founder John Adams emphasized that "a frequent recurrence to the fundamental principles of the constitution, and a constant adherence to those of piety, justice, moderation, temperance, industry, and frugality, are absolutely necessary to preserve the advantages of liberty, and to maintain a free government."[71] Despite concessions to slavery made out of necessity, the affirmation of equality at the time of the Revolution logically pointed to its extension to all human beings. Notwithstanding his own hypocrisy, Jefferson himself intended the principle of equality to apply universally to all human beings.[72] Indeed, the Founders themselves recognized the incompatibility between the principles of the Revolution and the practice of slavery, as when Jefferson stated in the *Notes in the State of Virginia*:

> And can the liberties of a nation be thought secure when we have removed their only firm basis, a conviction in the minds of the people that these liberties are the gift of God. That they are not to be violated but with his wrath? Indeed I tremble for my country when I reflect that God is just: that his justice cannot sleep for ever: that considering numbers, nature and natural means only, a revolution of the wheel of fortune, an exchange of situation, is among the possible events that it may become probable by supernatural interference! The Almighty has no attribute which can take side with us in such a contest.[73]

Lincoln often cited this passage in support of his interpretation of the Founders' recognition that slavery was wrong. Though he admired and revered the Founders for what they had attained, as a philosopher statesman he was by no means uncritical of them. In the Lyceum address, he went so far as to question the motives of the revolutionary generation. He would subsequently explain that we are not "bound to follow implicitly in whatever our fathers did. To do so, would be to discard all the lights of current experience—to reject all progress—all improvement."[74]

As noted, progress in this sense is not a matter of historical inevitability that supersedes the principles of the founding, but of prudent deliberation that recurs to fixed principles and extends them under new circumstances in a manner that accords with their inner logic and dictates. In "Notes on Ancient and Modern Confederacies," written at the time of the Founding, James Madison, the father of the Constitution, clearly recognized the logical incompatibility between slavery and equality when he stated: "Where slavery exists, the Republican Theory becomes still more fallacious."[75]

The Founders work was noble, yet unfinished. Quoting Henry Clay, his "beau ideal of a statesman," Lincoln thus explained: "I desire no concealment of my opinions in regard to the institution of slavery. I look upon it as a great evil; and deeply lament that we have derived it from the parental government; and from our ancestors. But here they are and the question is, how can they be best dealt with?"[76]

The circumstances of the Civil War opened new possibilities for dealing with slavery that did not exist in peacetime. Lincoln was not disingenuous when he claimed to be defending the principles of the founding before the war, while subsequently claiming to be doing something new during the war. By eliminating an entrenched institution and forever changing the status quo, the freeing and arming of the slaves may be seen as revolutionary in a certain sense of the term. However, it should not be viewed as a revolution in the broader sense as a radical departure of the founding. Black freedom was achieved through constitutional means and in accordance with the inner logic of the principles of the regime.

The continuity between old and new is vividly seen in Lincoln's special message to Congress on December 1, 1862, which anticipated the final Emancipation Proclamation a month later on January 1, 1863:

> The dogmas of the quiet past, are inadequate to the stormy present. The occasion is piled high with difficulty, and we must rise with the occasion. As our case is new, so we must think anew, and act anew. We must disenthrall our selves, and then we shall save our country.
>
> Fellow-citizens, *we* cannot escape history. We of this Congress and this administration, will be remembered in spite of ourselves. No personal significance, or insignificance, can spare one or another of us. The fiery trial through which we pass, will light us down, in honor or dishonor, to the latest generation. We *say* we are for the Union. The world will not forget that we say this. We know how to save the Union. The world knows we do know how to save it. We—even *we here*—hold the power, and bear the responsibility. In

giving freedom to the *slave*, we *assure* freedom to the *free*—honorable alike in what we give, and what we preserve. We shall nobly save, or meanly lose, the last best, hope of earth. Other means may succeed; this could not fail. The way is plain, peaceful, generous, just—a way which, if followed, the world will forever applaud, and God must forever bless.[77]

In the same passage, the emancipation is referred to as a saving (conserving) act that is also "new." The "dogmas" of the quiet past (of the status quo ante) that allowed compromises with slavery no longer apply in wartime, when the very survival of the nation is at stake. The conflict had reached a point where the preservation of the Union necessitated destroying the malignant cause that had jeopardized its very existence. The newness referred to the new constitutional means made possible under the extraordinary circumstances of war. Nonetheless, the policy was consistent with the moral imperatives of the Declaration. Thinking anew and acting anew did not mean overthrowing the Constitution and the principles of the Declaration.

After preparing his audience to accept the "radical" step of emancipation, a measure consistent with the proper understanding of the regime's principles and wartime circumstances, Lincoln explains how the old and new are nonetheless inseparably linked as seen above: "In *giving* freedom to the *slave*, we *assure* freedom to the *free*."

The Gettysburg Address similarly describes the Civil War in terms of "a new birth of freedom" whereby the nation is redeemed from the original sin of slavery. The "new birth," however, fulfills the promise of the "ancient faith" in the Declaration. It perfects but does not abolish or radically depart from the old. Indeed, at Gettysburg, Lincoln recurs to the founding principles of the regime and the proposition that all men are created equal. Distinguishing Lincoln's "new birth of freedom" from Wilson's New Freedom, Jason Jividen explains that the former "consisted in a rededication to the natural rights principles of the Declaration. Wilson's New Freedom consists in something very different, a profound and far-reaching restructuring of the American regime that required a self-conscious and deliberate break with the principles Lincoln sought to restore."[78] To be sure, Lincoln clarified "the central idea" of equality in the American Decalogue by preaching its utter incompatibility with slavery and pointing to its ultimate fulfillment in black freedom and a multiracial democracy.

Lincoln was correct in maintaining that universal equality was latent to a coherent understanding of the very founding principles of the regime. Given the continuity between the spirit of seventy-six and the

Emancipation Proclamation, he did not undertake a refounding of the American regime. This "refounding thesis" overstates the newness without sufficient reference to the first principles of the regime and Lincoln's consistent recurrence to them. Thus, his statesmanship during the war was neither revolutionary in the sense of radically breaking with the principles of the founding nor simply conservative in preserving the status quo ante. Given the magnitude and duration of the Civil War, the act of preservation required something emergent and new, which was nonetheless derived from the old as both foreshadowed and intimated by it.

Now that we have clearly defined statesmanship and considered alternative interpretations of Lincoln's leadership, it remains to consider more specifically the character or Nature of Lincoln's philosophical statesmanship in terms of the aforementioned six dimensions: (1) wisdom, (2) prudence, (3) duty, (4) magnanimity, (5) rhetoric, (6) patriotism. In what follows, each chapter will focus on one of these crucial elements of Lincoln's philosophical statesmanship.

1
WISDOM

$\mathcal{T}$he Bible as well as Greek philosophy underscores the importance of wisdom to good governance. The book of Proverbs, attributed to the wise statesman Solomon, proclaims, "Without vision the people perish." As taught by Solomon, the statesman's wisdom consists primarily in vision, a rare and elusive quality that transcends managerial expertise or technical know-how. Indeed, Lincoln's political greatness cannot be understood apart from his intellectual vision or wisdom, a virtue that also includes the outstanding mental abilities of apprehension, judgment, and foresight. His prodigious intellectual gifts were developed through a life of self-discipline, reflection, and learning. They were placed in the service of an honorable ambition that ministered to the common good.

Lincoln was a supreme autodidact. With less than a year of formal schooling, he taught himself how to read and write. Through close and persistent study of great works like Euclid's *Elements*, Shakespeare's dramas, and the Bible, he attained a mastery of logic, moral reasoning, and the English language.[1] His verbal and logical skills were honed further through his legal practice.[2] He became adept at reducing a case in terms of its core principle and of persuading juries through tersely reasoned arguments, talents that would serve him well in mobilizing support for the Union cause.

Lincoln provided a telling description of his own philosophical cast of mind in a childhood recollection to a Connecticut clergyman in 1860: "I remember how, when a mere child, I used to get irritated when anybody talked to me in a way I could not understand. I don't think I ever got angry at anything else in my life. But that always disturbed my temper, and has ever since. I can remember going to my little bedroom, after hearing the neighbors talk of an evening with my father, and spending no small part of the night walking up and down, and trying to make out what was the exact meaning of some of their, to me, dark sayings. I could not sleep though I often tried to, when I got on such a hunt after an idea, until I had caught it; and when I thought I had got it, I was not satisfied until I had repeated it over and over, until I had put it in language plain enough, as I thought, for any boy I knew to comprehend. This was a kind of passion with me, and it has stuck by me, for I am never easy now, when I am handling a thought, till I have bounded it north and bounded it south and bounded it east and bounded it west."[3] This habit continued with Lincoln throughout his adult life. The sixteenth president's account of the desire to know as a pathos and mania that grips the soul and stirs within it a relentless search for truth was understood by Plato in similar terms over two thousand years earlier as the mark of a true philosopher.[4]

In addition to rational intelligence, Lincoln also possessed many of the traits associated with emotional intelligence, defined by Daniel Goleman as "self-awareness, self control and empathy, and the arts of listening, resolving conflicts and cooperation."[5] Goleman correctly points out that "the brightest among us can founder on the shoals of unbridled passions and unruly impulses; . . . people with high IQ's can be stunningly poor pilots in their private lives."[6] This observation certainly applies to our political leaders as well as private citizens.

Various life experiences as a farm hand, a rail-splitter, a flatboat rider, a store clerk, a postman, a surveyor, a militia captain, a politician, and a circuit-riding lawyer familiarized him with different personalities within his frontier microcosm. He would understand and appreciate the habits of the heart of the people whom he would govern.

Doris Kearns Goodwin summarizes Lincoln's political genius in terms of his ability "to form friendships with men who had previously opposed him; to repair injured feelings that, left untended, might have escalated into permanent hostility; to assume responsibility for the failures of subordinates; to share credit with ease; and to learn from mistakes."[7] In managing the strong egos of his cabinet, Lincoln showed that "kindness, sensitivity, compassion, honesty, and empathy . . . can also be impressive political resources."[8] To be sure, the qualities Goodwin describes above have less to do with IQ and more to do with emotional intelligence.

Lincoln's use of storytelling, jokes, and self-deprecating humor also reveals how his emotional intelligence could serve as a valuable political asset. He had an "extraordinary ability to convey practical wisdom in the form of humorous tales his listeners could remember and repeat."[9] A friend wrote that he "used his stories as much for producing conviction in the minds of his hearers as for creating merriment."[10] Humor was both therapeutic and instructional for Lincoln. He used it to disarm political opponents, lighten the mood, and to explain or illustrate a political point more clearly. For example, in response to those who questioned his lenient policy of pardoning so many deserters, he explained: "it would frighten the poor devils to death to shoot them." Here Lincoln's humor elicits compassion for the condemned man while still acknowledging his flaws. Humor also preserved harmony in the cabinet. When Lincoln heard that his secretary of defense called him a fool, he remarked: "Well, I guess I had better go over and see Stanton about this. Stanton is usually right."[11] Aware of his cabinet members' egos and peccadilloes, the president did not allow his own pride to get in the way of their broader service to the country.

Able to keep his own emotions within appropriate boundaries, Lincoln was "uncommonly tenderhearted," with "extraordinary empathy—the gift or curse of putting himself in the place of another, to experience what they were feeling, to understand their motives and desires."[12] This emotional intelligence partly explains his genuine sympathy toward fellow human beings held in bondage. In a letter dated August 24, 1855, to his best friend Joshua Speed, he recalled being horrified by the sight of shackled slaves on a trip down South. He experienced it viscerally and described it as "a continual torment to me; and I see something like it every time I touch the Ohio, or any other slave-border." It is "a thing which has, and continually exercises, the power of making me miserable."[13] Tenacious yet tenderhearted, Lincoln would prosecute the war to victory while also spending three hours each day reviewing and overturning the execution orders of Union soldiers guilty of desertion. He would intervene personally in sparing three hundred Sioux braves from execution, overturning a vengeful reprisal that would have punished the entire tribe for the actions of a few miscreants.[14]

While IQ and EQ (emotional intelligence) are necessary to wisdom, they are not sufficient. Because intelligence is common to both the vicious and the virtuous, wisdom involves something more than sheer cognitive ability. It also involves something more than emotional savvy and self-control. The wicked may also possess self-control along with the uncanny ability to read, manipulate, and play on others' emotions like a master fiddler. As the ancients recognized, one's inner disposition ultimately determines whether or not the intellect is directed toward serving base or noble ends.

In a word, wisdom proceeds from a righteous or good character. Aristotle and Aquinas identified it with *right reason*. They understood it as a virtue or habit of mind and character that perfects the intellectual faculty by disposing it to know *what is true* and to choose and *what is good*. The wise comprehend a noble vision and realize it through right actions. Indeed, "philosophy" literally means the love of wisdom in Greek.

Aristotle and Aquinas divided wisdom into two types depending on whether intelligence was directed to knowing rightly (theoretical wisdom) or to acting rightly (practical wisdom). To summarize, theoretical wisdom is the virtue of right reasoning in the realm of knowing and understanding; and practical wisdom is the virtue of right decision making in the realm of action—that is, in morals and politics. This work shows that Lincoln possessed both theoretical and practical wisdom.

Lincoln's theoretical wisdom consisted in his noble vision of human nature and politics, and his corresponding ability to provide a rational account of democratic government based on the principles of equality and consent. It is displayed through his profound understanding and articulation of the "philosophical basis" of politics in his speeches and writings.[15] William Herndon, Lincoln's law partner, described the sixteenth president's philosophical cast of mind in terms similar to Lincoln's own childhood recollection above. "Not only were nature, man, and principle suggestive to Mr. Lincoln," Herndon explained, "not only had he accurate and exact perceptions, but he was causative; his mind apparently with an automatic movement, ran back behind facts, principles, and all things to their origin and first cause—to the point where forces act as one as effect and cause."[16] Consistent with this philosophical disposition, Lincoln traced the ultimate legitimacy of political order to a first, underlying cause, as when he proclaimed, "I believe the declaration that 'all men are created equal' is the great fundamental principle upon which our free institutions rest."[17] To be sure, Lincoln was no shallow pragmatist who avoided theory; rather, he was truly "a man of ideas" as Allen C. Guelzo has recognized.[18] Probing beyond the rhetorical surface of an argument, he situated politics in the context of an overarching order and traced public policies to their first principles and underlying causes, determining ultimately whether or not they were in conformity with the transcendent "laws of nature and nature's God" in the Declaration.

Consider, for example, how Lincoln defined our national ordeal in philosophical terms as a clash over the meaning of first principles of self-government. Pondering the elusive meaning of liberty, he observed:

> The world has never had a good definition of the word liberty, and the American people, just now, are much in want of one. We all declare for liberty; but in using the same *word* we do not all mean the same *thing*. With some the word liberty may mean for each man to do as he pleases with himself, and the product of his labor; while with others the same word may mean for some men to do as they please with other men, and the product of other men's labor. Here are two, not only different, but incompatable [*sic*] things, called by the same name—liberty. And it follows that each of things is, by the respective parties, called by two different and incompatable names—liberty and tyranny.[19]

To be sure, Lincoln's quest for a coherent definition of liberty to undergird American republicanism was quite Socratic. Lincoln follows the philosophical method of the Greeks by beginning inquiry with commonly held opinions about norms like justice, happiness, and virtue. Just as Aristotle observed that there were differences opinions about happiness as either pleasure, wealth, honor or virtue, so Lincoln observes that there are differences of opinion about the meaning of liberty. The differences in opinion about the norms of happiness or liberty, however, do not mean that for either Aristotle or Lincoln that truth is relative. On the contrary, the truth about happiness and liberty emerges through rational inquiry about the meaning and Nature or essence of these norms. Though Lincoln was not a professional philosopher per se, he was highly philosophical in probing the moral foundations and first principles of republican government.

In turn, Lincoln's practical wisdom or prudence consisted in his ability to apply universal moral principles under the particular circumstances of time and place. In describing this virtue, Aristotle points to the example of the Greek statesman "Pericles and men like him [who] have practical wisdom . . . can see what is good for themselves and for mankind, and these are, we believe, the qualities of men capable of managing households and states."[20] More specifically, Lincoln displayed the virtue of prudence by applying and extending the principle of equality under the constitutional, social, and political contingencies of the Civil War era.

Given his combined theoretical and practical wisdom, Lincoln may justifiably be characterized as a philosopher statesman, thus the title of this book.[21] The remainder of this chapter will reveal Lincoln's theoretical wisdom while the next will consider his practical wisdom through a case study of Emancipation Proclamation as a model of prudent statesmanship.

Just as Plato's political philosophy was written in response to the disorders of Athenian democracy and the death of Socrates, so Lincoln's noble vision of politics was articulated in response to rival proslavery interpretations of public life that rejected the principles of equality and consent as axiomatic to democracy. Indeed, the finest southern minds of the Civil War era deftly used their intellectual abilities to justify slavery and the doctrine of states' rights in defense of it. These intellectual efforts coincided with a change in southern public opinion on slavery. By the mid-nineteenth century, southern public opinion no longer viewed slavery as a necessary evil that ought to be contained and placed on a path of ultimate extinction as the Founders had hoped; but rather as a positive blessing to master, slave, and society alike that should be embraced and perpetuated indefinitely. Historians have adduced a number of reasons to

explain this change: the profitability of cotton; the dread of slave insurrec-
tions; the loss of political power in Congress; insecurity over abolition in
the British Empire; reaction against abolitionist rhetoric; southern honor
in defense of its "peculiar institution"; poor southern whites' fear of losing
their guaranteed racial supremacy over blacks.

Indeed, the new attitude toward slavery was forthrightly proclaimed
by John C. Calhoun, mastermind of the South, in a speech on February
6, 1837: "But let me not be understood as admitting even by implication
that the existing relations between the two races in the slave-holding
States is an evil,—far otherwise; I hold it to be a good, as it has thus far
proved itself to be to both. . . . [It is] instead of an evil, a good—a positive
good."[22] Calhoun was joined by other leading minds of the South like
George Fitzhugh of Virginia and James H. Hammond of South Carolina,
who provided a comprehensive defense of slavery and a corresponding
critique of free labor and free society.

Today, we take for granted that slavery and democracy are utterly incompatible. In so doing, we reveal our debt to Lincoln, whose theoretical
wisdom demonstrated their incompatibility and whose practical wisdom
put an end to the institution. However, as southerners deftly pointed
out at the time, slavery was part and parcel of the ancient republics
of Rome and Greece. Citing this historical precedent, Fitzhugh wrote:
"We do not agree with the authors of the Declaration of Independence,
that governments 'derive their just powers from the consent of the governed.' . . . All governments must originate in force, and be continued by
force. . . . The ancient republics were governed by a small class of adult
male citizens who assumed and exercised the government without the
consent of the governed. The South is governed just as those ancient
republics were."[23]

Hammond of South Carolina propounded what became known as
the "mudsill" theory of labor. In an audacious speech before the Senate
entitled "Cotton Is King," on March 5, 1858, he explained: "In all social
systems there must be a class to do the menial duties, to perform the
drudgery of life. That is, a class requiring but a low order of intellect and
but little skill. . . . It constitutes the very mud-sill of society and of political government."[24] In short, the mudsill theory maintained that every
society inevitably rested on some bottom caste to perform menial labor.
The North no less than the South possessed such an underclass. In the
South, the bottom caste was occupied by Negro slaves, but in the North
the rung was occupied by wage slaves. Central to the mudsill theory
was the belief that the position of this underclass was permanently fixed

without the possibility of social or economic mobility. Proponents of the theory went so far as to claim that the care and condition of Negro slaves in the South was superior to that of wage slaves in the North. The former, it was argued, were paternalistically cared for by their masters while the latter were abandoned to the callous fortunes of the free market. As a paternalistic extension of the family, slavery was extolled by Southern leaders as a benevolent and enlightened institution that civilized and ameliorated the savage condition of the African race.

The repudiation of equality was by no means unique to the South. Senator Pettit of Indiana, a disciple of Calhoun, referred to it as "a self-evident lie."[25] And Stephen A. Douglas, Lincoln's political nemesis from Illinois, interpreted equality as perfectly compatible with white supremacy and slavery: "I believe this government was made on the white basis. I believe it was made by white men, for the benefit of white men and their posterity for ever, and I am in favour of confining citizenship to white men, men of European birth and descent, instead of conferring it upon negroes, Indians and other inferior races."[26] Indeed, Lincoln warned that the proslavery teachings of his time had wrought a dangerous transformation in public opinion throughout the North as well as the South:

> I assert that Judge Douglas and all his friends may search the whole records of the country, and it will be a matter of great astonishment to me if they shall be able to find that one human being three years ago had ever uttered the astounding sentiment that the term "all men" in the Declaration did not include the negro. Do not let me be misunderstood. I know that more than three years ago there were men who, finding this assertion constantly in the way of their schemes to bring about the ascendancy and perpetuation of slavery, *denied the truth of it*. I know that Mr. Calhoun and all the politicians of his school denied the truth of the Declaration. I know that it ran along in the mouths of some Southern men for a period of years, ending at last in that shameful though rather forcible declaration of Pettit of Indiana, upon the floor of the United States Senate, that the Declaration of Independence was in that respect "a self-evident lie," rather than a self-evident truth.[27]

According to Lincoln, the denial of equality as a "self-evident lie" constituted a radical innovation and betrayal of the principles of the founding. "If [this] had been said in old Independence Hall, seventy-eight years ago," he observed, "the very door-keeper would have throttled the man, and thrust him into the street."[28]

The repudiation of equality culminated with the "Cornerstone speech" of Alexander Stephens, vice president of the Confederacy, on March 21, 1861, in Savannah, Georgia. Stephens triumphantly proclaimed inequality and racial supremacy as the new moral foundation of the Confederacy:

> Those ideas [of Jefferson in the Declaration], however, were fundamentally wrong. They rested upon the assumption of the equality of races. This was an error. It was a sandy foundation, and the government built upon it fell when the "storm came and the wind blew."
>
> Our new government is founded upon exactly the opposite idea; its foundations are laid, its corner-stone rests, upon the great truth that the negro is not equal to the white man; that slavery subordination to the superior race is his natural and normal condition. This, our new government, is the first, in the history of the world, based upon this great physical, philosophical, and moral truth.[29]

Stephens's defense of human inequality and white supremacy was likely derived from the "scientific" theories of the French aristocrat Count Gobineau in *The Inequality of Human Races*, a work that attributed racial mixing as the cause of the downfall of every great civilization throughout history.[30] Partially translated into English in 1856, *The Inequality of Human Races* was subsequently used as a propaganda tool by the Confederacy to persuade London and Europe of the "great, physical, philosophical and moral truth" of human inequality.

As a philosopher statesman, Lincoln intellectually engaged his proslavery rivals in a battle of ideas and responded to them in kind. William Herndon noted that "George Fitzhugh's *Sociology for the South*, which attacked the mobility of market societies as an 'abyss of misery and penury,' succeeded in arousing 'the ire of Lincoln more than most proslavery books.'"[31] In response, Lincoln sought to vindicate "the ancient faith" of the Declaration against the radical innovation of proslavery doctrines. Indeed, he viewed the debate over slavery as a debate over the very moral foundations of the American regime and its future as a free or slaveholding republic: "It is equally impossible to not see that that common object [of proslavery opinion] is to subvert, in the public mind, and in practical administration our old and only standard of free government, that 'all men are created equal,' and to substitute for it some different standard. What that substitute is to be is not difficult to perceive. It is to deny the equality of men, and to assert the natural, moral, and religious right of one class to enslave another."[32]

Lincoln's grasp and articulation of the correlative relationship between equality, consent, and democracy is crucial to his theoretical wisdom.[33] He clearly revealed how these three principles were logically related to each other. Just as there are first principles or axioms in the realm of logic (for example, the law of noncontradiction) that cannot be proved but are presupposed in all further reasoning, so Lincoln noted that the self-evident truth of equal consent is a starting point or principle for all further reasoning and reflection about politics and democracy.[34] Equality was the "central idea" of the American regime and "the father of all moral principle."[35] In 1859, he explained:

> One would start with great confidence that he could convince any sane child that the simpler propositions of Euclid are true; but, nevertheless, he would fail, utterly, with one who should deny the definitions and axioms. The principles of Jefferson are the definitions and axioms of free society. And yet they are denied, and evaded, with no small show of success. One dashingly calls them "glittering generalities"; another bluntly calls them "self evident lies"; and still others insidiously argue that they apply only to "superior races."[36]

In view of the proslavery philosophy of the time, Lincoln was in earnest when he declared: "But soberly, it is now no child's play to save the principles of Jefferson from total overthrow in this nation."[37]

Lincoln's philosophical defense of equality as a first principle of self-government relied on the argument from definition, which, according to Richard M. Weaver, "includes all arguments from the nature of a thing. Whether the genus is an already recognized convention, or whether it is defined at the moment by the orator or whether it is left to be inferred from the aggregate of its species, the argument has a single postulate. The postulate is that there exist classes which are determinate and therefore predicable. . . . Whatever is a member of the class will accordingly have the class attributes."[38]

Philosophically, Lincoln understood equality in terms of our common humanity—that is, the common properties or Nature of human beings as a class or species in contrast to the irrationality of beasts and the perfect rationality of God. The unalienable right to self-governance followed from this common humanity. For "if the negro is a man," Lincoln rhetorically asked, "is it not to that extent, a total destruction of self-government, to say that he too shall not govern *himself*?"[39] Relying on the argument from definition, he affirmed the common humanity of the African American against the dehumanizing teachings of the Democratic Party:

The Republicans inculcate, with whatever ability they can, that the Negro is a man, that his bondage is cruelly wrong, and that the field of his oppression ought not to be enlarged. The Democrats deny his manhood; deny, or dwarf to insignificance, the wrong of his bondage; so far as possible crush all sympathy for him, and cultivate and excite hatred and disgust against him; compliment themselves as Union-savers for doing so; and call the indefinite outspreading of his bondage "a sacred right of self-government."

In Euclidean fashion, Lincoln then derived consent from the axiom of the equality. In the following passage from Peoria, October 16, 1854, he tersely describes consent and equality as logical corollaries of democracy:

The doctrine of self-government is right—absolutely and eternally right—but it has no just application, as here attempted. Or perhaps I should rather say that whether it has such just application depends upon whether a negro is *not* or *is* a man. If he is *not* a man, why in that case, he who *is* a man may, as a matter of self-government, do just as he pleases with him. But if the negro *is* a man, is it not to that extent, a total destruction of self-government, to say that he too shall not govern *himself*? When the white man governs himself that is self-government; but when he governs himself, and also governs *another* man, that is *more* than self-government—that is despotism. If the negro is a *man*, why then my ancient faith teaches me that "all men are created equal;" and that there can be no moral right in connection with one man's making a slave of another.[40]

Practically speaking, the denial of equality involved not only the rejection of the slave's equal dignity, but also the master's equal depravity. In a word, the equal dignity and depravity of human nature were both relevant to democracy. On the one hand, all human beings are equal in their common dignity as rational and free beings who participate in the natural law.[41] On the other hand, they are equal in their common depravity as fallible beings prone to selfish interests and the abuse of power. Patriot Sam Adams expressed this truism about our common humanity at the time of the Revolution: "The Legislature has no right to absolute arbitrary power over the lives and fortunes of the people: Nor can mortals assume a prerogative, not only too high for men, but for Angels; and therefore reserved for the exercise of the Deity alone."[42] In the twentieth century, American theologian, Reinhold Niebuhr put it this way: "Man's capacity for justice makes democracy possible; but man's inclination to injustice makes democracy necessary."[43]

Given the common dignity and depravity of human nature, no one is entitled to absolute rule over another without that other's consent. In the same Peoria speech of 1854, Lincoln explained: "no man is good enough to govern another man, *without that other's consent.* I say this is the leading principle—the sheet anchor of American republicanism."[44] To be sure, the conclusion that "no man is good enough to govern another man, without that other's consent"[45] follows from the premise that all human beings are equally fallible and prone to abuse power. Consequently, no one can be entrusted with absolute power, not even the wisest and most virtuous, which is tantamount to governing another without another's consent. Lincoln humorously pointed to man's inclination for selfishness in his seventh and last debate with Douglas at Alton, when he observed: "The Bible says somewhere that we are desperately selfish. I think we would have discovered that fact without the Bible."[46]

To govern another without his or her consent is to rule another absolutely. It is to treat another as less than fully human by denying one the use of his or her intellect and free moral agency in the governing of oneself. Lincoln tersely explained how claims to govern another without consent rested on a fundamental assertion of inequality in kind whereby some were elevated to the status of godlike supremacy and others were debased to the level of a beast. He correctly recognized that the crux of proslavery arguments depended on the dehumanization of the African race. In denying the African American's common humanity, Stephen Douglas and others were "blowing out the moral lights around us; teaching that the negro is no longer a man but a brute; that the Declaration has nothing to do with him; that he ranks with the crocodile and the reptile; that man, with body and soul, is a matter of dollars and cents."[47] Lincoln's reference to how slavery debased human beings to a matter of "dollars and cents" shows his realistic appreciation of the extent to which financial self-interest may bias moral judgment in the master's determination of his slave's dignity and common humanity.

Because equality also denotes a symmetric relationship between two things, any principle used to justify the mastery of some over others could likewise be turned around to justify one's own enslavement. Lincoln expressed this symmetrical argument in Euclidean terms as well:

If A. can prove, however conclusively, that he may, of right, enslave B.
—why may not B. snatch the same argument, and prove equally, that

he may enslave A?—You say A. is white, and B. is black. It is *color*, then; the lighter, having the right to enslave the darker? Take care. By this rule, you are to be slave to the first man you meet, with a fairer skin than your own.

You do not mean *color* exactly?—You mean the whites are *intellectually* the superiors of the blacks, and, therefore have the right to enslave them? Take care again. By this rule, you are to be slave to the first man you meet, with an intellect superior to your own.

But, say you, it is a question of *interest*; and, if you can make it your *interest*, you have the right to enslave another. Very well. And if he can make it his interest, he has the right to enslave you.[48]

Notably, the above argument does not mention race as a principle that would validate slavery. Consistent with the argument from definition, the omission suggests that Lincoln did not view race as a defining characteristic of our common humanity. Race is incidental, not essential to what it means to be a human being. While Lincoln's argument mentions differences in intelligence, color, and interest, these inequalities are differences in degree between members of the same species, not differences in kind that would justify a title to absolute rule to govern another without his consent. Nearly a half century earlier, in his letter to Henri Gregoire of February 25, 1809, Jefferson concisely explained how differences in degree do not entitle the superior individual to a political mastery over another: "Because Sir Isaac Newton was superior to others in understanding, he was not therefore lord of the person or property of others."[49]

In addition to the argument from definition based on our common humanity and the symmetrical argument based on degree and kind, Lincoln invoked the biblical precept of the "Golden Rule" of Matthew 7:12, to "do unto others," as axiomatic to democracy: "As I would not be a *slave*, so I would not be a *master*. This expresses my idea of democracy. Whatever differs from this, to the extent of the difference, is no democracy."[50] The biblical principle of "do unto others" can also be expressed in terms of Kant's secular imperative to treat each person as an end in himself or herself, rather than as a means to something else. Slavery violates this principle of ends by treating other human beings as purely instrumental to the interests of the master. In a similar vein, Lincoln noted, "The democracy of to-day hold the *liberty* of one man to be absolutely nothing, when in conflict with another man's right of *property*. Republicans, on the contrary, are for both the *man* and the *dollar*; but in cases of conflict, the man *before* the dollar."[51]

Probing the ultimate moral foundations of public policy, Lincoln argued that proslavery theology was philosophically indistinguishable in principle from the doctrine of the divine rights of kings—the very antithesis of the Founders' republicanism. The principle of despotism was the same whether it came from a king over his subjects or a master over his slave: both claimed an absolute rule over another by denying the subject or the slave consent. Lincoln thus explained: "Those arguments that are made, that the inferior race are to be treated with as much allowance as they are capable of enjoying; that as much is to be done for them as their condition will allow. What are these arguments? They are the arguments that kings have made for enslaving the people in all ages of the world."[52] By this argument, "the King is to do just as he pleases with his white subjects, being responsible to God alone. By the former the white man is to do just as he pleases with his black slaves, beings responsible to God alone. The two things are precisely alike."[53] At bottom, the principle of divine right and slavery were the same: both types of rule entitle one to an absolute mastery of another without that other's consent. A philosophically consistent and coherent understanding of equality at the time of the Revolution thus required a repudiation of a master's claim to divine right in the form of racial superiority over the slave.

The intellectual battle over slavery was also waged in the pulpit. As Lincoln ironically observed in the Second Inaugural, "both [North and South] read the same Bible, and pray to the same God; and each invokes His aid against the other."[54] The teaching of Frederick Ross, a Presbyterian minister from Alabama, whose work *Slavery Ordained of God* Lincoln had read and rebutted, was characteristic of the South's proslavery theology. Ross proclaimed that "the relation of master and slave is not sin" and that "slavery [is] found to be in absolute harmony with the word of God." In sum, the South appealed to the following passages from the Bible in support of its proslavery theology: "Let every soul be subject unto higher powers. For there is no power but of God: the powers that be are ordained off God" (Romans 13:1); "Servants, be obedient to them that are your masters according to the flesh, with fear and trembling, in singleness of your heart, as unto Christ" (Ephesians 6:5–9); and "If you buy a Hebrew servant, he is to serve you for six years" (Exodus 21:2–5).[55]

One of the most commonly accepted biblical justifications in defense of slavery was based on a peculiar interpretation of Genesis 9:18–27, also known as "the Curse of Ham." Genesis 9 tells of an incident between Noah and his three sons, Ham, Japheth, and Shem. Some interpreted the three sons as the progenitors of the three races of humanity. Ham behaves inappropriately, and God not only chastises him for his impudence but also curses his descendants by making them servants of his brothers' descendants. Although scripture does not identify Ham or his descendants with a specific race, proslavery apologists interpreted God's retribution as sanctioning the perpetual enslavement of the African race. Indeed, in an 1859 speech, Jefferson Davis, future president of the Confederacy, invoked the divine authority of Genesis 9 as unanswerable proof that God ordained the servitude of the entire African race: "It is enough for us that the Creator, speaking through the inspired lips of Noah, declared that the destiny of all three races of men. Around and about us is the remarkable fulfillment of the prophecy, the execution of the decree, and the justification of the literal construction of the text."[56] Thus, on the eve of the Civil War, the future president of the Confederacy, Jefferson Davis, and the future vice president, Alexander Stephens, appealed respectively to the Bible and science in defense of slavery.

Given the Bible's moral authority in nineteenth-century America, the South's exploitation of it to justify slavery required a response. Thus, Lincoln's wisdom comes to light not only in his understanding of Euclidean logic, but also in his profound knowledge of the Bible in vindicating self-government against the claims of proslavery theology. In a previous work, *Abraham Lincoln's Political Faith*, I refer to Lincoln's noble vision of democratic government as biblical republicanism.[57] As an ultimate moral justification of democracy, biblical republicanism combined the traditions of unassisted reason, revelation in the Bible, and the republican teachings of the Founders on ordered liberty, especially as interpreted by Whigs like Joseph Story, Daniel Webster, and Henry Clay. The "ancient faith" of the Declaration constituted the creed of biblical republicanism.

According to Lincoln, the principles of the Declaration were both known by reason and confirmed by the teachings of the Christian faith. These principles serve as a universal normative standard, a rule and measure, to judge and guide the regime from generation to generation. Testifying to the potential harmony between faith and reason in providing political wisdom, the mature Lincoln remarked to his Springfield friend Joshua Speed: "take all of this book [the Bible] upon reason that you can, and the balance on faith, and you will live and die a happier and better man."[58] Consistent with this understanding, Lincoln's vision of equality relied on the complementary teachings of republicanism and revelation to vindicate self-government. The self-evident truth of equality was not only known by reason and affirmed by Euclidean logic; it was also confirmed by the biblical teaching of Genesis 1:27, of "man created in the image of

God." Thus, at Lewiston, Lincoln praised the "wise statesmanship" of the Founders for affirming the equal dignity of all human beings created in the image of God. A full quotation is warranted:

> This was their majestic interpretation of the economy of the Universe. This was their lofty, and wise, and noble understanding of the justice of the Creator to His creatures. [Applause.] Yes, gentlemen, to *all* His creatures, to the whole great family of man. In their enlightened belief, nothing stamped with the Divine image and likeness was sent into the world to be trodden on, and degraded, and imbruted by its fellows. They grasped not only the whole race of man then living, but they reached forward and seized upon the farthest posterity. They erected a beacon to guide their children and their children's children, and the countless myriads who should inhabit the earth in other ages. Wise statesmen as they were, they knew the tendency of prosperity to breed tyrants, and so they established these great self-evident truths, that when in the distant future some man, some faction, some interest, should set up the doctrine that none but rich men, or none but white men, were entitled to life, liberty and the pursuit of happiness, their posterity might look up again to the Declaration of Independence and take courage to renew the battle which their fathers began—so that truth, and justice, and mercy, and all the humane and Christian virtues might not be extinguished from the land; so that no man would hereafter dare to limit and circumscribe the great principles on which the temple of liberty was being built.[59]

Here Lincoln powerfully affirms the timeless truths of the Declaration as inclusive to all human beings. He consistently identifies equality with a principle of justice that enjoins recognition of each person's dignity as rational and free beings and the corresponding government guarantee of each person to the right to rise and to enjoy the fruits of his or her own labor.

Lincoln's biblical wisdom rebutted proslavery theology on its own grounds, appealing to the word and spirit of the Bible against human servitude. In sum, he pointed to the following biblical precepts against slavery: the teaching that man is created in the image of God (Genesis 1:27); the Golden Rule to do unto others (Matthew 7:12); the "Great Commandment" to love God and one's neighbor with all one's heart (Matthew 22:37–40); and labor as a common curse of entire human race (Genesis 3:19). As seen, Lincoln invoked the teaching of Genesis 1:27, that man is created in the image of God, when he declared that "nothing stamped with the Divine image and likeness was sent into the world to be trodden on, and degraded, and imbruted by its fellows."[60] He appealed to the Great Commandment in Matthew 22:37–40 when he stated, "'Give to him that is needy' is the Christian rule of charity; but Take from him that is needy is the rule of slavery."[61] And, applying the Golden Rule, he said: "This is a world of compensations and he who would *be* no slave, must consent to *have* no slave. Those who deny freedom to others, deserve it not for themselves; and, under a just God, can not long retain it."[62] His terse definition of democracy, "As I would not be a slave, so I would not be a master,"[63] was likewise an expression of the Golden Rule.

Lincoln's letter to a group of northern Baptist ministers, May 30, 1864, integrates many of his biblical arguments against proslavery theology:

To read in the Bible, as the word of God himself, that "In the sweat of *thy* face shalt thou eat bread,["] [Genesis 3:19] and to preach therefrom that, "In the sweat of *other mans* faces shalt thou eat bread," to my mind can scarcely be reconciled with honest sincerity. When brought to my final reckoning, may I have to answer for robbing no man of his goods; yet more tolerable even this, than for robbing one of himself, and all that was his. When, a year or two ago, those professedly holy men of the South, met in the semblance of prayer and devotion, and, in the name of Him who said "As ye would all men should do unto you, do ye even so unto them" [Matthew 7:12] appealed to the christian world to aid them in doing to a whole race of men, as they would have no man do unto themselves, to my thinking, they contemned and insulted God and His church, far more than did Satan when he tempted the Saviour with the Kingdoms of the earth [Matthew 4]. The devils attempt was no more false, and far less hypocritical. But let me forbear, remembering it is also written "Judge not, lest ye be judged" [Matthew 7:1].[64]

Lincoln's reference to those "professedly holy men of the South"[65] was likely a scathing jab at the Southern Presbyterian Church, which had recently endorsed the moral and religious right to slavery the same year: "we hesitate not to affirm that it is the peculiar mission of the Southern Church to conserve the institution of slavery, and make it a blessing to master and slave."[66] Lincoln further condemns slavery by equating it with robbery of one's goods and oneself.

Recalling Matthew 4, Lincoln compares southern ministers' manipulation of the Bible to Satan's twisting of scripture to tempt Christ in the desert: "If you are the son of God," he said, "throw yourself down; for scripture says: 'He has given his angels orders about you, and they will carry you in their arms in case you trip over a stone.'" The comparison provides a timeless lesson about the potential use and abuse of scripture in politics. Jesus responded to Satan's exploitation of the Bible not by rejecting or supplanting its authority, but by providing an alternative interpretation of scripture from the book of Deuteronomy: "Scripture also says, 'Do not put the Lord your God to the test.'" Following Jesus's own example, Lincoln upholds the authority of the Bible while warning against its exploitation for wicked ends. After this scornful reply, he tempers his above remarks with Christ's injunction in Matthew 7:1 "Judge not, lest ye be judged." Here as elsewhere, we see how in replying to the Baptist minister, Lincoln combined seemingly opposite traits, by being righteous without being self-righteous.

Lincoln's philosophical statesmanship, his comprehensive vision of man and government, involved not only a negative critique of slavery, but also a positive prescription of free labor and free society. The principles of the Declaration not only affirmed our common humanity, they also guaranteed a right to property, economic liberty, and social mobility. Like the Founders, he saw political and economic freedom as intertwined. Political liberty, equality, and consent had an economic counterpart. The inalienable right to liberty in the Declaration guaranteed a right to property in oneself and a corresponding right to enjoy the fruits of one's labor without having them stolen by another. "The legitimate object of government," Lincoln explained, "is to do for a community of people whatever they need to have done, but cannot do at all, or cannot so well do, for themselves in their separate and individual capacities. In all that the people can individually do well for themselves, government ought not to interfere."[67] Lincoln's vision of government thus eschews both a strict libertarianism that distrusts, in principle, any positive role of government in securing the common good beyond the minimalist state; and a progressivism that has no principled limit to government intervention, thereby leading to "the nanny state." Government has a legitimate yet limited purpose in protecting inalienable rights, providing ladders of opportunity, and in promoting the conditions of freedom. Government empowers individuals to do things for themselves, to develop their abilities and to use them in the service of the common good rather than being dependent upon the state or privately self-absorbed.

The founding principles of the regime included a right to rise for all human beings. In a democratic society of equals, a black man was entitled to the same opportunity of advancement as a white man. Lincoln thus declared:

"I want every man to have the chance—and I believe a black man is entitled to it—in which he *can* better his condition—when he may look forward and hope to be a hired laborer this year and the next, work for himself afterward, and finally to hire men to work for him! That is the true system."[68]

As with his vindication of equality and republican government, Lincoln's moral justification for free labor drew from the traditions of reason, revelation, and the Founders' republicanism. As a philosopher statesman, he articulated a theology of labor whereby God ordained "the burden of work, the individual's duty to engage in it, and the moral right to enjoy the fruits of his labor."[69] Throughout his public life, he consistently invoked Genesis 3:19 to confirm the inalienable right to enjoy the fruits of one's labor. An early speech on the tariff, dated December 1, 1847, is exemplary of this theology of labor in combining biblical and republican teachings on free labor and the right to rise:

> In the early days of the world, the Almighty said to the first of our race "In the sweat of thy face shalt thou eat bread" [Genesis 3:19]; and since then, if we except the *light* and the *air* of heaven, no good thing has been, or can be enjoyed by us, without having first cost labour. And, inasmuch [as] most good things are produced by labour, it follows that [all] such things of right belong to those whose labour has produced them. But it has so happened in all ages of the world, that *some* have laboured, and *others* have, without labour, enjoyed a large proportion of the fruits. This is wrong, and should not continue. To [secure] to each labourer the whole product of his labour, or as nearly as possible, is a most worthy object of any good government.[70] (emphasis added)

Written more than a decade before the Civil War, this passage reveals the consistency of Lincoln's view of free labor and its centrality to his vision of democratic government. As a consequence of sin, labor was divinely ordained as the universal predicament of human nature. Government must take its bearings from this moral imperative in securing "to each labourer the whole product of his labour, or as nearly as possible."

Lincoln pitted Genesis 3:19 against the biblical defense of slavery in Genesis 9, "the Curse of Ham" cited above by Jefferson Davis. In a fragment on free labor in 1859, he explained: "As Labor is the common *burthen* of our race, so the effort of *some* to shift their share of the burthen on to the shoulders of *others*, is the great, durable, curse of the race. Originally a curse for transgression upon the whole race, when, as by slavery, it is concentrated on a part only, it becomes the double-refined curse of God upon his creatures."[71]

In line with his view of the potential harmony between reason and revelation, Lincoln further appealed to natural theology or unassisted reason in confirmation of the biblical teaching of Genesis 3:19 on free labor. "If anything can be proved by natural theology," he explained, "it is that slavery is morally wrong. God gave man a mouth to receive bread, hands to feed it, and his hand has a right to carry bread to his mouth without controversy."[72] Lincoln's reference to natural theology was likely based on William Paley's book *Natural Theology*, which he had read around the same time it appears in his speeches and writings in 1859. Paley famously referred to God as a divine watchmaker. *Natural Theology* affirmed God's existence and wisdom without recourse to authority through reasonable inference of the manifest contrivance, design, and purpose in Nature. In sum, Paley provided an enlightenment version of Aquinas's five cosmological ways to consider the existence of God as the first cause of an ordered universe. Paley explains: "There cannot be design without a designer; contrivance without a contriver; order without choice; arrangement, without any thing capable of arranging. . . . Arrangement, disposition of parts, subserviency of means to an end, relation of instruments to an use, imply the presence of intelligence and mind."[73] Sources corroborate that Lincoln read Paley's *Natural Theology* "in the years preceding his election to the Presidency."[74] Indeed, his allusions to natural theology coincide within this time frame.

For example, in his address before the Wisconsin State Agricultural Society, 1859, Lincoln vindicated free labor against the mudsill theory by humorously appealing to natural theology. Notably, his vision of free labor and free society in this speech includes universal education as a crucial ladder of opportunity:

> Free labor argues that as the Author of man makes every individual with one head and one pair of hands, it was probably intended that heads and hands should cooperate as friends, and that that particular head should direct and control that pair of hands. As each man has one mouth to be fed, and one pair of hands to furnish food, it was probably intended that that particular pair of hands should feed that particular mouth—that each head is the natural guardian, director, and protector of the mouth and inseparably connected with it; and that being so, every head should be cultivated and improved by whatever will add to its capacity for performing its charge. In one word, free labor insists on universal education.[75]

Lincoln's theology of labor is also articulated in his two lectures on discovery and invention, 1859, which were written around the time of his candidacy for the Republican Party. These lectures provided a comprehensive account of the genealogy of discovery and invention from creation to Lincoln's own time: "Man is not the only animal who labors; but he is the only one who *improves* his workmanship. This improvement, he effects by *Discoveries*, and *Inventions*. His first important discovery was the fact that he was naked; and his first invention was the fig-leaf-apron. This simple article—the apron—made of leaves, seems to have been the origin of *clothing*—the one thing for which nearly half of the toil and care of the human race has ever since been expended."[76] Throughout, Lincoln copiously references the Bible in support of his genealogy. The ability to improve on labor through discovery and invention was a defining characteristic of human nature ordained by God. Revealing throughout history how "necessity served humanity as the mother of invention," Lincoln recounted the innovation of tools, transportation, food, agriculture, wind, water, and steam power. Whether or not one is ultimately persuaded by this account, it speaks volumes about Lincoln's philosophical cast of mind that on the eve of the critical election of 1860 in defense of free labor, he speculated both philosophically and theologically about the origins and development of human industry and enterprise.

In addition to the Bible and natural theology, Lincoln also drew on the republican teachings of the Founders in defense of free labor. He emphasized that popular government by definition was incompatible with feudal hierarchies and fixed conditions of labor to the land—as in the case of both European serfdom and American slavery. Indeed, the British government's violation of property rights and its stifling of the social, political, and economic opportunities of the colonists were fundamental grievances justifying the Revolution. As James Otis, one of the leading spokesmen for the rights of the North American colonies against the British, noted in 1764, "no man can take my property from me without my consent: if he does, he deprives me of my liberty and makes me a slave. . . . Now what liberty can there be, where property is taken away without consent? "[77] Otis's belief that "white and black" subjects were entitled to the rights of life, liberty, and property reveals the extent to which Lincoln's statesmanship should be viewed as a continuation and extension of the founding rather than a radical innovation or transformation of it. In view of the relationship between economic and political liberty, it is telling that the final draft of the Emancipation Proclamation included an injunction to "labor faithfully for reasonable wages."[78]

A just government must recognize the inalienable right of property, thereby guaranteeing what Gabor Boritt has aptly described as "the right to rise" in his important work *Abraham Lincoln and the Economics of the American Dream.*[79] A truly free society is a dynamic one where individuals may improve their condition on the basis of talent and ability rather than having their lot permanently fixed by accidents of birth. Equality logically dictates that neither undue burdens be imposed on some nor unmerited privileges on others simply because of their birth, as was the case with divine right monarchy and the feudal hierarchies of Europe. Slavery and serfdom were both caste systems that prevented talented individuals from rising above the station of their birth. Depriving another of the fruits of his or her labor would, in effect, be "a right to absolute arbitrary power over the lives and fortunes" of another, as Sam Adams explained at the time of the Revolution.[80]

As Harry Jaffa has profoundly shown, Lincoln's defense of the right to rise was based on the understanding of equality as a principle of fairness or distributive justice.[81] All human beings should have an equal opportunity to compete in the race of life for status, rewards, and advancement. In this competition, the privileges and burdens of citizenship should be distributed equally regardless of race, creed, gender or color. Though government should not interfere in this race by imposing undue burdens on one group or by privileging another, Lincoln nonetheless believed that it had a positive function in providing certain ladders of opportunity to assist poor and disadvantaged citizens in rising up. In sum, Lincoln viewed equality as a principle of justice that included four related guarantees: (1) equality of rights; (2) equal consent; (3) equality before the law; and (4) equal opportunity—the "right to rise."[82]

Throughout his public life, Lincoln associated equality of opportunity with "universal education." In March 9, 1832, in his first run for public office he stated:

> Upon the subject of education, not presuming to dictate any plan or system of respecting it, I can only say that I view it as the most important subject which we as a people can be engaged in. That every man receive at least, a moderate education, and thereby be enabled to read the histories of his own and other countries, by which he may duly appreciate the value of our free institutions, appears to be an object of vital importance, even on this account alone, to say nothing of the advantages and satisfaction to be derived from all being able to read the scriptures and other works, both of a religious and moral nature, for themselves.[83]

Meaningful equality of opportunity thus requires a civic education, allowing the educated "to appreciate the values of our free institutions" as well as receive moral and religious instruction.

More than three decades later, in his Proclamation of Amnesty and Reconstruction, December 8, 1863, Lincoln reaffirmed the importance of providing educational opportunities to the freedmen: "And I do further proclaim, declare, and make known that any provision which may be adopted by such State government in relation to the freed people of such State, which shall recognize and declare their permanent freedom, provide for their education, and which may yet be consistent, as a temporary arrangement, with their present condition as a laboring, landless, and homeless class, will not be objected to by the national Executive."[84]

In defending free labor and equality of opportunity, Lincoln provided one of the most enduring expressions of the American Dream. This vision was highly consistent with Franklin's earlier articulation of the American Dream in his revealing essay addressed to "Those who would Remove to America" in 1784. Written as a republican manifesto to dispel European misconceptions about the New World, this remarkable letter provides a window into America's self-understanding of equality of opportunity at the time of the founding from the quintessential American:

> Much less is it adviseable for a Person to go [to America] who has no other Quality to recommend him but his Birth. In Europe it has indeed its Value, but it is a Commodity that cannot be carried to a worse Market than to America, where People do not enquire concerning a Stranger, *What is he?* But *What can he do?* If he has any useful Art, he is welcome and if he exercises it and behaves well, he will be respected by all that know him; but a mere man of Quality, who on that Account wants to live upon the Public, by some Office or Salary, will be despis'd and disregarded. The Husbandman is in honor there, & even the Mechanic, because their Employments are useful.[85]

Franklin's description of the American people's belief in the dignity of work as patterned on their belief in God as the Divine craftsman of creation reveals the extent to which Lincoln's theology of labor was building upon the republican teachings of the Founders.[86] "The People have a Saying," Franklin noted, "that God Almighty himself [is] a Mechanic, the greatest in the Universe; and [that] he is respected and admired more for the Variety, Ingenuity and Utility of his Handiworks, than for the Antiquity of his Family."[87]

In defending the American Dream, Lincoln, like Franklin, testified to his own experience as self-made man as proof that opportunity and advancement were still possible in a free society: "We know, Southern men declare that their slaves are better off than hired laborers amongst us. How little they *know*, whereof they *speak*! There is no permanent class of hired laborers amongst us. Twentyfive years ago, I was a hired laborer. The hired laborer of yesterday, labors on his own account to-day; and will hire others to labor for him to-morrow. Advancement—improvement in condition—is the order of things in a society of equals."[88] Contrary to the mudsill theory's belief that labor was permanently fixed, Lincoln explained, "The prudent, penniless beginner in the world, labors for wages awhile, saves a surplus with which to buy tools or land, for himself; then labors on his own account another while, and at length hires another new beginner to help him. This, say its advocates, is *free* labor—the just and generous, and prosperous system, which opens the way for all—gives hope to all, and energy, and progress, and improvement of condition to all."[89]

Ever the student of human nature, Lincoln explains that free labor offers the proper motivation of hope for individual striving, advancement, and improvement. The promise of reward for hard work is a powerful incentive and spur to progress:

> Free labor has the inspiration of hope; pure slavery has no hope. The power of hope upon human exertion, and happiness, is wonderful. The slave-master himself has a conception of it; and hence the system of *tasks* among slaves. The slave whom you can not drive with the lash to break seventy-five pounds of hemp in a day, if you will task him to break a hundred, and promise him pay for all he does over, he will break you a hundred and fifty. You have substituted *hope*, for the *rod*. And yet perhaps it does not occur to you, that to the extent of your gain in the case, you have given up the slave system, and adopted the free system of labor.[90]

In his annual message to Congress on December 3, 1861, Lincoln profoundly delved into the relationship between labor and popular government. The subordination of labor to capital undermines the principles of consent and equality. It degrades labor to a tool or possession that has no regard for the dignity of the laborer—that is, the free will, intelligence, and enterprise of the laborer. Lincoln argued that capital is the fruit of labor, not its permanent master. As philosopher statesman, he publicly articulated what is known as the labor theory of value, which regards labor as "the prior engine of human activity."[91]

It is assumed that labor is available only in connexion with capital; that nobody labors unless somebody else, owning capital, somehow by the use of it, induces him to labor. This assumed, it is next considered whether it is best that capital shall *hire* laborers, and thus induce them to work by their own consent, or *buy* them, and drive them to it without their consent. Having proceeded so far, it is naturally concluded that all laborers are either *hired* laborers, or what we call slaves. And further it is assumed that whoever is once a hired laborer, is fixed in that condition for life. Now, there is no such relation between capital and labor as assumed; nor is there any such thing as a free man being fixed for life in the condition of a hired laborer. Both these assumptions are false, and all inferences from them are groundless. Labor is prior to, and independent of, capital. Capital is only the fruit of labor, and could never have existed if labor had not first existed. Labor is the superior of capital, and deserves much the higher consideration.[92]

Lincoln's defense of the right to strike, without which free labor would be meaningless, followed from his view of the priority of labor over capital: "And I am glad to know that there is a system of labor where the laborer can strike if he wants to! I would to God that such a system prevailed all over the world."[93]

Contrary to both Marxists, who envisioned the ultimate destruction of the bourgeois class, and southern mudsill theorists, who preached the necessary subordination of labor to capital, Lincoln's "economic philosophy meant that labor and capital should work together rather than in conflict" or exploitation.[94] Free labor meant that capital and labor could bargain freely over wages. In effect, the denial of the right to strike was a denial of the laborer's right of equal consent. Without such a right, the condition of labor would be permanently fixed and completely subject to the whims of capital. Though a terrible scourge to the African race, slavery was also a threat to free society and free labor everywhere. Lincoln explained that to the extent that the principle of slavery is accepted as legitimate "white free labor that *can* strike will give way to slave labor that *cannot!*"[95] He thus denounced the "effort to place *capital* on an equal footing with, if not above *labor*, in the structure of government."[96]

Finally, because the Civil War was at once a constitutional and moral struggle, Lincoln's wisdom is also displayed in his critique of secession as incompatible with the very Nature of democratic government. Like his defense of equality, Lincoln's refutation of secession relied on Euclidean arguments from definition. The very Nature of majority rule excluded the idea of secession: "If the minority will not acquiesce, the majority must, or the government will cease. There is no other alternative; for continuing the government is acquiescence on one side of the other."[97]

Like Hamilton in the *Federalist Papers*, Lincoln argued that popular governments, by their very Nature, tended to vacillate between the extremes of tyranny and anarchy.[98] In establishing a Constitution of ordered liberty, the Founders sought to avoid these extremes. Relying on the argument of definition, Lincoln thus identified "the central idea of secession as "the essence of anarchy." He explained that "a majority, held in restraint by constitutional checks, and limitations, and always changing easily, with deliberate changes of popular opinions and sentiments, is the only true sovereign of a free people. Whoever rejects it, does, of necessity, fly to anarchy or to despotism. Unanimity is impossible; the rule of a minority, as a permanent arrangement, is wholly inadmissable; so that, rejecting the majority principle, anarchy, or despotism in some form, is all that is left."[99] To allow a minority to set aside the will of a constitutionally elected majority and to dissolve the government without that majority's consent undermines the very essence or Nature of popular government.

Lincoln's argument from the Nature of the American Union was yet another example of how he used the argument from definition to rebut secession. By definition, the Constitution of 1787 created a "more perfect Union" to remedy the defects of the preceding government under the Articles of Confederation. Part of this more perfect Union included the "vital element of perpetuity." "Perpetuity is implied, if not expressed, in the fundamental law of all national governments."[100] To allow a state to unilaterally withdraw from the Union violated the principle of perpetuity and was therefore incompatible with the more perfect Union intended by the Founders.

It bears repeating that for Lincoln, preserving the Union meant preserving the founding principles for which it stood—namely, those principles enshrined in the Declaration. The inseparability of liberty and Union was a fundamental tenet of Whig and Republican Party ideology made famous by Daniel Webster in his reply to Hayne: "Liberty and Union, now and forever, one and inseparable." Indeed, the Republican Party had reaffirmed the principles of the Declaration in its 1860 platform. Notably, the platform further stated that the principles of the Declaration are "embodied in the Federal Constitution," thereby testifying to Lincoln and the Republican Party's view that the Declaration had a constitutional status as well as a moral status.

Moreover, the platform speaks to Lincoln and the Republican Party's self-understanding as the legitimate heirs of the Founders in regard to the policy of restricting slavery and placing it on a course of ultimate extinction. Contrary to Taney's innovative ruling in *Dred Scott* that the Constitution guaranteed a national right to property in a slavery, Article 8 of the Republican platform declares: "That the normal condition of all the territory of the United States is that of freedom: That, as our Republican fathers, when they had abolished slavery in all our national territory, ordained that 'no persons should be deprived of life, liberty or property without due process of law,' it becomes our duty, by legislation, whenever such legislation is necessary, to maintain this provision of the Constitution against all attempts to violate it; and we deny the authority of Congress, of a territorial legislature, or of any individuals, to give legal existence to slavery in any territory of the United States."[101]

Lincoln succinctly expressed his moral vision of the Union in his brief but revealing back-to-back speeches at Trenton, New Jersey, on February 21 and at Independence Hall on February 22, 1861, en route to his inauguration. The combined circumstances of the patriotic venue and the impending political crisis seemed to have prompted his cogent articulation about the meaning and ends of the American regime. Reflecting on the legacy of George Washington and the founding, Lincoln declared at Trenton: "I am exceedingly anxious that that thing which they struggled for; that something even more than National Independence; that something that held out a great promise to all the people of the world to all time to come; I am exceedingly anxious that this Union, the Constitution, and the liberties of the people shall be perpetuated in accordance with the original idea for which that struggle was made."[102] As noted, Lincoln's reference to the "original idea" of the Revolution was a reference to the founding principle of equality, "the father of all moral principle" that he likened to the "apple of gold" in the book of Proverbs.

In a similar vein, at Independence Hall a day later, Lincoln clearly reaffirmed the moral ends that would guide his presidential statesmanship:

> I have often pondered over the dangers which were incurred by the men who assembled here and adopted that Declaration of Independence—I have pondered over the toils that were endured by the officers and soldiers of the army, who achieved that Independence. I have often inquired of myself, what great principle or idea it was that kept this Confederacy so long together. It was not the mere matter of the separation of the colonies from the mother

land; but something in that Declaration giving liberty, not alone to the people of this country, but hope to the world for all future time. It was that which gave promise that in due time the weights should be lifted from the shoulders of all men, and that *all* should have an equal chance. This is the sentiment embodied in that Declaration of Independence.[103]

Delivered on the eve of secession, the two speeches at Trenton and Independence Hall vividly reveal Lincoln's moral vision of the Union and the American Dream. This vision included both a political and an economic dimension. It was formulated in response to the proslavery sophistries of the time that denied equality of rights and equality of opportunity. Lincoln's intellectual abilities and persistent study equipped him in a battle of ideas to vindicate the principles of the founding against radical innovation.

To summarize, Lincoln's theoretical wisdom consisted in his comprehensive vision of man and society and his corresponding ability to provide an ultimate moral justification of democratic government based on the principles of equality and consent. Because politics is the art of the possible, not the perfect, successful statesmanship also depends on the indispensable virtue of practical wisdom—that is, the ability to apply as much of this noble vision as possible within the actual limits of legal, social, and political circumstances. The next chapter thus considers Lincoln's practical wisdom or prudence.

2
PRUDENCE

*W*hile Lincoln's theoretical wisdom consisted in his ability to articulate and defend a vision of self-government, free labor, and free society on philosophical and theological grounds, his practical wisdom or prudence consisted in his ability to realize as much of this noble vision as possible given the prevailing laws, customs, and opinions. Prudence harmonizes universal principles of right reason with the particularities of time and place. The following chapter considers Lincoln's prudence as a crucial dimension of his statesmanship. More specifically, it will reveal the Emancipation Proclamation as a model of prudent statesmanship in furthering the principle of equality under a myriad of perilous social, legal, political, and military circumstances.[1]

The gulf between theory and practice in American politics was poignantly observed by Thomas Jefferson at the time of the founding. In *Notes on the State of Virginia*, he warned of a divine judgment on the nation for failing to practice what it preached (a passage often cited by Lincoln testifying to the Founders' principled opposition to slavery):

> And can the liberties of a nation be thought secure when we have removed their only firm basis, a conviction in the minds of the people that these liberties are of the gift of God? That they are not to be violated but with his wrath? Indeed I tremble for my country when reflect that God is just: that his justice cannot sleep for ever: that considering numbers, nature and natural means only, a revolution of the wheel of fortune, an exchange of situation, is among possible events: that it may become probable by supernatural interference! The Almighty has no attribute which can take side with us in such a contest.[2]

The failure of the Founders to realize universal equality at the time of the Revolution has lent credence to the belief, both then and now, that they never viewed equality as a universal norm that applied to all human beings. This was the argument not only of southern proslavery apologists, but also of Union Democrats like Stephen A. Douglas and Roger B. Taney who claimed that the principles of the Declaration were exclusive to the white race. The same argument is repeated today by proponents of "the refound-ing thesis" who maintain that the Constitution was so radically flawed that Lincoln had to create a new one in order to realize his egalitarian vision.

On the contrary, Lincoln argued that the compromises made by the Founders were a matter of *necessity* and not principle. Slavery had ex-isted in North America over a century before the Revolution. It was an entrenched institution. Notwithstanding successful efforts in the North at the time of the Revolution to abolish it, the institution precariously coexisted with freedom in America. Although concessions were indeed made to slavery, the Founders had treated it as necessary evil (an excep-tion to the rule of freedom) to be contained and placed on a course of ultimate extinction. The failure to end slavery at the time of the founding, however, did not abolish the principles of Declaration as norms to guide policy. Succeeding generations, Lincoln maintained, must strive to carry on the work begun by the Founders. This meant containing slavery and extending the principle of equality as much as possible.

By the mid-nineteenth century, however, Lincoln feared that slavery was becoming the rule rather than the exception. The institution was being placed on a new path of extension and indefinite perpetuation. It was one thing to tolerate slavery as a necessary evil; it was quite an-other to embrace it as either (a) a positive good as preached by Calhoun, Fitzhugh, Hammond, or (b) a matter of moral indifference as taught by Stephen Douglas and his doctrine of popular sovereignty, the right of territorial settlers to choose slavery without interference from the national government. Rather, the containment of slavery demanded a clear moral recognition of its inherent evil. Despite its pretext of moral neutrality, the doctrine of popular sovereignty had the same practical effect as the positive good theory by enabling its indefinite perpetuation. Lincoln de-nounced popular sovereignty as blind to "the monstrous injustice of slav-ery." The discretion given to territorial settlers to choose slavery was not simply a local matter; for it undermined the moral credibility of the entire nation. In Lincoln's words, it: "deprives our republican example of its just influence in the world—enables the enemies of free institutions, with plausibility, to taunt us as hypocrites—causes the real friends of freedom to doubt our sincerity, and especially because it forces so many really good men amongst ourselves into an open war with the very fundamental prin-ciples of civil liberty—criticising the Declaration of Independence, and insisting that there is no right principle of action but *self-interest*."[3] True to his philosophical vocation, in the speech above, Lincoln insists that policies must take their bearing from a "right principle of action"—that is, a guiding normative standard that recognizes the dignity and depravity of each human being. Popular sovereignty cannot serve as a legitimate principle since it is based on the naked self-interest of the territorial settlers without just regard for the common humanity of the slave and the principle of equal consent.

Conceding the point of fact that universal abolition did not occur at the time of the Revolution or afterward, Lincoln explained that in declaring "all men are created equal," the Founders "did not mean to assert the obvious untruth, that all were then actually enjoying that equality, nor yet, that they were about to confer it immediately upon them. In fact they had no power to confer such a boon. They meant simply to declare the *right* so that the *enforcement* of it might follow as fast as circumstances should permit. They met to set up a *standard maxim for free society*, which should be familiar to all, and revered by all; constantly looked to, constantly labored for" (emphasis added).[4] Indeed, from the mouth of a statesman, let alone a philosopher, it would be difficult to find a clearer articulation in American history of how norms guide policy and how leaders are morally obliged to affirm and apply principles of natural law under the circumstance notwithstanding.[5]

Appealing to revelation, Lincoln also used a biblical analogy to explain how timeless principles remain unchanged as normative standards to be approximated despite their imperfect realization:

> It is said in one of the admonitions of the Lord, "As your Father in Heaven is perfect, be ye also perfect." The Savior, I suppose, did not expect that any human creature could be perfect as the Father in Heaven; but He said, "As your Father in Heaven is perfect, be ye also perfect." He set that up as a standard, and he who did most towards reaching that standard, attained the highest degree of moral perfection. So I say in relation to the principle that all men are created equal, let it be as nearly reached as we can. If we cannot give freedom to every creature, let us do nothing that will impose slavery upon any other creature.[6]

Prudence of practical wisdom is the indispensable political skill of harmonizing principle and practice, of narrowing the gap between the possible and the actual, between the ideal and the real. It thus involves a consideration of both universal moral principles in decision making and the application or determination of these principles to a variety of legal, social, and political contingencies. For an act to be truly prudent it must be good in its intent, its action, and its consequences. As originally understood by

ancient and medieval political thinkers, and as practiced by Lincoln, prudence was right reason applied to the realm of practical matters—that is,
ethics and politics.[7] Put another way, a prudent statesman adopts suitable
means to attain just ends. Aquinas explains: "it belongs to prudence chiefly
to direct something aright to an end; and this is not done aright unless both
the end be good, and the means good and suitable."[8]

In sum, Lincoln's prudence sought to harmonize the moral obligation to the principles of the Declaration with his legal obligation to
the rule of law under the Constitution. Following the teachings of his
Whig predecessors, Webster and Clay, his statesmanship was guided by
inseparability of liberty and the Union as the regime's moral end. The
Emancipation Proclamation was a prudent mean adapted to this end.[9]
Recalling the metaphor of Proverbs, the Declaration was the moral centerpiece (the apple of gold) of the Union framed by the Constitution as its
picture of silver. Prudence dictated that neither the apple (the principles
of the Declaration) should be bruised nor the picture (the Union and
the rule of law) harmed. The two were mutually supportive in securing
ordered liberty.

Lincoln's protest in the Illinois legislature on March 3, 1837, against
a gag order seeking to suppress abolitionist literature provides an early
example of his prudence. Indeed, this protest was his first public stance
against slavery. At age twenty-eight, he was one of only six (out of over
eighty representatives) who voted against the measure. The rationale of
this principled minority who risked voter backlash in "the negrophobic"
state of Illinois was as follows:

> They believe that the institution of slavery is founded on both injus-
> tice and bad policy; but that the promulgation of abolition doctrines
> tends rather to increase than to abate its evils.
>
> They believe that the Congress of the United States has no power,
> under the constitution, to interfere with the institution of slavery
> in the different States.
>
> They believe that the Congress of the United States has the power,
> under the constitution, to abolish slavery in the District of Co-
> lumbia; but that that power ought not to be exercised unless at the
> request of the people of said District.[10]

While "slavery is founded on both injustice and bad policy," "the prom-
ulgation of abolition doctrines tend to increase than to abate its evil."
Here, Lincoln recognized that politics is the art of the possible, not the
perfect. The redress of an evil must take into consideration whether or

not the unintended consequences of policies will create a greater evil. While theory informs practice as a standard, the perfect realization of an ideal is neither possible nor practical given the limits of human nature and politics.

The virtue of prudence may be understood further as the mean between the two extremes of (a) political idealism, and (b) political pragmatism or shrewdness.[11] As will be seen, Lincoln's prudent harmonization of principle to practice avoids the pitfalls of both a utopian perfectionism that seeks to bring about a political kingdom of heaven on earth, and a moral realism that places power over principle.

The concern for abstract moral principles overrides all other considerations for the idealist. The quest for earthly perfection blinds him or her to the inherent limits of politics and human nature. As Jaffa explains: "The best form of government is not possible everywhere and may not at any time be possible anywhere. As an abstract truth it may nonetheless supply a direction to policy, and to the improvement of the laws. But there is a danger of tyranny in the attempt to treat the desirable as if it were always possible, when in fact it is not."[12]

Idealists tend toward the puritanical equation of law and morality in politics. All too often they are willing to use the coercive force of the state to impose unrealistic moral standards on a recalcitrant public. For example, though all can agree that alcohol may be harmful to both individuals and society, the policy of prohibition and its unintended consequences of aiding and abetting organized crime illustrates that not all vices should be repressed through the force of law.

As noted in the introduction, the radical abolitionists during Lincoln's time exhibited the defect of political idealism. Though their antislavery principles were correct in the abstract and shared by Lincoln, they failed to consider sufficiently the limits of politics. For example, William Lloyd Garrison, who repudiated the Constitution as a "covenant with death" and "an agreement with hell," proclaimed that "if slaves have a right to their freedom, it ought to be given to them, regardless of the consequences."[13] And Gerrit Smith, who helped finance John Brown's murderous raid on Harpers Ferry in the fall of 1859, likewise declared: "I insist that the Nation has a right and is therefore bound to abolish slavery. But if it will not do so, then let there be Disunion & Abolition will follow."[14] Indeed, the political immoderation of the abolitionists is epitomized by the motto "liberty without Union," self-righteously proclaimed by Wendell Phillips, "the national scold," on the eve of the Civil War:

> Not an Abolitionist, hardly an antislavery man, Mr. Lincoln consents
> to represent an antislavery idea. A pawn on the political chessboard,
> his value is in his position; with fair effort, we may soon change him
> for knight, bishop, or queen, and sweep the board. . . . The Republican
> party have undertaken a problem, the solution of which will force
> them to our position. . . . Not Mr. Seward's "Union and Liberty,"
> which he stole and poisoned from Webster's Liberty and Union.
> No: Their motto will soon be "Liberty first. Union afterwards."[15]

Hubris and bravado were by no means the sole possession of southern fire-eaters. As Michael Burlingame has shown, many of the leading
abolitionists were racist by today's standards.[16] Regardless of this alleged
hypocrisy, abolitionist rhetoric alienated conservative Unionists and provided a pretext for southern radicals to argue that the South's property
and rights were insecure in the hands of northern radicals who had no
regard for the Constitution and rule of law. Unfortunately, Phillips's bom-
bastic rhetoric has also perpetuated the illusion that Lincoln was "forced
into glory" by more principled abolitionists.[17]

Notwithstanding the purity of their principles, the abolitionists were
a radical fringe who could not carry a national election as president. The
fact that they pressured Lincoln does not mean that their immoderate
views carried the day. Though he shared antislavery principles with the
abolitionists and collaborated with them on national policy, their influence was not one of simple cause and effect. Lincoln was also pressured by border state men and war Democrats who opposed the views of
the abolitionists.[18] As clearly seen in the protest of 1837, his antislavery
principles were well established before he took office. Nonetheless, he
rejected the abolitionist plea for immediate, uncompensated emancipation. Lincoln's prudence, in part, consisted in his ability to take counsel
from the different factions within the war coalition and to balance them
in view of the common good. The question for Lincoln was how to best
advance the principles of the Declaration under the circumstances so
as to preserve both the Union and liberty.

While contrary to political idealism, prudence is often confused with
pragmatism, which also means cunning, or shrewdness. As mentioned
in the introduction, the pragmatist is one who subordinates principle to
self-interest, expediency, and/or success. If the idealist is uncompromising, inflexible, and rigid, the pragmatist, by contrast, is a shrewd com-
promiser, negotiator, and bargainer who views politics almost exclusively
in terms of quid pro quo. In short, the pragmatist is big on results, but

short on vision and principle. Whereas the idealist fixates on principles in their abstract purity, the pragmatist suffers from a moral obtuseness that evades moral absolutes in politics as subversive of the seemingly democratic goals of tolerance, compromise, and openness.

This is not to say that interest and expediency are necessarily contrary to the common good or that flexibility and compromise are unimportant to the statesman's prudential calculus. Ever sober about human nature, a prudent statesman well recognizes that most people will not act on altruistic motives alone. Accordingly, he or she must find ways to yoke interest to principle. Lincoln attempted to do this when he proposed a federally compensated emancipation plan that would unite the pecuniary interest of the slaveholder with the public good of ending slavery peaceably in the border states. Based on this calculus, he concluded that "less than one half-day's cost of this war would pay for all the slaves in Delaware, at four hundred dollars per head."[19]

The defect of political pragmatism was displayed by Stephen Douglas before the war and the war Democrats and conservatives during the war. All of these alike were indifferent to the "monstrous injustice" of slavery and saw no ultimate incompatibility between it and the Union. For example, Douglas's policy of popular sovereignty attempted to provide a moderate solution to the slavery problem in response to northern and southern disunionism. Douglas believed that this policy was most consistent with the Union's preservation and the principles of majority rule, democratic process, local autonomy, and diversity.

In an effort to diffuse political strife, popular sovereignty, however, sought to evade the question of slavery's inherent good or evil. The issue of slavery, Douglas contended, was relative to the subjective preferences and interests of local majorities. In a characteristically pragmatic manner, he distinguished sharply between legal rights, which were posited by the Supreme Court and could not be contested; and moral and religious rights which were divisive and should be kept entirely out of politics:

> I am now speaking of rights under the constitution, and not of moral or religious rights. I do not discuss the moral of the people of Missouri but let them settle that matter for themselves. I hold that the people of the slaveholding States are civilized men as well as ourselves, that they bear consciences as well as we, and that they are accountable to God and their posterity and not to us. It is for them to decide therefore the moral and religious right of the slavery questions for themselves within their own limits.[20]

Like modern legal realists and positivists, Douglas rejected the guiding imperatives of universal norms by arguing that law should reflect only "the community sense of what is expedient." The war Democrats and conservatives were likewise morally obtuse in seeking to restore the status quo ante in regard to slavery. In effect, they sought to preserve a Union without liberty—that is, without the promise of freedom for all.

Contrary to the idealists' equation of law and morality and the pragmatists' subordination of principle to expediency, Lincoln recognized that spheres of law and morality are related yet distinct. While law participates in morality, not all moral actions should be regulated by the coercive force of state authority. Only the most serious and injurious vices should be regulated and punished. It is particularly self-defeating and futile to impose moral principles on a community where the prevailing opinions, mores, history, local law, habits, and legal precedents promote the contrary. Such was the case with the existing institution of slavery in Lincoln's time, which was an ingrained way of life for over two hundred years, the basis of the South's economy, and protected by culture, mores, customs, and law. Though the proposition that all men are created equal "is true as an abstract principle," Lincoln prudently acknowledged that "it can't be practically applie[d] . . . in all cases."[21]

In the short term, Lincoln believed, the preservation of the Union took precedence over the immediate, unlawful abolition of slavery. Preserving the Union was the indispensable means, the sine qua non, to ending slavery. At Peoria, he went so far as to admit, "Much as I hate slavery, would consent to the extension of it rather than see the Union dissolved, just as I would consent to any great evil, to avoid a greater one."[22] Lincoln posed this dilemma in extreme terms to distinguish himself from the radical abolitionists. Like his protest in 1837, the argument is conditioned on the premise that the dissolution of the Union is "a greater evil." Though Lincoln posed the question in the abstract to reveal the priority of the Union, his statesmanship avoided both horns of the dilemma: disunion or a proslavery Union.

Given his sober view of human nature, Lincoln saw that few things in politics are purely good or purely evil. As a result, prudence necessarily involves choosing between the lesser of two evils. Consistent with his view of the free soil party in 1848, his remarks at Peoria in 1854 convey the prudent outlook that would guide his statesmanship during the war and on the Emancipation Proclamation. "The true rule," he explained, "in determining to embrace, or reject any thing, is not whether it have *any* evil in it; but whether it have more of evil, than of good. There are few things *wholly* evil, or *wholly* good. Almost every thing, especially of governmental policy, is an inseparable compound of the two; so that our best judgment of the preponderance between them is continually demanded."[23] Like Plato, Lincoln views statesmanship in terms of the art of measurement.

Seeking to preserve a moral Union under the rule of law, Lincoln's statesmanship was prudentially counterpoised to the extremes of both northern and southern disunionism: "Stand with anybody that stands RIGHT. Stand with him while he is right and PART with him when he goes wrong. Stand WITH the abolitionist in restoring the Missouri Compromise; and stand AGAINST him when he attempts to repeal the fugitive slave law. In the latter case you stand with the southern disunionist. What of that? you are still right. In both cases you are right. In both cases you oppose [expose?] the dangerous extremes. In both you stand on middle ground and hold the ship level and steady."[24]

Disunion before the war may have afforded abolitionists the solace of moral purity in a miniature northern republic uncontaminated from the blight of slavery, but it would likely have consigned millions of slaves down South to abject misery without the promise of freedom. Freed from the moral embrace of the Union, the South would be able to extend its slave empire in the Caribbean with impunity and to perpetuate slavery indefinitely without opposition from the North. Like the defunct Articles of Confederation, the fragmentation of the Union into separate republics was unlikely to secure ordered liberty.

In sum, Lincoln's prudent leadership assimilated the merits of both the idealist and pragmatist position while transcending their defects. Avoiding either extreme, he considered both universal principles and expediency in his decision making. Though willing to compromise on the existing institution of slavery as a matter of necessity and constitutional duty, he nonetheless held firm to the core principle of the Republican Party to restrict slavery in the territories. For this reason, as president elect, he opposed the Crittenden Compromise—a proposed measure by the Thirty-Sixth Congress that intended to prevent war and placate the South by extending the Missouri Compromise line, and slavery north of this line, to the West. Lincoln would thus risk war rather than surrender the party's core antislavery principle. A month after the election, in a private letter to a political ally, he explained: "Prevent, as far as possible, any of our friends from demoralizing themselves, and our cause, by entertaining propositions for compromise of any sort, on *slavery extention*[.]" There is no possible compromise upon it, but which puts us under again, and leaves all our work to do over again. Whether it be a Mo. line, or

Eli Thayer's Pop. Sov. it is all the same. Let either be done, & immediately filibustering and extending slavery recommences. On that point hold firm, as with a chain of steel."[25]

Now that prudence has been clearly defined, it remains to consider more specifically the variables Lincoln had to weigh and measure in seeking to preserve both "liberty and Union" through the Emancipation Proclamation. Though ending slavery was a noble aim in principle, precipitous actions could undermine the Union's very preservation, leading to the triumph of the Confederacy and the indefinite perpetuation of slavery for generations to come. Some of the possible consequence of an ill-conceived emancipation included: loss of the border states as part of the war coalition; public backlash against the war effort; desertion of troops; demoralization of the military; a rebuke by the Supreme Court; feeble enforcement that would negate its intended effect; a Wall Street panic; foreign intervention; political defeat at the polls in the midterm elections of 1863; and racial strife in the form of either a slave insurrection or angry reprisals against blacks, or both. One of these factors by itself, or a combination of them, could result in a Confederacy victory and the indefinite perpetuation of slavery. As the saying goes, "The road to hell is paved with good intentions."

Indeed, the defeat of the Confederacy, on which all other goals depended, relied on Lincoln's ability as a statesman to maintain a broad coalition in support of the Union within government and among the public at large. This included a precarious coalition of radical Republicans from the North who favored immediate emancipation, conservative Republicans who were more cautious, and war Democrats, primarily from the border-slave states, who opposed black freedom.

Prudence also dictated a consideration of whether or not the Constitution authorized an Emancipation Proclamation at all. Prior to the Thirteenth Amendment, the Constitution's federal division of power made it illegal for the national government to interfere with the domestic institutions of states, including slavery. From his earliest statements on the subject to his First Inaugural Address in 1861, Lincoln had consistently declared that the Constitution prohibited the federal government from interfering with state slavery. As much as he hated slavery, he had sworn an oath to uphold the Constitution, and that meant upholding its concessions to slavery as a state institution. An Emancipation Proclamation in defiance of the Constitution would only confirm the suspicion of southerners and northern moderates alike that the Republican Party was composed of lawless fanatics who had no respect for the rule of law and the federal division of power. Moreover, if justified on a flimsy legal basis, the act would be vulnerable to judicial review, thereby discrediting the administration. It should be remembered that Roger B. Taney, the author of *Dred Scott*, still presided over the Supreme Court and needed only the slightest pretext to strike down an act declaring the slaves free. Indeed, Taney had already challenged the president's authority by declaring his suspension of habeas corpus unconstitutional in *ex parte Merryman*, 1861.[26] Support from the bench was tenuous at best. Those sympathetic to Taney's states' rights views still had a majority. The retired justice Curtis, who wrote a scathing dissent in *Dred Scott*, 1857, wrote a pamphlet making clear his position that the Constitution did not support an executive decree freeing the slaves.

Prudence further dictated that Lincoln consider the effect of an emancipation on the border states who remained loyal to the Union but who still had slaves and were teetering on the verge of secession. Located between the North and South, the states of Kentucky, Maryland, and Missouri were crucial to the Union's military and political success. At least Lincoln believed so, as when he said, "to lose Kentucky is to lose the whole game"; and that although, "we hope to have God on our side . . . we must have Kentucky."[27] In an effort to appease the border states, at the beginning of war in July of 1861, the Thirty-Seventh Congress enacted the Crittenden-Johnson Resolution (not to be confused with the Crittenden Compromise of the Thirty-Sixth Congress). The Crittenden-Johnson Resolution narrowly defined Union war aims in terms of preserving the Union without interfering with the institution of slavery. However, only four months later in December, the same Congress defeated the resolution by large margins, which testifies to the extent to which slavery, the root cause of the rebellion, was likely to become a casualty of war.

Not surprisingly, the two members of Lincoln's cabinet from the border states, Attorney General Bates and Postmaster Montgomery Blair, expressed grave reservations about an emancipation. The latter noted that it "would cost the Administration the fall elections."[28] *New York Times* editor Henry J. Raymond, who would later become a campaign manager for Lincoln in 1864, warned that "any attempt to make this war *subservient* to the sweeping abolition of Slavery, will revolt the Border States, divide the North and West, invigorate and make triumphant the opposition party, and thus defeat *itself* as well as destroy the Union."[29] Indeed, the Emancipation Proclamation exacted a political price during the midterm elections when the Republicans lost thirty-one seats in the Thirty-Eighth Congress.[30]

Lincoln's policy for dealing with the Border slave states was characteristically prudent in taking into consideration moral principle, the rule of law, self-interest, and public support of the measure. While the Constitution prevented the use of coercion to abolish slavery in the border states, it did not preclude moral suasion on the part of the president and financial incentivizes to black freedom. Lincoln thus proposed a federally compensated emancipation plan whereby the national government would assume part of the financial burden of freeing the slaves in the border states. With the utmost urgency, he appealed to the patriotism of the border states, calling for the "loftiest views and boldest acts."[31] If these higher appeals did not move the border states, he would appeal to their self-interest in explaining that "less than one half-day's cost of this war would pay for all the slaves in Delaware, at four hundred dollars per head."[32] In sum, slaveholders would be compensated, emancipation would be gradual, and it would require the consent of the states involved. Consistent with his lifelong commitment to education, Lincoln also believed that "education for young blacks should be included in the plan."[33]

Beginning in March of 1862, Lincoln appealed directly to the border state representatives on at least four occasions. He was rebuffed each time. On July 12, 1862, the third such occasion, he stated to the representatives: "Believing that you of the border-states hold more power for good than any other equal number of members, I feel it a duty which I can not justifiably waive, to make this appeal to you. I intend no reproach or complaint when I assure you that in my opinion, if you all had voted for the resolution in the gradual emancipation message of last March, the war would now be substantially ended."[34] Lincoln then warned that slavery was likely to become a casualty of war in any event and urged the border states to take advantage of the opportunity before it passed: "The incidents of war can not be avoided. If the war continue long, as it must, if the object be not sooner attained, the institution in your states will be extinguished by mere friction and abrasion—by the mere incidents of the war. It will be gone, and you will have nothing valuable in lieu of it."[35] Two days later, on July 14, the border state men rejected his plea. After exhausting all efforts to persuade the border states, a week later, on July 21, 1862, Lincoln revealed a preliminary draft of the Emancipation Proclamation to his cabinet.

As commander in chief, Lincoln was also bound to consider the effect an emancipation edict would have on the army's morale, which was already low after the disastrous defeat at Second Bull Run in late August of 1862. His response to the abolitionist plea of Charles Sumner is noteworthy: "I would do it if I were not afraid that half the officers would fling down their arms and four more states would rise.[36] The military situation was complicated further by the fact that General George B. McClellan, Lincoln's general in chief at the time, was a war Democrat who was notably hostile to Republican antislavery policies. Politicking behind the scenes, McClellan wrote to "an influential Democratic friend" in November of 1861: "Help me dodge the nigger question. . . . *I* am fighting to preserve the integrity of the Union. . . . To gain that end we cannot afford to raise up the negro question."[37]

When Lincoln visited McClellan at Harrison's Landing in July of 1862, the audacious general presented his commander in chief with a letter stating his opposition to abolitionist policies and predicting disastrous consequences for the Union army should they be enacted. He lectured the president that "neither confiscation of property . . . nor forcible abolition of slavery should be contemplated for a moment. Military power should not be allowed to interfere with the relations of servitude, either by supporting or impairing the authority of the master. . . . A declaration of radical views, especially upon slavery, will rapidly disintegrate our present Armies."[38]

McClellan was not alone. During the war, some Union officers had actually returned fugitive slaves to the Confederacy during cease-fires, citing their constitutional obligation to do so. Other soldiers in the field threatened to desert if the cause of the Union was identified with abolitionism. After General Fremont unilaterally proclaimed martial law and emancipation in Missouri on August 30, 1861, a Union regiment threw down their arms and deserted. Upon hearing of Fremont's proclamation, Lincoln's friend from Kentucky Joshua Speed wrote to the president saying, "It will hurt us in K[entucky]." Speaking for the border states, Speed advised Lincoln that: "The war should be waged upon high points and no state law be interfered with—our Constitution & laws both prohibit emancipation of slaves among us—even in small numbers—If a military commander can turn them loose by thousands by mere proclamation—It will be a most difficult matter to get our people to submit to it."[39] Indeed, Fremont's emancipation elicited protests from border states, who feared "the Pandora's box of a slave rebellion."[40] Much to the chagrin of radicals, Lincoln asked Fremont to "modify" his emancipation so that it would accord with the Confiscation Act passed earlier the same month by Congress and signed by Lincoln without comment. This so-called First Confiscation Act authorized the confiscation and freeing of slaves used by Confederates in the war effort.[41] It did not, however, authorize generals in the field to free slaves upon the mere suspicion of their master's disloyalty, as Fremont had done.

In his annual message to Congress on December 3, 1861, Lincoln once again made the case for gradual compensated emancipation. After hinting that emancipation could be undertaken legally on military grounds, he cautiously addressed fears about a slave insurrection: "In considering the policy to be adopted for suppressing the insurrection, I have been anxious and careful that the inevitable conflict for this purpose shall not degenerate into a violent and remorseless revolutionary struggle. I have, therefore, in every case, thought it proper to keep the integrity of the Union prominent as the primary object of the contest on our part, leaving all questions which are not of vital military importance to the more deliberate action of the legislature."[42] Though it makes clear that the Union's preservation was the "primary object," it also reveals that Lincoln was contemplating emancipation as a war measure at this time.

On April 13, 1862, General David Hunter freed the slaves in Fort Pulaski and Cockspur Island in the coastal areas of Georgia that were under his control. Less than a month later, on May 9 Hunter issued a second, more sweeping emancipation that freed all the slaves in the states of South Carolina, Georgia, and Florida, "only small portions of which were actually under Union control," according to James Oakes.[43] As with Fremont's proclamation a year earlier, Lincoln revoked General Hunter's military emancipation. In his proclamation of May 19, 1862 the president emphasized that the authority to free the slaves was reserved to him alone as commander in chief: "I further make known that whether it be competent for me, as Commander-in Chief of the Army and Navy, to declare the Slaves of any state or states, free, and whether at any time, in any case, it shall have become a necessity indispensable to the maintenance of the government, to exercise such supposed powers are questions, which under my responsibility, I reserve to myself, and which I can not feel justified in leaving to the decision of commanders in the field."[44] Indeed, this remarkable statement anticipated the rationale of the Emancipation Proclamation four months later.

Though critical of Hunter's precipitous actions, Lincoln took the opportunity to reaffirm his core principles by also noting that he "valued [General Hunter] none the less for his agreeing with me in the general wish that all men everywhere could be free."[45] For those who could read between the lines, Lincoln was hinting that the slaves could be lawfully freed under his authority as commander in chief on the basis of military necessity and the law of war.[46] As Allen Guelzo explains in his magisterial and indispensable work *Lincoln's Emancipation Proclamation: The End of Slavery in America*, the president had intimated that both

General Fremont and General Hunter had "done the right thing in the wrong way."[47]

A Second Confiscation Act was passed by Congress in July of 1862. Preceding the Emancipation Proclamation, these congressional acts indicated that the war was being transformed in a more radical direction that would permit the federal government to strike directly at the existing institution of slavery in the states, a policy that had been constitutionally off-limits in ordinary, peacetime circumstances. Though Lincoln signed both Confiscation Acts, he had reservations about their constitutionality and permanence. These two laws were potentially suspect as an illegal bill of attainder—that is, a congressional act that punishes a person without the benefit of a trial. As such they were vulnerable to judicial review by Taney and the Supreme Court. The legal concerns about a bill of attainder would be eliminated, however, if an emancipation was justified under the president's more robust constitutional authority as commander in chief in wartime, as Lincoln would ultimately decide.

Notwithstanding the constitutionality of such an act, Lincoln had further reservations about the credibility of freeing the slaves without a decisive Union military victory to crown it. The stalling of McClellan's peninsular campaign and the disastrous Union defeat at Second Bull Run in August of 1862 did not bode well for the Union. With federal armies thwarted, how could an emancipation proclamation be enforced in rebel held territory? It certainly would not be self-executed. Because perceptions count in politics, Lincoln's secretary of state, William Seward of New York, urged him to delay a proclamation until a Union military victory, without which the act would be perceived as the "last measure of an exhausted government, a cry for help . . . our last shriek on the retreat."[48]

Prudence required that Lincoln also consider the social impact and consequences of freeing the slaves. This involved volatile considerations of racial adjustment. What would happen to the slaves after emancipation? Could they be assimilated given their servile condition and the prevailing opinion among the majority of the American public that they were an inferior race? Indeed, the North's opposition to slavery coexisted with an ingrained racism. Slavery was one thing, but having blacks as one's neighbors and fellow citizens was quite another. Moreover, freeing the slaves could trigger an insurrection that would claim much innocent blood and completely undermine public support at home and abroad for the Union cause.

Though firm on core principles, Lincoln consistently acknowledged the difficulty of dealing with the existing institution of slavery. At Peoria on October 16, 1854, he tempered his condemnation of slavery by speculating about the practical difficulties related to universal emancipation: "What next? Free them [the slaves], and make them politically and socially, our equals? My own feelings will not admit of this; and if mine would, we well know that those of the great mass of white people will not. Whether this feeling accords with justice and sound judgment, is not the sole question, if indeed, it is any part of it. A universal feeling, whether well or ill-founded, can not be safely disregarded."[49]

Notably, Lincoln is speculating about the possibilities of full social and political equality if slavery were to be abolished in the near future. He is not speaking about the intrinsic evil of the institution of slavery itself, which he had already condemned in no uncertain terms as a "monstrous injustice." In 1854, Lincoln viewed colonization as the best means to settling the racial question after slavery had been abolished. However, as one who was renowned for choosing his words carefully, his evasive use of language raises doubts in the mind of the careful reader or listener about whether or not he personally shared the prejudices of his time against black people. For example, he refers to the racial animus of "the great mass of white people" as a "feeling." Feelings, as opposed to truths, are often subjective. As such, this feeling may or may not "accord with justice and sound judgment." Lincoln's remarks about full social and political equality are qualified further by the addition of "and if mine would" to the sentence. That is to say his evasive language leaves doubt about whether or not he actually shares the same prejudice as "the great mass of white people" or whether he is just bowing to political necessity.

Whatever his personal views, Lincoln makes clear that moral right "is not the only question" involved in deciding whether or not to grant full social and political equality to blacks. A "universal feeling," he explains, "whether ill or well founded, cannot safely be regarded." In other words, in the context of the state of Illinois in 1854, public opinion was not yet prepared to support such a drastic measure. Taken together, these two speeches from October 1854 reveal Lincoln's prudence and his respect for the limits of politics. The earlier remarks educate the public about the evils of slavery and its ultimate incompatibility with popular government, while the subsequent remarks temper this moral condemnation by acknowledging the limits of public opinion in regard to full social and political equality for blacks at the time.

The success of the Emancipation Proclamation depended further on timing and Lincoln's ability to prepare public opinion for the momentous change to come. James Stoner describes Lincoln's task and that of all great statesmen as: "How to present unwelcome truth in a way that leads a substantial number of men and women to change how they act, how they vote, and what they uphold as law is a task worthy of a great statesman in a democracy."[50] Though Lincoln had revealed an early draft of the Emancipation Proclamation to his cabinet in July of 1862, he was still waiting for the opportune moment to act. He once remarked that what separated him from the radicals was an interval of six weeks.

In *Emancipating Lincoln*, Harold Holzer points to three examples of the president's masterful public relations campaign in support of the Emancipation Proclamation: (1) his remarks to a "Deputation of free Negroes"; (2) his correspondence with Horace Greeley, editor of the *New York Tribune*; and (3) his meeting with a Chicago Christian delegation.[51] In each case, Lincoln took careful steps to publicize his remarks. Historical hindsight now tells us that he addressed public concerns in order to broaden support for a measure that was already in the works.

On August 14, 1862, Lincoln received a "Deputation of Free Negroes" to the White House. After acknowledging the injustice of slavery to the black race as "the greatest wrong," he delivered a condescending speech in favor of voluntary colonization:

> Your race are suffering, in my judgment, the greatest wrong inflicted on any people. But even when you cease to be slaves, you are yet far removed from being placed on an equality with the white race. You are cut off from many of the advantages which the other race enjoy. The aspiration of men is to enjoy equality with the best when free, but on this broad continent, not a single man of your race is made the equal of a single man of ours. Go where you are treated the best, and the ban is still upon you. I do not propose to discuss this, but to present it as a fact with which we have to deal. . . . It is better for us both, therefore, to be separated.[52]

Seemingly insensitive and harsh, this message was primarily tailored for public consumption in view of the fact that Lincoln had arranged to have reporters to attend the meeting, which was something he never did.[53] The meeting was a public relations effort that sought to answer concerns and fears about what would be done with the slaves after emancipation. The proposed colonization plan, which would remain voluntary, was intended to "soften the blow" of the coming thunderbolt of emancipation. It bears mentioning that Lincoln had rejected Attorney General Edward Bates's proposal of a forced deportation of blacks after emancipation.[54]

Holzer notes that Lincoln "had exaggerated his commitment to colonization to prepare the country for unthreatening black freedom."[55] He
describes Lincoln's prudent actions in these concise terms: "Seemingly
alternatively to be inconsistent, harsh, humble, and ruthless, Lincoln was
more accurately patient, wise, prescient, and practical. . . . With his public
letters, recorded remarks, and shared secrets, Lincoln did nothing less than
succeed in making freedom palatable for whites and possible for blacks."[56]
Oakes likewise notes that "both the nature and the timing of the event suggest that Lincoln had another agenda besides the overt one of persuading a
handful of accomplished blacks to lead the way on voluntary emigration."[57]

Lincoln's less than enthusiastic commitment to colonization is seen
by the fact that only $38,000 of the $600,000 appropriated by Congress
was actually spent on colonization. After feeble attempts at colonization
in 1862 and 1863 both failed, Lincoln sent a rescue mission in February
of 1864 to the island of Vache "to bring back to this country such of the
colonists there as desire to return."[58] No further colonization efforts were
attempted after this debacle.

Lincoln's correspondence with Horace Greeley, editor of the *New York
Tribune*, was also part of his public relations campaign to broaden support
for the forthcoming emancipation. On August 20, 1862, Greeley wrote
an editorial entitled "The Prayer of Twenty Millions," which criticized
the president for his reluctance to emancipate: "We think you are unduly
influenced by the counsels . . . of certain fossil politicians hailing from
the Border Slave States."

Lincoln chose to respond to Greeley's editorial two days later on August
22 in a competing newspaper. The president selected his words carefully
knowing full well that they would be publicly scrutinized by all sides
of the political spectrum. He explained to Greely and the nation: "My
paramount object in this struggle is to save the Union and is not either
to save or to destroy slavery. If I could save the Union w/out freeing any
slave, I would do it; and if I could save it by freeing all the slaves, I would
do it; and if I could save it by freeing some of the slaves and leaving others alone, I would do it. . . . This does not change my personal wish that
all men can enjoy freedom everywhere."[59] In declaring that saving the
Union was his "paramount object," did Lincoln embrace a pragmatism
that subordinated principle to success?

The practical and realistic concern for the Union's preservation should
not obscure a momentous implication contained in the letter. As Guelzo
has perceptively noted, this was the first time a president had actually
claimed to possess the authority to free the slaves, a policy that had never
even been considered by former presidents. Moreover, as noted, a month

earlier, in July, Lincoln had already revealed a draft of the Emancipation Proclamation to his cabinet. He timed the measure so as to take full advantage of public support possible and so that its credibility bolstered by a Union victory. That victory came at Antietam, the hitherto bloodiest single day in American history, on September 17, 1862.

Lincoln's commitment to the principle of equality is not merely pragmatic if one recognizes that the goals of preserving the Union and ending slavery were implicitly linked in his mind. Throughout his public life, he consistently affirmed the noble vision of the inseparability of liberty and Union (conveyed by the apple of gold and picture of silver). For example, in a speech in Bloomington, Indiana, in 1854, he emphasized that "the Union must be preserved in the purity of its principles,"[60] a reference to the Declaration. At Peoria the same year, he reiterated this point: "Let us re-adopt the Declaration of Independence, and with it, the practices, and policy, which harmonize with it. Let north and south—let all Americans—let all lovers of liberty everywhere—join in the great and good work. If we do this, we shall not only have saved the Union; but we shall have so saved it, as to make, and to keep it, forever worthy of the saving."[61] In a revealing statement at a political rally in June of 1858, Lincoln left no doubt as to the inseparable connection between liberty, the Constitution, and the Union, by exhorting his audience to be "ever true to Liberty, the Union and the Constitution—true to Liberty, not selfishly, but upon principle—not for special classes of men, but for all men, true to the Union and the Constitution, as the best means to advance that liberty."[62] And in his annual message to Congress December 6, 1864, Lincoln applauded Maryland's emancipation of the slaves in these terms: "Maryland is secure to Liberty and Union for all the future. The genius of rebellion will no more claim Maryland."[63] This terse statement not only reveals the connection in Lincoln's mind between preserving the Union and ending slavery, but it also reveals the extent to which he viewed slavery as principal cause or "the genius of the rebellion."

As someone who chose his words carefully, Lincoln's reference to "Paramount Object" also merits attention in revealing an implicit link between ending slavery and preserving the Union. Consistent with Lincoln's intent, the word "paramount" does not mean "exclusive" "sole" or "only," but "primary" or "of high priority." As seen in his special message to Congress, December 31, 1861, Lincoln similarly referred to preserving the Union as his "primary object." He believed that the long-term preservation of the Union must take precedence over the emancipation of slavery in the short term. To be sure, the triumph of the Confederacy and the dissolution of the Union would render the slavery question moot and lead to the unintended consequence of its indefinite perpetuation. Since Lincoln further believed that preserving the Union meant preserving the principles for which it stood, the Union's preservation under a Republican administration meant the enactment of policies that would work toward its ultimate extinction. Thus, the dispute between Lincoln and the abolitionists is not over ending slavery or not, but over timing and the particular means that were best conducive to attain the long-term goal of freedom for all.

The defeat of the Confederacy, on which all other goals depended, relied on the support of both war Democrats and Republicans. Lincoln defined the Union's cause in the broadest terms possible so that both members of the coalition could support it despite their differences over slavery's ultimate fate. However, so long as Lincoln was at the helm of the ship of state, the antislavery principles of the Republican Party, renamed the Union Party during the election of 1864, would remain the touchstone in the long term.

Lincoln's remarks to a delegation of Chicago Christians on September 13, 1862, were also part of his public relations effort to prepare the country for his preliminary draft of the emancipation document, which he would issue on September 22, the following week after the Battle of Antietam on September 17 the same year. Lincoln's reply is noteworthy because it highlights many of the prudential concerns and contingencies surrounding emancipation:

> What *good* would a proclamation of emancipation from me do, especially as we are now situated? I do not want to issue a document that the whole world will see must necessarily be inoperative, like the Pope's bull against the comet! Would *my word* free the slaves, when I cannot even enforce the Constitution in the rebel States? Is there a single court, or magistrate, or individual that would be influenced by it there? And what reason is there to think it would have any greater effect upon the slaves than the late law of Congress, which I approved, and which offers protection and freedom to the slaves of rebel masters who come within our lines? Yet I cannot learn that that law has caused a single slave to come over to us. And suppose they could be induced by a proclamation of freedom from me to throw themselves upon us, *what should we do with them?* How can we feed and care for such a multitude?[64]

Lincoln's reference to "the Pope's bull against the comet" humorously compares the futility of an unenforceable decree of emancipation to Pope Callixtus's III's excommunication of Halley's Comet in 1456.[65]

In practical matters, the "good" must always involve a deliberation about circumstances and unintended consequences. Lincoln scolds the religious advocates of emancipation for making the same mistake in practical reasoning as did the free soil party years earlier when they similarly declared their duty, leaving the consequences to God. In both cases, the antislavery forces simply appealed to the Bible or a religious norm in defense of their policy, without further consideration of the circumstances in which the principle is to be applied.

A literal appeal to the text of the Bible could not resolve the question of slavery since both sides invoked scripture in support of their position. Despite sophistic twisting to the contrary, Lincoln believed that a deeper meditation on God's justice and a proper interpretation of the Bible in both spirit and letter revealed its incompatibility with slavery. Granted that slavery was wrong according to the Bible and the norms of the Christian religion, nothing in the Bible or the teachings of Christianity answered the practical questions of *who* had the authority to emancipate—the president, Congress, or the courts. As Lincoln was at pains to show, even if the Bible were unequivocally opposed to slavery, this recognition nonetheless left a number of important questions unanswered. It did not answer *when* the act should be done: immediately or after a Union victory? *Who* would enforce it? *Where* should it apply—in rebel territory or the Border States as well? *What effect* would it have on the military? *Would* it make foreign intervention on the side of the Union or Confederacy more or less likely? Moreover, it did not answer the question of *what* to do with the freedmen after the act. *How* would they make the transition to freedom? *Who* would care for them?

In view of these considerations, Lincoln assured the Christian delegation that he sought to do God's will while sternly reminding them that religious precepts cannot always be applied literally to politics without prudential mediation: "it is my earnest desire to know the will of Providence in this matter. *And if I can learn what it is I will do it!* These are not, however, the days of miracles, and I suppose it will be granted that I am not to expect a direct revelation. I must study the plain physical facts of the case, ascertain what is possible and learn what appears to be wise and right."[66]

As with his proclamation revoking Hunter's emancipation in the spring of 1862 and his letter to Greeley of August the same year, Lincoln intimates to the Chicago Christian denomination that a proclamation may be constitutionally justified under his authority as commander in chief in time of war:

Understand, I raise no objections against it on legal or constitutional grounds; for, as commander-in-chief of the army and navy, in time of war, I suppose I have a right to take any measure which may best subdue the enemy. Nor do I urge objections of a moral nature, in view of possible consequences of insurrection and massacre at the South. I view the matter as a practical war measure, to be decided upon according to the advantages or disadvantages it may offer to the suppression of the rebellion.[67]

In *Emancipation and Reconstruction*, Michael Perman states the crux of Lincoln's prudent deliberation in freeing the slaves: "The question was therefore how and when a moral stance could be translated into practical policy so as to guarantee its success. That Lincoln was cautious, even opportunistic, does not necessarily mean that he lacked earnestness and sincerity in pressing for Emancipation."[68] Given his constitutional scruples, Lincoln maintained that the emancipation was a necessary and reasonable means (a war measure) taken by the nation's chief executive to impair the South's ability to make war. It would encourage slaves to escape from their southern masters and to support the approaching Union army.

The Union victory at Antietam on September 17, 1862, answered Seward's concerns about freeing the slaves without battlefield success. The victory bolstered the credibility of the Emancipation Proclamation at home and in the eyes of the world. The identification of the Union cause with the freeing of the slaves was intended to discourage foreign intervention on the side of the Confederacy by Great Britain and other European countries. The Union army would become hereafter an army of liberation. In turn, Lincoln sought to neutralize General McClellan's opposition to his policy by first replacing him as general in chief and then cashiering him altogether after the midterm elections in the fall of 1862.

A year later, on September 2, 1863, in a memo to Secretary of Treasury Salmon Chase, Lincoln tersely explained the legal basis of the Emancipation Proclamation as a war measure under his authority as commander in chief. He warned Chase that it would be both unconstitutional and imprudent to extend the measure beyond this rationale to the border slave states where military necessity did not apply. The memo is worth quoting in revealing Lincoln's prudent regard for the contingencies discussed above and Chase's corresponding blindness to them. In sum, Lincoln provides the radical Chase with a needed lesson about prudence in politics:

Knowing your great anxiety that the emancipation proclamation shall now be applied to certain parts of Virginia and Louisiana which were exempted from it last January, I state briefly what appear to me to be difficulties in the way of such a step. The original proclamation has no constitutional or legal justification, except as a military measure. The exemptions were made because the military necessity did not apply to the exempted localities. Nor does that necessity apply to them now any more than it did then. If I take the step must I not do so, without the argument of military necessity, and so, without any argument, except the one that I think the measure politically expedient, and morally right? Would I not thus give up all footing upon constitution or law? Would I not thus be in the boundless field of absolutism? Could this pass unnoticed, or unresisted? Could it fail to be perceived that without any further stretch, I might do the same in Delaware, Maryland, Kentucky, Tennessee, and Missouri; and even change any law in any state? Would not many of our own friends shrink away appalled? Would it not lose us the elections, and with them, the very cause we seek to advance?[69]

As a war measure that applied only to belligerents, the Emancipation Proclamation exempted the border slave states who remained loyal to the Union. It thus was consistent with Lincoln's intimation in the letter to Greeley of "freeing some of the slaves and leaving others alone." Critics like Lerone Bennett who contend that Lincoln was insincere in his opposition to slavery because the Emancipation Proclamation did not apply to the border states fail to mention not only the constraints of the rule of law at the time, but also Lincoln's many efforts to abolish slavery legally through gradual, compensated emancipation with the consent of these states. As noted, in March of 1862, Lincoln steered a joint resolution through Congress that offered financial aid to any border state that would take measures toward gradual, compensated emancipation. He argued that one million dollars, or less than half a day's cost of the war, would buy all the slaves in Delaware at four hundred dollars a head. Congress approved the measure, but the Border States would not consent. Ever persistent, Lincoln invited border state men to the White House, appealing to them on at least four separate occasions to accept his plan. Notably, they refused each time.

Critics also lament the dry legal language of the Emancipation Proclamation. Richard Hofstadter famously ridiculed the document as having "all the moral grandeur of a bill of lading." Yet Lincoln considered the Emancipation Proclamation his "greatest act." He explained, "If my name ever goes into history, it will be for this act, and my whole soul is in it."[70] Soaring rhetoric was inappropriate to the legal purposes of the Emancipation Proclamation, which was ingeniously written to survive the Court's review. The text notably refrained from language that would alarm moderates, including the word "abolition," with its highly suspect radical implications to most Americans at the time. Holzer correctly notes that "Lincoln had couched his thunderbolt in the muffled language of a legal writ."[71] To quell public fears about reprisals against whites, the final act also enjoined the freedmen to "abstain from all violence, unless in necessary self-defense." The subdued language and circumstances of the Emancipation Proclamation made it palatable to a broader white public that was reluctant to grant black freedom.

Once the constitutional grounds were established and public opinion cultivated in support of the measure, Lincoln's soaring rhetoric was subsequently placed in the service of sustaining the act. The Gettysburg Address is perhaps the most celebrated example. Its proclamation of a "new birth of freedom" seeks to persuade the American public to ratify the final Emancipation Proclamation as a fulfillment of the promise of equality made by the founding and the Declaration.

Finally, the dry language of the act should not obscure an important and controversial provision: authorization of the enlistment of black soldiers in the Union army. In the United States, military service was traditionally a path to citizenship. The recruitment of black soldiers was a bold yet practical step toward black freedom as Frederick Douglass recognized: "Once let the black man get upon his person the brass letters U.S.; let him get an eagle on his button, and a musket on his shoulder and bullets in his pocket and there is no power on earth which can deny that he has earned the right to citizenship in the United States."[72]

In sum, Lincoln's practical wisdom consisted in his ability to realize the principles of the Declaration under the circumstances. The Emancipation Proclamation is exemplary in this regard as prudential means that furthered the end of both liberty and Union. Lincoln's prudence is further understood in contrast to the defects of moral idealism of the abolitionists who advocated "liberty without Union" and the political pragmatism of Douglas and war Democrats, who, in effect, advocated "Union without liberty." Counterpoised to each extreme, Lincoln guided the ship of state on a steady course through rough waters. His prudence enabled him to preserve both the apple of gold and the picture of silver.

3

DUTY

*T*he parameters of statesmanship are circumscribed by constitutional and moral duty. Despotism is synonymous with the habitual transgression of these boundaries. Unlike the leadership of a radical reformer, a statesman is necessarily tied to a position of power in government and bound to a public trust with official obligations and responsibilities.[1] As the highest elected official of the nation, the president swears a solemn oath "to preserve, protect and defend the Constitution of the United States." An evaluation of Lincoln's statesmanship must therefore consider the performance of his oath-bound duty. To what extent has a leader honorably fulfilled the public trust, as opposed to shrinking from it through cowardice, betraying it through an abuse of power, or enfeebling it through incompetence?

Notably, Lincoln interpreted the duties of his office as both a source of *empowerment* and *constraint*. William Lee Miller, in his masterful study *President Lincoln: The Duty of a Statesma*n, correctly observes that upon taking office "the moral situation of Abraham Lincoln was abruptly transformed."[2] From that moment, he became "an oath bound head of state" with "an awesome new battery of powers and an immense new layer of responsibilities, obligating, constraining, and empowering him."[3] Duty can be understood in terms of this dual sense of command and prohibition. Empowerment without restraint is a recipe for despotism; restraint without empowerment is a prescription for impotence. The Union and the Constitution would have been imperiled by either extreme. The sometimes conflicting and vague requirements of duty required a prudent determination of what was appropriate in the given situation. In his special message to Congress, July 4, 1861, Lincoln posed the enduring problem of maintaining ordered liberty in this way: "Is there, in all republics, this inherent, and fatal weakness?" "Must a government, of necessity, be too *strong* for the liberties of its own people, or too *weak* to maintain its own existence?"[4] The questions reveal the extent to which the sixteenth president also viewed the Civil War as a test of the viability of republican government. Could liberty and the rule of law survive the impending crisis, or were tyranny and anarchy inevitable? What did official duty both command and forbid under these extreme circumstances? An early draft of Lincoln's Farewell Address to Springfield reveals his thoughtful contemplation of the awful weight of responsibility thrust on him as president elect: "A duty devolves upon me which is, perhaps, greater than that which has devolved upon any other man since the days of Washington."[5]

In sum, Lincoln's performance of duty was guided by his effort to harmonize moral and legal obligation. Unlike his political rivals, who saw duty exclusively in terms of allegiance to abstract moral imperatives or as blind submission to the Supreme Court, he sought to reconcile prudently the moral principles of the Declaration with the rule of law established by the Constitution. In terms of the metaphor from Proverbs, he was duty bound to preserve both the picture of silver (the Constitution) and the apple of gold (the Declaration).

This chapter will first consider Lincoln's courageous embrace of duty during the secession crisis in contrast to his predecessor's evasion of it. It will then reveal his view of oath-bound duty in the First Inaugural Address and the extent to which it both empowered and constrained him as a statesman. Lincoln's effort to reconcile moral and legal obligation was complicated further by the Supreme Court's opinion in *Dred Scott*, 1857, which had declared the central plank of the Republican Party's platform, the policy of restricting slavery in the territories, unconstitutional. Finally, because Lincoln's two terms were spent as a war president, the remaining part of the chapter will assess how he performed his duty as commander in chief who was guided by the belief "that measures, otherwise unconstitutional, might become lawful, by becoming indispensable to the preservation of the constitution, through the preservation of the nation."[6]

Lincoln's view of oath-bound duty is revealed more clearly in contrast to some of the competing views held by both North and South during the Civil War era. To say the least, the call of duty was understood differently by the various actors in the drama of the Civil War. As a former officer of the United States Army, Robert E. Lee renounced his duty and allegiance to the Constitution when he took up arms against the federal government. And whereas Stephen A. Douglas saw it as the duty of all good citizens to submit to the Supreme Court's decision in *Dred Scott*, the abolitionist William Lloyd Garrison believed that it was his duty to reject all compromises with slavery regardless of the consequences, even if it meant disunion. Finally, peace Democrats or Copperheads saw it as their duty to return the country to the status quo ante with slavery mostly intact. Their motto: "the Constitution as it is" and "the Union as it was." At the end of four years of bloody struggle, over seven hundred thousand Americans gave their lives for the sake of duty.

In contrast to each of the views above, Lincoln's prudential understanding of duty was informed by a consideration of both moral and legal norms as well as exigent circumstances. As noted in the previous chapter, he eschewed the moral idealism of some of the more radical abolitionists who viewed duty in Kantian terms as the rigid adherence to the dictates of abstract moral principle regardless of consequences. Garrison clearly expressed this Kantian understanding of duty in 1832 when he exclaimed:

> You must perform your duty, faithfully, fearlessly and promptly, and leave the consequences to God: that duty clearly is, to cease from giving countenance and protection to southern kidnappers. Let them separate, if they can muster courage enough—and the liberation of their slaves is certain. Be assured that slavery will very speedily destroy this Union, *if it be let alone;* but even if the Union can be preserved by treading upon the necks, spilling the blood, and destroying the souls of millions of your race, we say it is not worth a price like this, and that it is in the highest degree criminal for you to continue the present compact. Let the pillars thereof fall—let the superstructure crumble into dust—if it must be upheld by robbery and oppression.[7]

Indeed, Garrison's view of duty is best captured by the Latin motto "*Fiat iustitia ruat caelum*" (Let justice be done though the heavens fall).

On the other hand, Lincoln also rejected a pragmatic view of duty that placed short-term considerations of political expediency and success over principle. In his official capacity to preserve the Union, the president observed both constitutional and moral limits. He was willing to sacrifice personal ambition and the power of office in cases where compromise would have destroyed his own moral integrity and/or the constitutional integrity of the nation.

Lincoln clearly explained the extent to which oath-bound duty both *constrained* and *empowered* him as president in a letter to Albert Hodges, editor of the *Frankfort Kentucky Commonwealth* on April 4, 1864:

> I am naturally anti-slavery. If slavery is not wrong, nothing is wrong. I can not remember when I did not so think, and feel. And yet I have never understood that the Presidency conferred upon me an unrestricted right to act officially upon this judgment and feeling. It was

in the oath I took that I would, to the best of my ability, preserve, protect, and defend the Constitution of the United States. I could not take the office without taking the oath. Nor was it my view that I might take an oath to get power, and break the oath in using the power. I understood, too, that in ordinary civil administration this oath even forbade me to practically indulge my primary abstract judgment on the moral question of slavery. I had publicly declared this many times, and in many ways. And I aver that, to this day, I have done no official act in mere deference to my abstract judgment and feeling on slavery. I did understand however, that my oath to preserve the constitution to the best of my ability, imposed upon me the duty of preserving, by every indispensable means, that government—that nation—of which that constitution was the organic law.[8]

The president's remarks to Hodges above bear comparison to his similar statement to Horace Greeley two years earlier, August 22, 1862, as seen in chapter 2. In both cases, Lincoln consistently distinguished between his *"official* duty" and his "personal wish" in regard to a policy of emancipation. Though his oath prevented him from indulging his "primary abstract judgment on the moral question of slavery" "in ordinary civil administration," the same oath also obligated him to preserve the Constitution and government "by every indispensable means."[9]

James Buchanan's evasive view of his duty also provides a glaring contrast to Lincoln's willingness to use all the constitutional means at his disposal to preserve the Union. About a month after Lincoln's election and just weeks before South Carolina's secession, the lame-duck president Buchanan began his annual message of December 3, 1860, by blaming northern abolitionist agitation as the cause of the impending crisis: "The long-continued and intemperate interference of the Northern people with the question of slavery in the Southern States has at length produced its natural effects.... The immediate peril arises ... from ... the incessant and violent agitation of the slavery question throughout the North for the last quarter of a century."[10] While Buchanan acknowledged his oath-bound duty as president "to take care that the laws be faithfully executed," he argued further that the Constitution did not provide him with the lawful means to fulfill this responsibility:

What, in the meantime, is the responsibility and true position of the Executive? He is bound by solemn oath, before God and the country, "to take care that the laws be faithfully executed," and from this obligation he can not be absolved by any human power. But what if the performance of this duty, in whole or in part, has been rendered impracticable by events over which he could have exercised no control? Such at the present moment is the case throughout the State of South Carolina so far as the laws of the United States to secure the administration of justice by means of the Federal judiciary are concerned.[11]

Though Buchanan did make a case for the Union's perpetuity, he also denied, on grounds of strict construction, that the Constitution granted him, or any other branch of the federal government, the authority to coerce a state back into the Union: "Has the Constitution delegated to Congress the power to coerce a State into submission which is attempting to withdraw or has actually withdrawn from the Confederacy? . . . After much serious reflection I have arrived at the conclusion that no such power has been delegated to Congress or to any other department of the Federal Government." William Lee Miller correctly describes this speech as a "declaration of impotence." Upon hearing of Buchanan's willingness to surrender Fort Moultrie in South Carolina to the rebels, Lincoln allegedly remarked, "If that is true they ought to hang him."[12]

Buchanan's failure to deal decisively with threat of secession differed markedly from the actions of his Democratic predecessor, Andrew Jackson, during the nullification crisis. Though, as a Whig, he had criticized some of Jackson's policies, Lincoln nonetheless consulted his predecessor's arguments in his proclamation regarding nullification, December 10, 1832, as an important source for his first inaugural speech. Miller correctly explains, "Where Buchanan sought avoidance and found restriction and therefore excuse, this new president [Lincoln] would accept responsibility and find necessity and therefore empowerment."[13]

Lincoln's First Inaugural, March 4, 1861, provides a clear example of how oath-bound duty both *constrained* and *empowered* him during the impending crisis. The speech begins on a conciliatory note by reiterating Lincoln's oft-repeated pledge not to touch the existing institution of slavery: "I have no purpose, directly or indirectly, to interfere with the institution of slavery in the States where it exists. I believe I have no lawful right to do so, and I have no inclination to do."[14] As an antislavery moderate, Lincoln had consistently distinguished legally between the *existing institution* of slavery and *its extension* in the territories. The federal division of power under the Constitution prohibited the national government from interfering with the *existing institution* in the states. Put another way, it created "a firewall" between the states and the federal government on slavery.[15] Constitutionally speaking, the institution fell under the authority of the states' domestic police powers and was therefore off-limits to federal interference. Though Lincoln hated slavery ("I have always hated slavery, I think as much as any Abolitionist"), as president he swore an oath to uphold the Constitution, which meant recognizing its concessions toward the institution. Prior to the exigencies of war, duty thus constrained him in regard to the *existing institution*.

After acknowledging that the Constitution denied him authority to touch the *existing institution* of slavery, Lincoln further conceded his duty to uphold the fugitive slave provision of Article IV, Section 2: "No person held to Service or Labour in one State, under the Laws thereof, escaping into another, shall, in Consequence of any Law or Regulation therein, be discharged from such Service or Labour, but shall be delivered up on Claim of the Party to whom such Service or Labour may be due." By contrast, radicals, such as Lincoln's future secretary of treasury Salmon P. Chase, refused to acknowledge the odious obligations associated with this constitutional provision. As head of his party, however, Lincoln disagreed. He reminded his fellow Republicans of their oath-bound duty: "All members of Congress swear their support to the whole Constitution—to this provision as much as to any other. To the proposition, then, that slaves whose cases come within the terms of this clause, "shall be delivered up," their oaths are unanimous."[16]

Critics of Lincoln both yesterday and today cite these concessions to the *existing institution* of slavery and to the fugitive slave provision as proof that he was a pragmatist willing to "sell-out" his antislavery principles in exchange for peace at any price. Lincoln, then and now, fails to live up to this absolute standard that ignores the constitutional obligations to slavery. Indeed, the abolitionist Wendell Phillips ridiculed Lincoln as "the Slave Hound of Illinois" because of his support for the fugitive slave provision.[17] To judge Lincoln by this standard, however, blatantly disregards the duty of elected officials by ignoring an explicit provision of the Constitution and settled precedent.

Years earlier, in 1848, Lincoln chided the free soil party for its rigid moral idealism. He recognized that the splinter party's unwillingness to support Zachary Taylor, a slaveholder with antislavery views, would lead to the election of a proslavery Democrat. The practical reasoning of the free soil movement was flawed since its conception of duty appealed only to religious and moral principles in their abstract without regard for political and legal circumstances and the unintended consequences of their actions. With reference to Garrison, Lincoln stated:

The "Free Soil" men in. . . . declaring that they would "do their duty and leave the consequences to God," merely gave an excuse for taking a course that they were not able to maintain by a fair and full argument. To make this declaration did not show what their duty was. If it did we should have no use for judgment, we might as well be made without intellect, and when divine or human law does not clearly point out what *is* our duty, we have no means of finding out what it is by using our most intelligent judgment of the consequences.[18]

Over a decade later, as president, Lincoln similarly lectured a group of Chicago ministers about their narrow view of duty that only considered abstract moral claims apart from the legal, social, and political contingencies of the time:

I hope it will not be irreverent for me to say that if it is probable that God would reveal his will to others, on a point so connected with my duty, it might be supposed he would reveal it directly to me; for, unless I am more deceived in myself than I often am, it is my earnest desire to know the will of Providence in this matter. *And if I can learn what it is I will do it!* These are not, however, the days of miracles, and I suppose it will be granted that I am not to expect a direct revelation. I must study the plain physical facts of the case, ascertain what is possible and learn what appears to be wise and right.[19]

As with his criticism of the abolitionist cause in 1848, Lincoln here rejects a Kantian idealism that considers only the dictates of moral principles in their abstract purity. Though he well recognized the evil of slavery in principle, this abstract recognition did not mandate immediate emancipation contrary to constitutional obligations, nor did it tell him specifically what course of action was best suited for realizing this principle given the present situation. While the inherent goodness or evil of slavery in principle continued to guide his deliberations as a statesman, he also maintained that the specific determination or application of this principle to politics involved prudential mediation and the consideration of its consequences.

As noted, considerations of duty not only constrained Lincoln, but they also empowered him. His concessions to slavery at the beginning of the First Inaugural were by no means his last words on the subject. They should not obscure what was both implicitly and explicitly claimed in the remaining parts of his speech. Indeed, Lincoln remained inflexible on the core principles of the Republican Party in defiance of the Supreme Court's opinion in *Dred Scott*: the duty and right to restrict slavery in the territories. His indomitable will and firm determination to preserve the Union are conveyed vividly in an early draft of the speech, which was subsequently toned down in the final version: *"All the power at my disposal* will be used to hold, occupy and possess the property and places belonging to the government"* (emphasis added).[20]

Throughout his public life, he had consistently argued that the moral imperatives of the Declaration, the text of the Constitution, the Founders' intentions, and ample legal and historical precedent authorized the federal restriction of slavery in the territories. In the case of territorial slavery, constitutional duty and moral right strongly converged. Lincoln tersely summarized the crux of the argument in his First Inaugural: "One section of our country believes slavery is *right*, and ought to be extended, while the other believes it is *wrong*, and ought not to be extended."[21]

In defense of his claim to restrict slavery in the territories, Lincoln cited Article IV, Section 3 of the Constitution: "The Congress shall have Power to dispose of and make all needful Rules and Regulations respecting Territory or other Property belonging to the United States." In addition, he often appealed to Article 6 of the Northwest Ordinance of 1787: "There shall be neither slavery nor involuntary servitude in the said territory." Indeed, this federal act fortuitously ensured that Illinois, Indiana, Wisconsin, Michigan, and Ohio would enter the Union as free states.

Lincoln's Cooper Union address, February 27, 1860, which was delivered a year before his First Inaugural, provided a masterful exposition of the Founders' intent to restrict territorial slavery. His exhaustive research on the subject concluded that of the thirty-nine Founders who voted for the Constitution, thirty-six either voted at some time in their public life for the federal restriction of slavery or expressed clear convictions in support of this policy.[22] Indeed, Cooper Union revealed Lincoln's intellectual prowess as the standard bearer of the Republican Party and as a viable candidate for his party's presidential nomination. He concluded the speech with a rousing call to magnanimous *duty* that would guide his presidency: "Neither let us be slandered from our duty by false accusations against us, nor frightened from it by menaces of destruction to the Government nor of dungeons to ourselves. LET US HAVE FAITH THAT RIGHT MAKES MIGHT, AND IN THAT FAITH, LET US, TO THE END, DARE TO DO OUR DUTY AS WE UNDERSTAND IT."[23] The concluding words of the Cooper Union address left no doubt in the mind of the country that Lincoln considered it a "DUTY" to restrict slavery. As Harold Holzer has shown, the speech was widely published and distributed as a manifesto of Republican political ideology.

Consonant with the stated principles of the Cooper Union address and its attendant view of duty, during the secession winter (the interval between his election in November and his inauguration in March), Lincoln worked behind the scenes to defeat any compromises on the question of slavery extension.[24] In a revealing private letter to Elihu Washburne, December 3, 1860, the president elect gave these instructions: "Prevent, as far as possible, any of our friends from demoralizing themselves, and our cause, by entertaining propositions for compromise of any sort, on "*slavery extention*" There is no possible compromise upon it, but which puts us under again, and leaves all our work to do over again. . . . On that point hold firm, as with a chain of steel."[25] Lincoln thus risked war rather than surrendering the core principle of the Republican Party. His actions in this regard are exemplary of the statesman committed to *courageous duty* and principle, rather than a pragmatist bent on results at the cost of both.

The call to duty at Cooper Union included the important qualification, "AS WE UNDERSTAND IT." This qualification was in response to the *Dred Scott* decision of 1857, which had declared the central plank of the Republican Party's platform—the restriction of territorial slavery—unconstitutional. In effect, *Dred Scott* made it a "*duty*" on the part of public officials to protect, perpetuate, and extend slavery. In an egregious overreach of judicial power, Taney used his authority as chief justice to vindicate the extreme proslavery of the Constitution, by claiming that "the right of property in a slave is distinctly and expressly affirmed in the Constitution."

There were three key elements to Taney's opinion: (1) the denial of black citizenship and the further sweeping assertion that the black man had "no rights that the white man was bound to respect; and that the negro might justly and lawfully be reduced slavery for his benefits"; (2) the denial of the federal right to restrict slavery in the territories; and (3) the affirmation of a national right to property in a slave under the Fifth Amendment's due process clause. In effect, Taney reversed the free soil motto of "freedom national and slavery local" by transforming slavery into a national institution.[26] If the right to property in a slave state was indeed a fundamental, national right as safeguarded by the Fifth Amendment as Taney claimed, then policies that proposed its restriction in the territories (perhaps even in the free states as well) were constitutionally suspect. In defiance of Taney's opinion, Article 7 of the Republican Party platform of 1860 condemned *Dred Scott* as a radical betrayal of the founding and the rule of law: "That the new dogma that the constitution of its own force carries slavery into any or all of the territories of the United States, is a dangerous political heresy, at variance with the explicit provisions of that instrument itself, with cotemporaneous exposition, and with legislative and judicial precedent, is revolutionary in its tendency and subversive of the peace and harmony of the country."[27] Lincoln and the Republicans would not regard *Dred Scott* as a settled or controlling precedent on slavery. The stage was thus set for a clash between the judiciary and the Republican Party over the interpretation of the Constitution and the requirements of official duty in regard to the Court's ruling.

In earlier speeches, Lincoln demonstrated that the text of the Constitution failed to support Taney's claim of a national right to property in a slave under the Fifth Amendment. An inspection of the document revealed that the right to property in slave states was neither "distinctly" nor "expressly affirmed in the Constitution." Nor was the word property ever mentioned in connection the word slavery or slave, as Taney asserted. On the contrary, Lincoln argued that the Founders deliberately avoided using the term "slave" or "slavery" in the Constitution and instead substituted euphemistic terms and evasive language such as "persons held to labor" in order to convey their moral dubiousness about the institution. Indeed, Madison, the so-called father of the Constitution, candidly stated in his *Notes of the Debates in the Federal Convention* that "he thought it wrong to admit in the Constitution that there could be property in men."[28] And contrary to Taney, who asserted that the Founders maintained that the negro could "justly and lawfully be reduced slavery," Madison noted that although these same terms were originally included in an early draft of the fugitive slave provision, they were deleted and replaced with "held to Service or Labour in one State, under the Laws thereof." Most notably, Madison explained that the change was made "in compliance with the wish of some who thought the term ["legal"] equivocal, and favoring the idea that slavery was legal in a moral view."[29] That is to say, the words were deliberately changed to avoid the impression of a moral embrace of slavery.

In sum, Lincoln interpreted the concessions at the Constitutional Convention in regard to slavery as a matter of "necessity" without which the Constitution could not have been ratified. While these compromises were indeed legally binding, they were to be regarded as exceptions to the rule of freedom. The compromises in the Constitution were not, as Taney claimed, an enumeration of a fundamental national right to chattel slavery.

At Peoria in 1854, Lincoln used a folksy metaphor to describe the Founders' anomalous view of slavery and the Constitution. The Founders bow to the necessity of slavery at the Constitution, Lincoln explained, was much like a patient who was ashamed and fearful of a cancerous growth that could not be immediately remedied without killing him, but who nonetheless hoped that at some future date it could be safely removed:

> The argument of "Necessity" was the only argument they ever admitted in favor of slavery; and so far, and so far only as it carried them, did they ever go. They found the institution existing among us, which they could not help; and they cast blame upon the British King for having permitted its introduction. BEFORE the constitution, they prohibited its introduction into the north-western Territory—the only country we owned, then free from it. AT the framing and adoption of the constitution, they forbore to so much as mention the word "slave" or "slavery" in the whole instrument. In the provision for the recovery of fugitives, the slave is spoken of as a "PERSON HELD TO SERVICE OR LABOR." In that prohibiting the abolition of the African slave trade for twenty years, that trade is spoken of as "The migration or importation of such persons as any of the States NOW EXISTING, shall think proper to admit," &c. These are the only provisions alluding to slavery. Thus, the thing is hid away, in the constitution, just as an afflicted man hides away a wen or a cancer, which he dares not cut out at once, lest he bleed to death; with the promise, nevertheless, that the cutting may begin at the end of a given time.[30]

As a statesman, Lincoln was compelled to reconcile his duty to the rule of law with his opposition to the Court's opinion in *Dred Scott*. He had to defend the Republican Party from the charge that it was a purely sectional party made of lawless radicals like John Brown.[31] Indeed, Stephen A. Douglas had accused Lincoln and the Republicans of dereliction of duty and perjury for their opposition to *Dred Scott*. According to Douglas, Lincoln's actions in this regard were an incitement to anarchy and mob rule:

> If the decision of the Supreme Court, the tribunal created by the constitution to decide the question, is final and binding, is he not bound by it just as strongly as if he was for it instead of against it originally. Is every man in this land allowed to resist decisions he does not like, and only support those that meet his approval? What are important courts worth unless their decisions are binding on all good citizens? It is the fundamental principles of the judiciary that its decisions are final. It is created for that purpose so that when you cannot agree among yourselves on a disputed point you appeal to the judicial tribunal which steps in and decides for you, and that

decision is then binding on every good citizen. It is the law of the land just as much with Mr. Lincoln against it as for it. And yet he says that if that decision is binding he is a perjured man if he does not vote for a slave code in the different territories of this Union. Well, if you (turning to Mr. Lincoln) are not going to resist the decision, if you obey it, and do not intend to array mob law against the constituted authorities, then, according to your own statement, you will be a perjured man if you do not vote to establish slavery in these territories.[32]

Here Douglas emphasizes constitutional duty in terms of blind obedience to the Supreme Court as the ultimate arbiter of the Constitution. By contrast, in his first public reply to *Dred Scott* in Springfield, June 26, 1857, Lincoln sought to reconcile his opposition to this opinion with his respect for the rule of law by citing Andrew Jackson's precedent for constitutional interpretation: "If the opinion of the Supreme court covered the whole ground of this act, it ought not to control the co-ordinate authorities of this Government. The Congress, the executive and the court, must each for itself be guided by its own opinion of the Constitution. Each public officer, who takes an oath to support the Constitution, swears that he will support it as he understands it, and not as it is understood by others."[33] Thus, while Lincoln would abide by the Court's decision in regard to the narrow question of whether or not Dred Scott was free, he would not accept it as a settled precedent.

In the same speech at Springfield, Lincoln offered exacting criteria for accepting the Court's opinion as a settled precedent. Though seemingly high by today's standards, Lincoln's criteria is perhaps just as revealing about our habitual willingness to submit to the Court's abuse of power when other constitutional means are at our disposal to resist it:

If this important decision had been made by the unanimous concurrence of the judges, and without any apparent partisan bias, and in accordance with legal public expectation, and with the steady practice of the departments throughout our history, and had been in no part, based on assumed historical facts which are not really true; or, if wanting in some of these, it had been before the court more than once, and had there been affirmed and re-affirmed through a course of years, it then might be, perhaps would be, factious, nay, even revolutionary, to not acquiesce in it as a precedent.[34]

In sum, Lincoln found *Dred* Scott wanting in all of these respects.

This background helps us appreciate Lincoln's view of duty in the First Inaugural Address where he reiterated opposition to *Dred Scott*. To acquiesce in the Court's abuse of power was to abandon popular government in exchange for government by the judiciary: "the candid citizen must confess that if the policy of the government, upon vital questions, affecting the whole people, is to be irrevocably fixed by decisions of the Supreme Court, the instant they are made, in ordinary litigation between parties, in personal actions, the people will have ceased, to be their own rulers, having, to that extent, practically resigned their government, into the hands of that eminent tribunal."[35] His explicit declamation in the First Inaugural that he would not recognize *Dred Scott* as an authoritative precedent left no doubt that he would remain firm on the Republican Party's moral right and lawful duty to restrict slavery in the territories.

Lincoln further defied the Court's ruling in *Dred Scott* by suggesting that he would extend federal protection to free blacks who were mistakenly claimed as fugitives. After acknowledging his duty to return fugitive slaves per Article IV, Section 2, he turned to the privileges and immunities clause of the same article, rhetorically asking: "Again, in any law upon this subject, ought not all the safeguards of liberty known in civilized and humane jurisprudence to be introduced, so that a free man be not, in any case, surrendered as a slave? And might it not be well, at the same time, to provide by law for the enforcement of that clause in the Constitution which guarantees that 'the citizens of each State shall be entitled to all privileges and immunities of citizens in the several States'?"[36] In defiance of *Dred Scott*, Lincoln suggested that it was his duty as president to extend federal protection to free blacks in order to safeguard them from abuses of the Fugitive Slave Act. Thus, while the fugitive slave provision of Article IV in the Constitution constrained Lincoln in regard to slavery, the privileges and immunities clause of the same article empowered him to extend black freedom in this regard.

Herman Belz correctly describes Lincoln's "rhetorical inquiry" in the First Inaugural as a "significant move" that "advanced a civil rights proposal that was deeply offensive to southern and border state opinion."[37] "In addition to setting a dangerous precedent," Belz explains, "Lincoln's proposal would strike at the inequality of the races, the fundamental principle on which slavery rested." During the war, Lincoln acted on his civil rights rhetoric in the First Inaugural by having his administration confer birthright citizenship on free blacks. This was done through an opinion of Attorney General Bates on November 29, 1862, which declared, "that every free person born in the United States was, 'at the moment of birth, *prima facie* a citizen.'"[38] Because military service in the United States has always provided a path to citizenship, it is perhaps no coincidence that Bates's opinion was issued two months before the final Emancipation Proclamation's provision for black enlistment in the Union army.

The First Inaugural also explained how the president's oath-bound duty obliged him to resist secession. Appealing to the argument from definition, Lincoln first claimed that perpetuity is implied in all fundamental laws: "I hold, that in contemplation of universal law, and of the Constitution, the Union of these States is perpetual. Perpetuity is implied, if not expressed, in the fundamental law of all national governments. It is safe to assert that no government proper, ever had a provision in its organic law for its own termination. Continue to execute all the express provisions of our national Constitution, and the Union will endure forever—it being impossible to destroy it, except by some action not provided for in the instrument itself."[39] Indeed, one of the stated goals of the Articles of Confederation, which outlined the form of government that preceded the Constitution, was to maintain a "perpetual Union." As a fundamental law that defined the legal relations between the states and the Union, the Constitution did not include a provision for its own termination.

He then took up the southern states' rights doctrine of the Constitution as a contract that could be unilaterally dissolved by any member. If the Constitution was indeed a contract, asked Lincoln, "can it . . . be peaceably unmade, by less than all the parties who made it? One party to a contract may violate it—break it, so to speak; but does it not require all to lawfully rescind it?" Again, using the argument from definition, he noted: "Plainly, the central idea of secession, is the essence of anarchy."[40] Majority rule, not the tyranny of one or a few, is the governing principle in a democratic republic. Lincoln concluded that whoever rejects the principle of majority rule is compelled to embrace either despotism or anarchy as the only practical alternative.

Regarding the Declaration as the formal cause of America's collective identity, Lincoln further contended that the Union preceded the Constitution:

> Descending from these general principles, we find the proposition that, in legal contemplation, the Union is perpetual, confirmed by the history of the Union itself. The Union is much older than the Constitution. It was formed in fact, by the Articles of Association in 1774. It was matured and continued by the Declaration of Independence in 1776. It was further matured and the faith of all the

then thirteen States expressly plighted and engaged that it should be perpetual, by the Articles of Confederation in 1778. And finally, in 1787, one of the declared objects for ordaining and establishing the Constitution, was *"to form a more perfect union."*[41]

Though an incipient Union was formed by the Articles of Association of 1774 and the Articles of Confederation, Lincoln clearly views 1776 as a critical moment in the Union's maturation. Though not first chronologically, the Declaration was philosophically prior as the formal cause or governing principle of the Union, just as the soul is the essence of a human being. Put another way, the Declaration, in Lincoln's view, represented the animating spirit that breathed life into the Union and the Constitution.

Thus, the "more perfect Union" of 1787 replaced "the less than perfect" Union under the Articles of Confederation. The latter was less than perfect in view of its failure to fulfill its stated goal of perpetuity. Given this object, Lincoln asked, "if destruction of the Union, by one, or by a part only, of the States, be lawfully possible, the Union is *less* perfect than before the Constitution, having lost the vital element of perpetuity."[42] In conclusion, Lincoln argued "that no State, upon its own mere motion, can lawfully get out of the Union,—that *resolves* and *ordinances* to that effect are legally void; and that acts of violence, within any State or States, against the authority of the United States, are insurrectionary or revolutionary, according to circumstances."[43]

Though the Constitution implies perpetuity and provides no legal basis for secession, Lincoln conceded that the South may nonetheless appeal outside the Constitution by invoking the right to revolution. However, the Declaration itself notes that the right to revolution cannot be justified on the basis of "light and transient causes" but only in regard to a "long train of abuses and usurpations." According to Lincoln, the factual basis did not justify a right to revolution/secession. The South could point to no specific enumerated right in either the Constitution or the Bill of Rights that had been violated by the Republican Party. On the contrary, Lincoln consistently had acknowledged his official duty to uphold the established provisions and precedents in regard to slavery, even the odious fugitive slave provision. He thus rhetorically asked, "Think, if you can, of a single instance in which a plainly written provision of the Constitution has ever been denied. If, by the mere force of numbers, a majority should deprive a minority of any clearly written constitutional right, it might, in a moral point of view, justify revolution—certainly would, if such right were a vital one. But such is not our case. All the vital rights of minorities, and of individuals, are so plainly assured to them, by affirmations and negations, Warranties and prohibitions, in the Constitution, that controversies never arise concerning them."[44]

Certainly, there were differences of constitutional opinion over the extension of slavery, including the Court's novel interpretation in *Dred Scott*, which was not yet settled precedent. Counseling prudence, Lincoln explained that "no organic law can ever be framed with a provision specifically applicable to every question which may occur in practical administration." Since it is impossible to settle every disputed question through a direct appeal to the text of the Constitution and precedent, differences of opinion on constitutional issues should be resolved within the legal framework of the Constitution and through the amendment process rather than an appeal to secession. Voters dissatisfied with policies should seek recourse to the ballot box instead of bayonets.

Contrary to Buchanan's "declaration of impotence," Lincoln then cited his oath in Article II as the basis of his obligation to preserve the Union and enforce federal law:

> I therefore consider that, in view of the Constitution and the laws, the Union is unbroken; and, to the extent of my ability, I shall take care, as the Constitution itself expressly enjoins upon me, that the laws of the Union be faithfully executed in all the States. Doing this; and I shall perform it, so far as practicable, unless my rightful masters, the American people, shall withhold the requisite means, or, in some authoritative manner, direct the contrary. I trust this will not be regarded as a menace, but only as the declared purpose of the Union that it *will* constitutionally defend, and maintain itself.[45]

Here Lincoln refers to his public charge in Article II, Section 3 that the president "shall take Care that the Laws be faithfully executed." As the only elected representative of the entire nation, the president is entrusted to administer the government and to enforce the laws. Nowhere does this public charge call on him to oversee the dismemberment of the Union. On the contrary, his duty requires him to perpetuate the Constitution inviolably to his successor: "The Chief Magistrate derives all his authority from the people, and they have conferred none upon him to fix terms for the separation of the States. . . . His duty is to administer the present government, as it came to his hands, and to transmit it, unimpaired by him, to his successor."[46]

With reference to the rebel siege of Fort Sumter, Lincoln made clear that his official duty as chief executive both obligated and authorized him to enforce the laws and to protect federal property: "the power confined to me will be used to hold, occupy, and possess the property and places belonging to the government."[47] This phrasing studiously avoided belli- cose language like "invasion" or "force" that could alienate remaining loyal states teetering on the brink of secession. Acting on the vision of statesmanship in the Cooper Union address, as chief executive, Lincoln would perform his duty with the faith that "right makes might." In con- cluding his argument, he framed his duty in a manner that placed future responsibility for war on those who had seceded. In performing its duty, the government would not be the aggressor: "In *your* hands, my dissat- isfied fellow countrymen, and not in *mine*, is the momentous issue of civil war. The government will not assail *you*. You can have no conflict, without being yourselves the aggressors. *You* have no oath registered in Heaven to destroy the government, while *I* shall have the most solemn one to 'preserve, protect and defend' it."[48] Unlike his predecessor, this president would use all the constitutional tools at his disposal to pre- serve the Union in accordance with the "original idea" of equality in the Declaration. William Lee Miller explains that "in Lincoln's view this war was . . . a war not of choice, but of duty, a war not of conquest but of the most quintessential national self-defense."[49]

War opens new challenges to the Constitution that do not exist in peacetime.[50] Before Lincoln was inaugurated on March 4, 1861, seven states from the lower South had already seceded from the Union and formed the Confederacy. The rebels had seized public property, forts, arsenals, and mails. President Buchanan passively watched the dismem- berment of the Union, choosing to hand the problem over to his suc- cessor. During "the Eighty Days" between his inauguration on March 4, 1861, and the assembling of Congress in special session on July 4, 1861, Lincoln undertook a series of extraordinary measures to suppress the rebellion. These included suspending the writ of habeas corpus, block- ading the South, calling forth state militias, and spending money with- out congressional authorization. Though Congress would approve these measures subsequently, questions remain why Lincoln did not convene Congress earlier. In waging the Civil War, the Lincoln administration further enacted conscription, arrested Maryland legislators, evacuated parts of Missouri, passed an income tax, established military tribunals, and unleashed Sherman to make "Georgia howl." The justification of the Emancipation Proclamation "as a fit and necessary war measure for sup- pressing the rebellion" was just as controversial. Given his broad use of executive power during the Civil War, some wondered whether the Constitution would survive Lincoln's efforts to save it.

In defense of his actions, at times, the president appealed to the extraconstitutional maxim *"salus populi suprema lex"*: the welfare of the people is the supreme law. Most notably, in suspending the writ of habeas corpus (a due process safeguard that guarantees the accused the right to have a judge review the grounds of one's arrest), Lincoln rhetorically asked: "are all the laws, *but one*, to go unexecuted, and the government itself go to pieces, lest that one be violated?"[51] This "all the laws, *but one*" argument highly resembles John Locke's doctrine of prerogative—that is, the "Power to act according to discretion, for the publick good, without the prescription of the Law, and sometimes even against it."[52]

In view of Lincoln's broad exercise of power during the Civil War, Clinton Rossiter went so far as to claim that the sixteenth president provides an example of a constitutional dictatorship.[53] However, as Herman Belz has shown and as will be argued here, the Constitution itself includes sufficient flexibility to justify Lincoln's extraordinary measures without speculation about the need for a constitutional dictatorship.[54] Mark Neely likewise notes that Lincoln and the Republican Party "struggled to steer clear of saying that the Constitution was not made for war and that it should be put aside temporarily as a national inconvenience."[55] Though the motto *inter arma silent leges* (law is silent in the midst of arms) was invoked occasionally, Neely notes that "such statements were unusual."[56] In sum, the "Republicans continued to embrace the Constitution and appeal to it."[57]

Under the Constitution, Lincoln could have summoned Congress to convene at an earlier time, but he did not do so for at least three likely reasons: (1) elections were still taking place in some states. At this time in the nation's history, there was no uniform election date; (2) the capital had not been fully secured and was encircled by the slave states of Maryland and Virginia, thereby making it vulnerable to a Confederate preemptive strike or siege; (3) the absence of Congress provided an opportunity to deal more decisively with the immediate crisis until the situation was stabilized.

In justifying the broad measures to suppress the rebellion, Lincoln appealed to duty in his special message to Congress, July 4, 1861. Reiterating his oath-bound duty in the First Inaugural, he summarized the facts of the situation: "Finding this condition of things, and believing it to be an imperative duty upon the incoming Executive, to prevent, if possible, the consummation of such attempt to destroy the Federal Union, a choice of means to that end became indispensable. This choice was made; and was declared in the Inaugural address."[58] Lincoln then claimed that his actions were undertaken as a matter of "popular demand" and "public necessity" to meet the crisis: "These measures, whether strictly legal or not, were ventured upon, under what appeared to be a popular demand, and a public necessity; trusting, then as now, that Congress would readily ratify them. It is believed that nothing has been done beyond the constitutional competency of Congress."

Though acknowledging that his actions may not have been strictly legal, Lincoln suggested that they still may be justified as a matter of necessity based on the principle of *salus populi suprema lex*—the welfare of the people is the supreme law. Particularly controversial at the time was Lincoln's suspension of the writ of habeas corpus, which was challenged by none other than Chief Justice Roger B. Taney in the case of *ex parte Merryman*. The writ of habeas corpus is a cornerstone of due process that protects against arbitrary arrest. Its origins can be traced back to British constitutionalism and the effort to bridle the king's power. Sir William Blackstone in his *Commentaries on the Laws of England* referred to "the Great Writ" as "the glory of English law." Habeas provides the accused with the right to have a judge review the grounds of his or her arrest, and, if they are found wanting, to release him or her immediately. In sum, it tests the legality of detention.[59]

Lincoln framed his special message in response to Taney, who had declared his suspension of the writ of habeas corpus unconstitutional in the then recently decided case of *ex parte Merryman*, 1861.[60] Much overlooked in this message is the extent to which Lincoln sought to rebut Taney's accusation of dereliction of duty. Taney concluded his opinion in *Merryman* with a direct challenge to the president: "It will then remain for that high officer, in fulfilment of his constitutional obligation to 'take care that the laws be faithfully executed,' to determine what measures he will take to cause the civil process of the United States to be respected and enforced."[61]

Contrary to the charge of dereliction, Lincoln argued that duty obligated him to suspend the writ of habeas corpus: "Soon after the first call for militia, it was considered a duty to authorize the Commanding General, in proper cases, according to his discretion, to suspend the privilege of the writ of habeas corpus; or, in other words, to arrest, and detain, without resort to the ordinary processes and forms of law, such individuals as he might deem dangerous to the public safety. This authority has purposely been exercised but very sparingly."[62] With reference to Taney's challenge, he further explained, "Nevertheless, the legality and propriety of what has been done under it, are questioned; and the attention of the country has been called to the proposition that one who is sworn to 'take care that the laws be faithfully executed,' should not himself violate them."[63]

Lincoln then makes three arguments in his response to Taney's allegation that he violated his oath bound duty in suspending the writ and in ignoring the Court's ruling: (1) a hypothetical extraconstitutional argument based on prerogative; (2) a constitutional argument based on Article I, Section 9; and (3) a separation of powers inquiry about who has the authority to suspend the writ. Indeed, Lincoln's legal skill in making this three-pronged argument warrants Frank J. Williams's characterization of him as "Attorney General-in-Chief."[64]

The first part of his argument is a hypothetical appeal to prerogative. Lincoln concisely expressed this argument in terms of his question: "are all the laws, *but one*, to go unexecuted, and the government itself go to pieces, lest that one be violated?" As noted, his justification here highly resembles the political philosopher John Locke's teaching on prerogative, which is to be exercised only in extreme circumstances when a crisis renders the ordinary operation of laws either impossible or disastrous. In explaining the power of prerogative, Locke points to the necessity of burning down nearby houses (clearly illegal in ordinary circumstances) in order to contain the danger of a raging fire that would imminently consume an entire neighborhood or city. Because prerogative calls for quick decisive action in times of crisis, Locke vests it with the federative branch (an office that resembles the American presidency in combining the powers of executive and foreign affairs) instead of the slower and more deliberative legislative branch.

Despite his professed strict constructionism, Jefferson reiterated Locke's view of prerogative in a September 1810 letter, written shortly after his presidency, in defense of his actions in acquiring the Louisiana Purchase: "A strict observance of the written laws is doubtless *one* of the high duties of good citizen, but it is not the *highest*. The laws of necessity, of self-preservation, of saving our country when in danger, are of higher obligation. To lose our country by a scrupulous adherence to written law, would be to lose the law itself, with life, liberty, property and all those who are enjoying them with us; thus absurdly sacrificing the end to the means."[65] Like Locke and Jefferson, Lincoln maintained that while observance of the written law is a certainly a duty, its strict observance in time of crisis is trumped by a greater duty and obligation to preserve the very survival of the nation. Consistent with the views of Locke and Jefferson on prerogative, Lincoln contended that the breaking of the law, "to a limited extent" in at the beginning of the rebellion when Congress was out of session was necessary to prevent the country from going "to pieces."

After conceding that a law *might have been* broken, Lincoln cleverly argued that under the circumstances, in either case, whether he obeyed or disobeyed Taney's ruling, the president's oath would inevitably have been broken:

> The whole of the laws which were required to be faithfully executed, were being resisted, and failing of execution, in nearly one-third of the States. Must they be allowed to finally fail of execution, even had it been perfectly clear, that by the use of the means necessary to their execution, some single law, made in such extreme tenderness of the citizen's liberty, that practically, it relieves more of the guilty, than of the innocent, should, to a very limited extent, be violated? To state the question more directly, are all the laws, *but one*, to go unexecuted, and the government itself go to pieces, lest that one be violated? Even in such a case, would not the official oath be broken, if the government should be overthrown, when it was believed that disregarding the single law, would tend to preserve it?[66]

As a lawyer, Lincoln was famous for conceding his opponents premises yet nonetheless winning the case. Here he uses this same tactic by conceding Taney's premise that he broke the law, yet concluding that he was justified in doing so nonetheless. In obeying Taney's ruling, Lincoln's oath would have been broken since "all the laws but one" would have failed of execution. A strict adherence to the oath in this case was ambiguous since it would have been broken in either scenario. What then was at stake is the lesser of two evils, breaking one law in a limited sense or allowing the country to go to ruin. Duty demanded assigning greater weight to the higher obligation under the circumstances: to break the one law in order to save the country.

However, a careful reading of Lincoln's extraconstitutional appeal to prerogative reveals that it is hypothetical. This is made clear by his use of the conditional and subjunctive in the last sentence: *"Even in such a case*, would not the official oath be broken, if the government should be overthrown [?]"* (emphasis added).[67] That is to say, *even if* Lincoln conceded Taney's premise that a law was broken, he was nevertheless justified in so doing on extraconstitutional grounds of prerogative.

After presenting the hypothetical argument, Lincoln abruptly denies the factual basis of Taney's claim that he broke the law in suspending the writ of habeas corpus. Remarkably, Lincoln now suggests that "no law was broken" since Article I, Section 9 of the Constitution authorizes the suspension of the writ of habeas in cases of rebellion or invasion. This

second part of Lincoln's argument thus provides a constitutional defense
of his actions:

> But it was not believed that this question was presented. It was not
> believed that any law was violated. The provision of the Constitu-
> tion that "The privilege of the writ of habeas corpus, shall not be
> suspended unless when, in cases of rebellion or invasion, the public
> safety may require it," is equivalent to a provision—is a provision—
> that such privilege may be suspended when, in cases of rebellion,
> or invasion, the public safety *does* require it. It was decided that we
> have a case of rebellion, and that the public safety does require the
> qualified suspension of the privilege of the writ which was autho-
> rized to be made.[68]

Lincoln reaches his conclusion through a broad construction of the
text and the Founders' intent. The fact that the text of the Constitution
expressly allows for exceptions to the suspension of the writ in times of
rebellion and invasion implies that the Constitution itself distinguishes
between its operation in times of peace and crisis. By providing for these
exceptions, the Founders clearly recognized that the same legal safeguards
in peacetime were inapplicable during an invasion or rebellion. Since there
was undeniably a rebellion, the suspension of the writ was authorized.

The third part of the argument raises a question concerning separation
of powers, that is, *who* is authorized to suspend the writ—the Congress
or the president? The suspension clause is located in Article I, Section
9, which deals mostly, but not exclusively, with the powers of Congress.
In view of its placement in Article I, Taney emphasized in *Merryman*
that only Congress could suspend the writ. Lincoln, on the contrary, did
not view the placement of the clause in Article I as decisive. Instead, he
claimed that the Constitution was actually silent as to which branch may
suspend the writ. Of greater saliency, according to Lincoln, was the fact
that the provision was included in the case of "dangerous emergency."
It would have been imprudent on the part of the Founders, Lincoln argued, to have vested the power solely in Congress.[69] He thus explained:
"Now it is insisted that Congress, and not the Executive, is vested with
this power. But the Constitution itself, is silent as to which, or who, is to
exercise the power; and as the provision was plainly made for a dangerous
emergency, it cannot be believed the framers of the instrument intended,
that in every case, the danger should run its course, until Congress could
be called together; the very assembling of which might be prevented,
as was intended in this case, by the rebellion."[70] The third part of the

argument defended the executive's authority to suspend the writ based on a reasonable inference about the Founders' intent in terms of both the Constitution's expressed word and its silence.

In contemplating Lincoln's duty as a statesman, it must not be forgotten that his combined national strategy of preserving a Union and ending slavery depended foremost on the Union's military success. This, in turn, hinged on his role as commander in chief in wartime. As seen in the previous chapter, the Emancipation Proclamation, which advanced the twin goals of saving the Union and ending slavery, was justified as a "war measure" under the president's authority as commander in chief. Indeed, Lincoln revoked Fremont's prior emancipation because it was "not within the range of military law or necessity."

In *Tried by War: Abraham Lincoln as Commander in Chief*, James M. McPherson shows that "Lincoln was a hands-on commander in chief who persisted through a terrible ordeal of defeats and disappointments to final triumph—and tragedy—at the end."[71] While Lincoln seems not to have read Clausewitz's classic work *On War*, his actions as a war president were consistent with the Prussian strategist's main thesis: "The political objective is the goal, war is the means of reaching it, and means can never be considered in isolation from their purpose. . . . Therefore, it is clear that war should never be thought of as something autonomous but always as an instrument of policy."[72]

Lincoln's statesmanship thus cannot be divorced from his actions as war president. As a commander in chief, he had to manage the complicated interplay of politics and the military. His actions in this regard included removing a string of generals like McClellan, Pope, Burnside, and Hooker before he found Grant, who would relentlessly pursue the strategic objective of destroying the rebel army. It included prodding McClellan to act rather than hesitate and wage a defensive war: "And, once more let me tell you, it is indispensable to *you* that you strike a blow. . . . The country will not fail to note—is now noting—that the present hesitation to move upon an intrenched enemy, is but the story of Manassas repeated. I beg to assure you that I have never written you, or spoken to you, in greater kindness of feeling than now, nor with a fuller purpose to sustain you, so far as in my most anxious judgment, I consistently can. *But you must act.*"[73] He further reminded McClellan and other generals that the strategic objective of the war was to destroy the rebel army, disabusing them of the illusion that the war could be won simply by taking the capital of Richmond: "Your despatches of to-day received. God bless you, and all with you. Destroy the rebel army, if possible."[74]

Consistent with Clausewitz's teaching, Lincoln pursued a strategy of "concentration in time" that took advantage of the Union's superior numbers by attacking the enemy at various points simultaneously. He expressed this strategy in a letter to General Buell:

> I state my general idea of this war to be that we have the *greater* numbers, and the enemy has the *greater* facility of concentrating forces upon points of collision; that we must fail, unless we can find some way of making *our* advantage an over-match for *his*; and that this can only be done by menacing him with superior forces at *different* points, at the *same* time; so that we can safely attack, one, or both, if he makes no change; and if he *weakens* one to *strengthen* the other, forbear to attack the strengthened one, but seize, and hold the weakened one, gaining so much.[75]

As commander in chief, Lincoln prosecuted "a hard war" against the South, sending hundreds of thousands to their death. In a letter from July 1862, he conveyed his determination to win the struggle: "What would you do in my position? Would you drop the war where it is? Or, would you prosecute it in future, with elder-stalk squirts, charged with rose water? Would you deal lighter blows rather than heavier ones? Would you give up the contest, leaving any available means unapplied. . . . I shall not do *more* than I can, and I shall do *all* I can to save the government, which is my sworn duty as well as my personal inclination. I shall do nothing in malice. What I deal with is too vast for malicious dealing."[76] In this case of saving the government by all available means, Lincoln's "sworn duty" and "personal inclination" coincided. His pledge to doing "nothing in malice" anticipates the magnanimity of the Second Inaugural Address.

As noted, Lincoln understood his duty as obligating him to preserve both the picture of silver (the Constitution) and the apple of gold (the principles of the Declaration). His actions during the election of 1864 in sustaining the emancipation and the strides toward black freedom during the war further reveal how considerations of duty both informed and elevated his statesmanship. The fact that Lincoln even held an election in the midst of a civil war speaks to his regard for constitutional duty and democratic process. Under the pretext of a national emergency, he could have suspended elections, as Churchill did during World War II. Lincoln, however, risked personal ambition and political defeat by submitting to the election and the core principle of popular consent. He viewed the election as a test of the viability of self-government in a time of crisis. Recurring to the enduring problem of reconciling liberty and authority, Lincoln explained:

It has long been a grave question whether any government, not *too* strong for the liberties of its people, can be strong *enough* to maintain its own existence, in great emergencies. On this point the present rebellion brought our republic to a severe test; and a presidential election occurring in regular course during the rebellion added not a little to the strain. . . . But the election was a necessity. We can not have free government without elections; and if the rebellion could force us to forego, or postpone a national election, it might fairly claim to have already conquered and ruined us."[77]

Whereas the Constitution could be broadly interpreted to allow for the suspension of the writ of habeas corpus under exigent circumstances, it could not justify the suspension of an election. Moreover, Lincoln's claim that his extraordinary actions were justified by a popular necessity would have been completely hypocritical if he then disregarded the very principle of consent by suspending an election. Duty, as opposed to despotism, ultimately required public accountability for the president's actions.

Moral duty and personal honor converged in the case of Lincoln's decision to uphold the Emancipation Proclamation when it was politically expedient to retreat from promises made to the freedmen. The electoral fortunes of the Republican Party sunk to a low point in the summer of 1864. Grant's march toward Richmond, which resulted in massive casualties, was now stymied. The country was war weary. A growing peace movement sought to restore the status quo antebellum. In *Copperheads: The Rise and Fall of Lincoln's Opponents in the North*, Jennifer L. Weber demonstrates that "the peace movement was broad, and so influential by August 1864 that it very nearly took over the Democratic Party."[78] A third column movement of Copperheads, peace Democrats with southern sympathies who opposed the administration, plotted and undertook acts of espionage and subversion in the North. Lincoln referred to this movement as "the fire in the rear." Indeed, Weber persuasively argues that "the fire in the rear" was no mere fizzle, but a volatile blaze stoked by Union defeat on the battlefield. Also known as "butternuts" and "conservatives," the Copperheads fancied themselves strict-constructionists who sought a return to the status quo antebellum. Their motto, "The Constitution as it is, the Union as it was." They repudiated the suspension of habeas corpus, the draft, paper currency, the emancipation of the slaves, the induction of black troops, and the suppression of the press.[79] Though "their argument was based on constitutional principle, it was wrapped in racist rhetoric designed to appeal to people's basest fears."[80] Lincoln's suspension of the writ of habeas corpus and his use of military tribunals were aimed at preventing this third column from interfering with Union conscription efforts. In July of 1863, a year before the election, draft riots erupted. The rioters vented their racial animus by lynching blacks and burning down a black orphanage.

In 1864, the Democrats nominated former general George B. McClellan as their candidate. The alternatives provided in the party platforms could not be clearer. The Democratic platform urged a cessation of hostilities, attacked the Emancipation Proclamation as unconstitutional, and sought to restore the *Union as it was*, including slavery. By contrast, the Republican platform pledged to uphold the Emancipation Proclamation and extirpate slavery lawfully and definitively through a constitutional amendment.

The Republican Party, however, was not without internal divisions that threatened Lincoln's chances for reelection. Lincoln's secretary of treasury, Salmon P. Chase, schemed to replace him as candidate but was ultimately foiled by his boss's political acumen. To make matters worse, a miscegenation hoax perpetrated by the *New York World* newspaper sought to humiliate the Republican Party by pandering to racial hatred and fear over the Emancipation Proclamation. The article alleged that the Republican Party undertook emancipation as a social experiment to promote racial interbreeding.

In the summer of 1864, Lincoln was under pressure to revoke the Emancipation Proclamation and to sue for "peace at any price." In a letter dated August 22, his campaign manager, Henry Raymond, urged him to reconsider his demand that the end of slavery serve as a precondition of peace: "The tide is setting strongly against us. . . . Nothing but the most resolute and decided action on the part of the government and its friends, can save the country from falling into hostile hands. Two special causes are assigned to this great reaction in public sentiment,—the want of military successes, and the impression in some minds, the fear and suspicion in others, that we are not to have peace *in any event* under this administration until Slavery is abandoned."[81] Lincoln had pledged not to reclaim a word of the Emancipation Proclamation. In a reply to a war Democrat, Charles D. Robinson, on August 17, 1864, he exclaimed: "the promise, being made, must be kept.' I am sure you will not, on due reflection, say that the promise being made, must be *broken* at the first opportunity. I am sure you would not desire me to say, or to leave an inference, that I am ready, whenever convenient, to join in re-enslaving those who shall have served us in consideration of our promise. As matter of morals, could such treachery by any possibility, escape the curses of Heaven, or of any good man?"[82]

True to his word, and his honor, Lincoln ultimately decided to stand firm on this core principle rather than abandon it for the sake of political expediency. On August 23, he circulated a blind memo to his cabinet conceding defeat in the event that he lost the election. Lincoln's unwillingness to betray his promise to sustain the emancipation reveals that there were limits to both compromise and personal ambition. His willingness to sacrifice in this case is exemplary of a statesman who seeks to maintain his moral integrity rather than a pragmatist who sells it any price. Fortuitously, Sherman's capture of Atlanta in September of 1864 ensured Lincoln's success in the election. In his annual message to Congress, December 6 1864, Lincoln reaffirmed his pledge to uphold the Emancipation Proclamation:

> In presenting the abandonment of armed resistance to the national authority on the part of the insurgents, as the only indispensable condition to ending the war on the part of the government, I retract nothing heretofore said as to slavery. I repeat the declaration made a year ago, that "while I remain in my present position I shall not attempt to retract or modify the emancipation proclamation, nor shall I return to slavery any person who is free by the terms of that proclamation, or by any of the Acts of Congress." If the people should, by whatever mode or means, make it an Executive duty to re-enslave such persons, another, and not I, must be their instrument to perform it.[83]

Thus, the president would resign his office, if duty, perversely construed, would compel him "to re-enslave" those whom he had freed.

In sum, Lincoln's statesmanship was bound by considerations of duty that both empowered and constrained him as president. By the end of the Civil War, even William Lloyd Garrison, perhaps the most uncompromising of abolitionists, was able to appreciate how duty constrained Lincoln in his official capacity as president. "His freedom to follow his convictions of duty as an individual is one thing," but "as the President of the United States, it is limited by the functions of his office; for the people do not elect a President to play the part of a reformer or philanthropist, not to enforce upon the nation his own peculiar ethical or humanitary ideas."[84]

Far from despotic claims of absolute power and a moral idealism, Lincoln sought to justify his actions to the public through closely reasoned argument that appealed to the Constitution, precedent, his oath, and duty.

He risked holding an election and was willing to sacrifice his own personal ambitions to uphold the democratic process and his administration's pledge to uphold black freedom. Given "the zone of twilight" Lincoln operated in during the war, noted constitutional rights scholar Geoffrey Stone commends him for resisting "the temptation to enact a new Sedition Act."[85] And in *Lincoln's Constitution*, renowned constitutional scholar Daniel Farber provides the following assessment: "though the constitutional issue can hardly be free from doubt, on balance Lincoln's use of habeas in areas of insurrection or actual war should be considered constitutionally appropriate, at least in the absence of contrary action by Congress. When the war broke out, given the riots in Baltimore and the threat of secession by Maryland, that state could be considered a site of insurrection, particularly given its proximity to enemy territory and its control over access to Washington. Consequently, suspension of habeas could be justified as an emergency military measure."[86]

During the war, Lincoln would stretch the Constitution further (some would say break it) through the implementation of military tribunals. In his groundbreaking work on the topic, *The Fate of Liberty*, Mark Neely estimates that there were between thirteen thousand and thirty-eight thousand civilian arrests during the Civil War.[87] After 1862, most of these arrests were of either Confederate citizens or citizens of the border states, where allegiances were more divided. And despite the well-publicized Vallandigham case, military arrests for political dissent and opposition were rare.[88] In assessing Lincoln's duty as a statesman, it is noteworthy that he justified his extraordinary measures narrowly under the extreme circumstances of war and rebellion. These measures were aimed at maintaining conscription in the face of draft riots and at the Copperhead threat, which, as Jennifer Weber has shown, proved to be very real.[89] Accordingly, Lincoln distinguished between the Constitution in wartime and the Constitution peacetime. This crucial distinction limits his precedent to the extreme circumstances.

In sum, Lincoln's performance of his duty in terms of both limitation and empowerment reveals what Harvey Mansfield describes as "the ambivalence of executive Power."[90] Executive power is ambivalent because on the one hand it is potentially dangerous to republican institutions; while on the other, it is absolutely necessary to the country's survival in times of crisis. Mansfield explains: "The beauty of executive power, then, is to be both subordinate and not subordinate, both weak and strong. It can reach where the law cannot, and thus supply the defect of law, yet remain subordinate to law. This ambivalence in the modern

executive permits its strength to be useful to republics, without endan-
gering them."[91] As a source of both empowerment and restraint, Lincoln's
appeal to duty during the Civil War sought to prudently uphold the rule
of law under the extraordinary circumstances of the time. The challenge
of preserving the Union during its most dire crisis clearly reveals the
ambivalence of executive power inherent to the office of the president.
Succeeding generations of scholars and citizens continue to debate his
constitutional and presidential legacy in this regard.

4
MAGNANIMITY

*A*ristotle describes magnanimity or greatness of soul as "the crown of the virtues; for it makes them greater, and it is not found without them." Politically speaking, magnanimity is "the virtue that disposes us to do good to others on a large scale."[1] Aquinas, who synthesized Aristotle's teachings with Christianity, includes humility as part of this virtue. For Aquinas, true greatness of soul must take into account Christ's example of servant leadership in Matthew 20: "You know that the rulers of the Gentiles lord it over them, and their high officials exercise authority over them. Not so with you. Instead, whoever wants to become great among you must be your servant, and whoever wants to be first must be your slave—just as the Son of Man did not come to be served, but to serve, and to give his life as a ransom for many."

The following chapter will reveal Lincoln's political greatness in terms of Aquinas's view of magnanimity. Consistent with this teaching, Lincoln's character combined Christian humility and pagan greatness.[2] Throughout, I use the term *biblical magnanimity* to reflect Lincoln's reliance on the Bible as a source of insight and guidance in his private and public life. Informed by the Bible's teaching of servant leadership, humility, and higher purpose, Lincoln's political greatness also bears comparison to Hamilton's description of magnanimity in Federalist No. 71.[3]

Aquinas considers the virtue of magnanimity in Question 129 of the *Summa Theologica, II-II*.[4] As part of his wider synthesis between faith and reason, he seeks to reconcile Aristotle's conception of greatness of soul with Christian revelation. Following Aristotle, Aquinas defines magnanimity as a virtue or moral excellence concerning "great honors." Among "external goods," he notes, "honors takes precedence over all others." Aquinas likewise considers magnanimity to be "the ornament of all the virtues." It crowns, adorns, and displays resplendently the qualities of excellence embodied by the manly man of action.

Because "the essence of human virtue consists in safeguarding the good of reason in human affairs," the particular virtue of magnanimity "observes the mode of reason in great honors." The virtue of magnanimity strikes the rational mean between the vicious extremes of (1) vanity, whereby one overestimates the honor due to him; and (2) smallness of soul, whereby one underestimates it.

Aquinas modifies Aristotle's teaching on greatness of soul by incorporating the Christian norms of humility and charity into his understanding of magnanimity. The great-souled person does not seek honor as an end in itself but seeks to be worthy of honor insofar as he or she serves the public good and others who are in need.

Nonetheless, for Aquinas as well as Aristotle magnanimity concerns *great honors*, in contradistinction to "ordinary honors." Aquinas states: "But with regard to great honors there is magnanimity. Wherefore we must conclude that the proper matter of magnanimity is great honor, and that a magnanimous man tends to such things as are deserving of honor."[5] Indeed, the great-souled person is "intent only on great things." These are "few and require great attention." Unlike the restive activity of the small-souled person who gains satisfaction in accumulating petty honors, riches, and creature comforts, the great-souled person is stirred only when some momentous issue is at hand, one that is worthy of great honor. The epic task of founding or saving a regime draws him out of his self-imposed exile from mundane affairs.

To be sure, "the tending of things worthy of great honor" presumes great ambition. This trait, for better or worse, has defined the epic rulers of history—Alexander, Caesar, and Washington. Lincoln was no exception. William Herndon, his former law partner, memorably described his colleague's ambition as "a little engine that knew no rest." In point of fact, Lincoln candidly and frequently acknowledged his own thirst for distinction. In 1832, at the age of twenty-three, in his first run for political office, he confessed, "Every man is said to have his peculiar ambition. Whether it be true or not, I can say for one that I have no other so great as that of being truly esteemed of my fellow men, by rendering myself worthy of their esteem."[6] Is great ambition necessarily malignant? Does the thirst for distinction necessarily lead to the wellspring of despotism?

In describing his own ambition, Lincoln was most likely imitating his magnanimous role model—George Washington. In a letter dated October 26, 1788, Washington similarly stated: "It is said that every man has his portion of ambition. I may have mine, I suppose, as well as the rest, but if I know my own heart my ambition would not lead me into public life. My only ambition is to do my duty in this world as I am capable of performing it and to merit the good opinion of all man."[7] Indeed, Washington may be placed in the ranks of magnanimous statesmen like Pericles. Here as elsewhere, Lincoln self-consciously modeled his speech and deeds after the Founding Father.[8]

In his campaign biography of 1860, Lincoln recalled his election as captain of volunteers in the Black Hawk War as a "success which gave me more pleasure than any I have had since."[9] His greatness of soul flickered during his short stint in the Black Hawk War when he intervened to save the life of an Indian scout who had stumbled into his camp. He stood up to the blood lust of his fellow volunteers who wanted to kill the Indian, perhaps as a trophy to prove that they had seen action—as yet they had not. A lesser man would have given in to the rabble. Moreover, Lincoln could have held a grudge against the Indians since his grandfather was killed by one. A lesser man would have justified the execution to avenge family honor, as is practiced in far too many parts of the world today. However, at an early age, Lincoln displayed the strength of character to break the vicious cycle of hatred and revenge, and the moral fortitude to confront the ugly impulses of the mob.[10]

The theme of ambition also figures prominently in Lincoln's first great speech—the Lyceum address of 1838.[11] In it, he warns against the designs of a "towering genius" who would make common cause with the people to further his own ambition on the ruins of the nation's republican institutions. Consistent with Washington's warning in the Farewell Address, Lincoln foretold of a demagogue who would undermine the Union by exploiting sectional animosities for personal gain. His description is worth quoting in full:

> This field of glory is harvested, and the crop is already appropriated. But new reapers will arise, and *they*, too, will seek a field. It is to deny, what the history of the world tells us is true, to suppose that men of ambition and talents will not continue to spring up against us. And, when they do, they will naturally seek the gratification of their ruling passion, as others have *so* done before them. The question, then, is, can that gratification be found in supporting and maintaining an edifice that has been erected by others? Most certainly it cannot. Many great and good men, sufficiently qualified for any task they should undertake, may ever be found, whose ambition would aspire to nothing beyond a seat in Congress, a gubernatorial or a presidential chair; *but such belong not the family of the lion, or the tribe of the eagle*[.] What! think you these places would satisfy an Alexander, a Caesar, or a Napoleon? Never! Towering genius disdains a beaten path. It seeks regions hitherto unexplored. It sees *no distinction* in

adding story to story, upon the monuments of fame, erected to the memory of others. It *denies* that it is glory enough to serve under any chief. It *scorns* to tread in the footsteps of *any* predecessor, however illustrious. It thirsts and burns for distinction; and, if possible, it will have it, whether at the expense of emancipating slaves, or enslaving freemen. Is it unreasonable then to expect, that some man possessed of the loftiest genius, coupled with ambition sufficient to push it to its utmost stretch, will at some time, spring among us?[12]

Characteristic of those possessed by a longing for greatness, the towering genius will never be satisfied with the "ordinary honors" of "a seat in Congress, a gubernatorial or a presidential chair." However, the fact that there is no outlet for his great ambition (the field of glory has been harvested) leads him to seek other, less salutary outlets for his notoriety. Without the opportunity to build up, the towering genius must tear down, resorting to the most unscrupulous means to surpass the Founders' glory.

Lincoln's reference to Alexander and Caesar in the Lyceum address was no doubt influenced by his reading of *Plutarch*'s *Lives*. Notably, Plutarch couples these two conquerors as parallel Greek and Roman lives. Indeed, it was the *unbounded ambition* of Rome's leaders that led to the bitter rivalries among the triumvirates, civil war, and, ultimately, the loss of the republic. The inordinate desire for honor so vividly portrayed by Plutarch is diagnosed more profoundly by St. Augustine as the *libido dominandi*: the lust for power. In contrast to the magnanimous example of Washington, Lincoln depicts Alexander and Caesar as members of the "family of the lion" and "tribe of the eagle"—"noble" yet ruthless predators with an instinct to kill and lord over others. Indeed, this is the dark side of pagan manliness. And in the Lyceum address Lincoln applies its lesson to the circumstances of the American republic.

Psychohistorians have provocatively argued that Lincoln's description of the towering genius is self-referential; that he projected himself into the very role he was warning against; and that his subsequent actions during the Civil War prove that he was willing to gratify this master passion "at the expense of emancipating the slaves, or enslaving freemen."[13] This view was initially advanced by Edmund Wilson in *Patriotic Gore*. The root cause of Lincoln's disordered psyche can be attributed to a "towering ambition" that sought to outdo the legacy of the Founders at any cost. Ever since, the Lyceum address has been viewed as the psychological key that unlocks Lincoln's motives. In particular, Lincoln's description in the speech of "some man possessed of the loftiest genius" who "thirsts and burns for distinction; and, if possible . . . will have it, whether at the expense of emancipating the slaves or, enslaving freemen" has been interpreted as self-referential.[14]

In line with the "projection thesis," Dwight Anderson understands Lincoln's political leadership in terms of a demented psyche:

> Lincoln's personal psychology became bound up with the history of the nation through the influence of Mason Locke Weems's Life of Washington. This book, which Lincoln read repeatedly as a youth, offered him two contradictory models of political success. One was that of Washington himself, who according to Weems achieved his great stature because of his private virtues. The other was that of a "cunning, ambitious, unprincipled" man who would seek greatness on "the ruins of public liberty"—the figure against whom Washington warned the nation in his Farewell Address. Lincoln followed both models sequentially. At first he sought political success by upholding Washington's advice and example; failing there, he seized upon the alternative, eventually presiding over the destruction of Washington's Union, and becoming the very tyrant against whom Washington had warned. Sublimating guilt into political authority, Lincoln took Washington places as the father of his country.[15]

Anderson can be given credit for emphasizing the extent to which Washington served as a magnanimous role model for Lincoln and for pointing out the parallels between Washington's Farewell Address and Lincoln's Lyceum address. However, his account of Lincoln's leadership in terms of a demented psyche fails to recognize the sixteenth president's honorable ambition and his oath bound duty in seeking to reconcile moral obligation to the principles of the Declaration and legal obligation to the Constitution (chapter 3).

Regardless of whether or not Lincoln had himself in mind when he composed the Lyceum address (perhaps he was conducting a thought experiment in exploring his darker impulses), the speech nonetheless reveals a preoccupation with "the tending of things to great honor" so characteristic of magnanimity and its perversion by unbounded ambition. Indeed, one detects in the youthful yearnings of Lincoln an aspiration for greatness that rivals that of the Founders and the corresponding disappointment that "[the] field of glory is harvested." Twenty-three years later Lincoln could not have known that he would be confronted with the monumental task of preserving the Union, an honor that rivaled the glory of the founding. This great and honorable deed, however, would come at an awful cost to himself and to the nation.

The theme of ambition is likewise found in Lincoln's reading of Shakespeare. In a private letter to James Hackett, a Shakespearean actor, Lincoln listed his favorite plays as follows, "Lear, Richard Third, Henry Eight, Hamlet, and especially Macbeth. It is wonderful."[16] Not surprisingly, the common denominator among these plays is their vivid depiction of the protagonist's unbounded ambition. Did Lincoln see these tragedies as mirrors that reflected his own tyrannical longings or as cautionary tales of what to avoid?

Lincoln's self-described ambition was revealed throughout his adult life as well. After he had lost a senatorial bid in 1855, he pondered: "Twenty-two years ago Judge Douglas and I first became acquainted. We were both young then; he a trifle younger than I. Even then, we were both ambitious: I, perhaps quite as much so as he. With *me*, the race of ambition has been a failure—a flat failure; with *him* it has been one of splendid success."[17] Notably, Lincoln did not publish this candid statement. Perhaps it was too revealing; for it betrays more than a hint of envy toward his political rival and nemesis—Stephen A. Douglas. Notwithstanding his folksy demeanor, the sixteenth president was indeed conscious of his superiority over others. Historian David Donald observes that "Lincoln was not a modest man, and as John Hay astutely noted he quite inadvertently exhibited toward critics an 'intellectual arrogance and unconscious assumption of superiority' that mortally offended them."[18] At first glance, Lincoln's self-described ambition and conscious superiority over others may seem incompatible with Christian humility.

To be sure, Aquinas counts inordinate ambition and vainglory as vices that are contrary to the virtue of magnanimity. For Aquinas, it is not the desire for honor per se that is a vice; but rather "the inordinate love of honor."[19] Quoting the Roman historian Sallust, he explains that "the good as well as the wicked covet honors for themselves, but the one, i.e. the good, go about it in the right way, whereas the other, the wicked, through lack of the good arts, make use of deceit and falsehood."[20] Likewise, quoting Matthew 5:16 ("Let your light shine before men"), Aquinas notes that "the desire for glory does not, of itself, denote a sin: but the desire for empty or vain glory denotes as sin." Glory is vain when the one who seeks glory "does not refer the desire of his own glory to a due end, such as God's honor, or the spiritual welfare of his neighbor." Thus, the magnanimous man refers his gifts to God and uses them to "profit others." Aquinas explains that "a man ought so far to be pleased that others bear witness to his excellence, as this enables him to profit others."

According to Aquinas, the desire for honor can be inordinate in three ways: "First, when a man desires recognition of an excellence which he has not; this is to desire more than his share of honor. Secondly, when a man desires honor for himself without referring it to God. Thirdly, when a man's appetite rests in honor itself, without referring it to the profit of others."[21] In the first case, the mediocre person overestimates his talent; in the second, he attributes his gifts to his own self-sufficiency without reference to God; and in the third, he ignores his charitable obligation to use his gifts to serve the insufficiency of others. Thus understood, Aquinas makes clear that if the love of honor is not to derail into vainglorious pride, then the magnanimous man must remember his creaturely status and must rule for the sake of the political good, not for personal ambition alone.

Just as Aquinas counts vainglory as a vice, so he counts pusillanimity or smallness of soul as one too.[22] To despise honors is just as wrong as to covet them inordinately. Both irrational excesses are counterpoised to the rational mean of magnanimity that regards honor in due proportion. The pusillanimous man "shrinks from great things out of littleness of soul."[23] This smallness of soul prevents him from serving others. By contrast, magnanimity tends "to perfect works of virtue."

In contrast to pagan conceptions of manly greatness, Aquinas further emphasizes that magnanimity involves Christian humility. Consistent with the notion of servant leadership, honor must be directed toward the service or "the profit" of others. "These two limitations on a great man's attitude toward honor," Deutsch explains, "demonstrate the importance of the Christian virtues of humility and charity as clear norms for judging the rationality of a true statesman's attitude toward the great honors that *are* his due."[24]

In article 3 of Question 129 on Magnanimity, Aquinas considers the serious objection that magnanimity cannot be a virtue since it is contrary to the virtue of humility. "It belongs properly to humility," he explains, "that a man restrain himself from being borne towards that which is above him. For this purpose he must know his disproportion to that which surpasses his capacity. Hence knowledge of one's own deficiency belongs to humility, as a rule guiding the appetite."[25] Aquinas summarizes the objection against humility as part of magnanimity as being based on the supposition that a true virtue (humility) cannot be opposed to another virtue (magnanimity).

In response to the stated objection, Aquinas distinguishes between humility and magnanimity as different yet compatible virtues. A full quotation is warranted:

There is in man something which he possesses through the gift of God; and something defective which accrues to him through the weakness of nature. Accordingly magnanimity makes a man deem himself worthy of great things in consideration of the gifts he holds from God: thus if his soul is endowed with great virtue, magnanimity makes him tend to perfect works of virtue. . . . On the other hand, humility makes a man think little of himself in consideration of his own deficiency, and magnanimity makes him despise others in so far as they fall away from God's gifts: since he does not think so much of others as to do anything wrong for their sake. Yet humility makes us honor others and esteem them better than ourselves, in so far as we see some of God's gifts in them. Hence it is written of the just man (Ps. xiv. 4): *In his sight a vile person is contemned*, which indicates the contempt of magnanimity, *but he honoreth them that fear the Lord*, which points to the reverential bearing of humility. It is therefore evident that magnanimity and humility are not contrary to one another, although they seem to tend in contrary directions, because they proceed according to different considerations.[26]

Aquinas attributes the apparent contradiction between magnanimity and humility to their "contrary directions." That is to say, they appear to be at odds because they proceed from different considerations or standpoints. Magnanimity considers the person's worthiness of honor *in comparison to the deficiency of others*. Humility considers the agent's own deficiency *in comparison to the perfection of God*. In sum, "humility restrains the appetite from aiming at great things against right reason; while magnanimity urges the mind to great things in accord with right reason. Hence it is clear that magnanimity is not opposed to humility."[27]

Ken Deutsch further expounds Aquinas's teaching on magnanimity as a virtue of "social and political hope":

Through the realization of the "image of God" in the world, human persons with specific talents build up the world. Human beings are not totally wretched. Man is responsible for his good actions as well as his evil deeds. As a humble creature, man knows that his powers are gifts of God. Aquinas does not present a drama of God's grandeur as contrasted with puny man. The drama is shifted to man; it is concerned with the tension between human grandeur and limitations. Magnanimity, for Aquinas is a virtue of human social and political hope, to be realized through one's own human strength and honor must be viewed as the natural consequence of good deeds and not merely as an end in itself.[28]

A magnanimous man is worthy of honor insofar as he serves and ministers to honorable political goods that transcend his own personal ambition and reputation. This places a moral boundary on ambition. Aquinas explains: "If, however, one were to despise honors so as not to care to do what is *worthy of honor*, this would be deserving blame. Accordingly magnanimity is about honors in the sense that a man strives to do what is *deserving of honor* yet not so as to think much of the honor accorded by man" (emphasis added).[29] Aquinas's understanding of magnanimity thus recognizes the possibility of an honorable ambition tempered by humility and dedicated to humble, self-sacrificial service in a cause greater than oneself.

In sum, the conscious of superiority is not necessarily a vice for Aquinas if one's worthiness is understood in comparison to the deficiency of others and, at the same time, displays a humility in comparison to the perfection of God. Lincoln's honorable ambition observed this dynamic tension. His self-described "ambition" was not a vice to the extent that he acknowledged principles that were higher than his own reputation, and to the extent that he sought to be worthy of honor in the service of these higher principles.

Indeed, a more careful look at Lincoln's first campaign speech above shows that consonant with Aquinas's understanding of magnanimity and Washington's example, he sought to be "worthy" of the people's "esteem." In point of fact, his candid acknowledgments of personal ambition were consistently qualified by his commensurate fidelity to a nobler calling and a higher purpose.[30] "While pretending no indifference to earthly honors," he confessed, "I do claim to be actuated in this contest by something higher than anxiety for office." During the Lincoln-Douglas debates he reiterated the twin motives of ambition and principle:

> Ambition has been ascribed to me. God knows how sincerely I prayed from the first that this field of ambition might not be opened. I claim no insensibility to political honors; but today could the Missouri restriction be restored, and the whole slavery question replaced on the old ground of "toleration by *necessity*" where it exists, with unyielding hostility to the spread of it, on principle, I would, in consideration, gladly agree, that Judge Douglas should never be *out*, and I never *in*, an office, so long as we both or either, live.[31]

Lincoln's honorable ambition is also revealed in his remarks after losing the 1858 Senate election to Douglas. After his defeat, Lincoln explained to his friend Anson G. Henry: "I am glad I made the late race. It gave me a hearing on the great and durable question of the age, which I could have had in no other way; and though I now sink out of view, and shall be forgotten, I believe I have made some marks which will tell for the cause of civil liberty after I am gone."[32]

Further consistent with what Aquinas says about an honorable ambition in the service of higher aims, Lincoln consoled himself by reflecting on the similar setbacks, yet ultimate success, of Wilberforce and the British abolitionist movement:

> I have never failed—do not now fail—to remember that in the republican cause there is a higher aim than that of mere office. I have not allowed myself to forget that the abolition of the Slave-trade by Great Britain, was agitated a hundred years before it was a final success; that the measure had its open fire-eating opponents; its stealthy 'don't care' opponents; its dollar and cent opponents; its inferior race opponents; its negro equality opponents; and its religion and good order opponents; that all the opponents got offices, and their adversaries got none. But I have also remembered that though they blazed, like tallow-candles for a century, at last they flickered in the socket, died out, stank in the dark for a brief season, and were remembered no more, even by the smell.[33]

Facing his own political obscurity after losing to Douglas, Lincoln puts his own personal striving in perspective by acknowledging the greater significance of the antislavery cause for which he so nobly labored: "School-boys know that Wilbe[r]force, and Granville Sharpe, helped that cause forward; but who can now name a single man who labored to retard it? Remembering these things I can not but regard it as possible that the higher object of this contest may not be completely attained within the term of my natural life. But I can not doubt either that it will come in due time. Even in this view, I am proud, in my passing speck of time, to contribute an humble mite to that glorious consummation, which my own poor eyes may not last to see."[34]

In sum, Lincoln's magnanimity was measured by the noble political ends for which he lived and died—namely, the preservation of the Union and the principles for which it stood. Crowned by the Declaration (the apple of gold) and protected by the picture of silver (the Constitution), these noble ends were worth sacrificing for, and even dying for. The principles of the Declaration were sacred and worthy of honor given their status as rational participations in the Divine Law that governed the universe. For this reason, as seen, Lincoln described them in comparable terms as the nation's, "political faith," "ancient faith," "Old Faith," "the early faith of the Republic," "political religion."[35]

Lincoln was stirred to reenter public life by the momentous threat of slavery to a Union dedicated to these principles. "I was losing interest in politics," he explained, "when the repeal of the Missouri Compromise aroused me again."[36] In his first notable confrontation with the Little Giant at Peoria in 1854, Lincoln proclaimed the core principles that animated his statesmanship and called for a political renewal of these founding principles: "Let us readopt the Declaration of Independence and with it, the practices, and policy, which harmonize with it. . . . If we do this, we shall not only have saved the Union, but we shall have so saved it, as to make, and keep it, forever worthy of the saving."[37] Significantly, Lincoln demands not the preservation of any Union, but one that is "forever worthy of the saving." That is to say, a Union bound to the promise of freedom in the Declaration.

As noted, Lincoln's courageous declaration at Cooper Union to uphold the core principles of the Republican Party displayed the magnanimity that would guide his statesmanship: "Neither let us be slandered from our duty by false accusations against us, nor frightened from it by menaces of destruction to the Government nor of dungeons to ourselves. LET US HAVE FAITH THAT RIGHT MAKES MIGHT, AND IN THAT FAITH, LET US, TO THE END, DARE TO DO OUR DUTY AS WE UNDERSTAND IT."[38] Unwilling to capitulate to the demands of the South, he would perform his duty in preserving the Union based on the principles of the Declaration even if it meant war.

Indeed, before Lincoln's inauguration, seven states had seceded from the Union. In Independence Hall, Philadelphia, en route to the White House and threatened by an assassination plot, Lincoln courageously reaffirmed his commitment to a Union pledged to the principles of the Declaration and the equality of all human beings: "But, if this country cannot be saved without giving up that principle—I was about to say I would rather be assassinated on this spot than to surrender it."[39]

Some did not think Lincoln up to the task. His folksy demeanor gave the mistaken impression that he was a mediocrity or even a well-intentioned buffoon. In contrast to Washington's forbidding aloofness, the sixteenth president's humble origins, western accent, lack of refinement, coarse storytelling, and awkward appearance seemed the very opposite of aristocratic bearing and greatness. Upon initial impression, Edward Everett, one of the leading orators of the time, who would be honored as the primary speaker at Gettysburg, observed of Lincoln: "He is evidently a person of very inferior cast of character, wholly unequal to the crisis."[40] The patrician abolitionist Wendell Phillips likewise referred to him as a "first-rate second rate man."[41] And New York Lawyer George Templeton Strong concluded that "it is impossible to resist the conviction that he is unequal to his place."[42]

Others, however, recognized the underlying greatness behind Lincoln's unpolished exterior. William Tecumseh Sherman noted that "of all the men I ever met, he seemed to possess more of the elements of greatness combined with goodness than any other."[43] Sojourner Truth similarly recalled that she "never was treated by any one with more kindness and cordiality than was shown me by that great and good man."[44] Here then are two unlikely sources (a white Union general and a black female abolitionist) who reach the same conclusion about Lincoln's combined greatness and goodness. The intertwining of these two virtues are essential to understanding Lincoln's character as a statesman; for greatness without goodness corrupts into prideful self-assertion, while goodness without greatness lacks the wherewithal to prevail in monumental crises.

To appreciate further Lincoln's biblical magnanimity, we must consider the biblical faith that informed his political ethics and how the corresponding Christian norms of humility and charity held his desire for honor within moral boundaries. That Lincoln was an avid reader of the Bible is beyond dispute. The sincerity and depth of his mature biblical faith has been noted elsewhere by scholars.[45] Though he eschewed formal church membership and though he inclined to skepticism as a youth—at times vacillating between belief and unbelief—he nonetheless turned to the Bible for moral guidance and spiritual solace throughout his entire life—even during the period of his youthful questioning.

Moreover, Lincoln's faith extended beyond the use of religion for mere political utility. In a letter to his friend Joshua Speed, Lincoln bears witness to the role that Providence played in their lives: "I believe God made me one of the instruments of bringing your Fanny and you together, which union, I have no doubt He had fore-ordained. Whatever he designs, he will do for *me* yet. 'Stand *still* and see the salvation of the Lord' is my text just now."[46]

While the youthful Lincoln refers to his strong predestinarian beliefs in terms of both "superstition" and "fate," what he actually describes is likewise consistent with the Bible's description of trust in God's Providence. Lincoln describes the dynamic tension of faith as being existentially poised between the humble acceptance of God's will and an agnosticism concerning God's ultimate purpose. He thus quotes Exodus 14:13 to affirm his own trust in a living God who is overseeing events toward some ultimate good. Indeed, the biblical faith displayed in this early letter to Speed is consistent with Lincoln's mature articulation of his faith as president.

The letter to Speed displays Lincoln's self-understanding as "an instrument of God," a term he consistently used to describe his divine calling. Years later, as president, in response to the prayers of Mrs. Gurney, a Quaker woman who came to the White House in 1862 to provide him with spiritual consolation, he was moved to make the following confession of faith, one that further revealed his self-understanding as an instrument of God:

> In the very responsible position in which I happen to be placed, being a humble instrument in the hands of our Heavenly Father, as I am, and as we all are, to work out his great purposes, I have desired that all my works and acts may be according to his will, and that it might be so, I have sought his aid—but if after endeavoring to do my best in the light which he affords me, I find my efforts fail, I must believe that for some purpose unknown to me, He wills it otherwise.[47]

Lincoln's spontaneous confession of faith is also a poignant testimony of his humility before God. First, he acknowledges that all are called, albeit in different ways, to serve as "instruments of God." Second, in striving to work out God's "great purposes," he seeks God's aid. Third, he avoids self-righteousness by acknowledging the gulf between the human will and Divine Will. Finally, he submits to the Divine Will by accepting whatever purpose God has in store for him.

A subsequent private letter to Mrs. Gurney, dated September 4, 1864, reveals the importance of the prior meeting to Lincoln. Recalling their initial meeting two years past (cited above) and its inspiration to his servant leadership, he wrote:

> The purposes of the Almighty are perfect, and must prevail, though we erring mortals may fail to accurately perceive them in advance. We hoped for a happy termination of this terrible war long before this; but God knows best, and has ruled otherwise. *We shall yet acknowledge His wisdom and our own error therein.* Meanwhile we must work earnestly in the best light He gives us, trusting that so working conduces to the great ends He ordains. Surely He intends some great good to follow this mighty convulsion, which no mortal could make, and no mortal could stay.[48] (emphasis added)

To be sure, Lincoln's remarks to Mrs. Gurney in 1862 and his subsequent private letter to her in on September 4, 1864, clearly reveal a biblical magnanimity or servant leadership that is both humble and great.

The biblical faith animating Lincoln's servant leadership in the private letter to Mrs. Gurley is furthermore consistent with a private reflection entitled "Meditation on the Divine Will," which he wrote around the same time September 4, 1864. No one other than a sincere and relentless seeker of truth could have penned the following meditation:

> The will of God prevails. In great contests each party claims to act in accordance with the will of God. Both *may* be, and one *must* be wrong. God can not be *for*, and *against* the same thing at the same time. In the present civil war it is quite possible that God's purpose is something different from the purpose of either party—and yet the human instrumentalities, working just as they do, are of the best adaptation to effect His purpose. I am almost ready to say this is probably true—that God wills this contest, and wills that it shall not end yet. By his mere quiet power, on the minds of the now contestants, He could have either *saved* or *destroyed* the Union without a human contest. Yet the contest began. And having begun He could give the final victory to either side any day. Yet the contest proceeds.[49]

Lincoln's secretaries Nicolay and Hay, who discovered the Meditation after his assassination, noted that it "was not written to be seen of men. It was penned in the awful sincerity of a perfectly honest soul trying to bring itself in closer communion with its maker."[50]

While the Meditation is quite philosophical in its quest for ultimate meaning in the face of suffering, it also reveals an abiding faith in a just God who is free from contradictions as well as a humble servant's submission to the Divine Will. The Meditation springs from the same intellectual frame of mind that speculated about the "Doctrine of Necessity" as youth, which Lincoln described as the belief "that the human mind is impelled to action, or held in rest by some power, over which the mind itself has no control."[51]

Indeed, the same relentless pursuit of ultimate causes that led Lincoln to reject the emotionalism of frontier religion as a skeptical youth found expression in the Old School Presbyterian teaching of Reformed theology preached by Reverend Phineas Gurney at the New York Avenue Presbyterian Church in D.C. Gurney's Old School Presbyterianism appealed to the head as well as the heart. The meditation reveals that Lincoln's philosophical quest for order was compatible with faith in a living God who is the ultimate source or first cause of all things.

In sum, these private writings manifest the following core elements of Lincoln's biblical faith: humble submission and service to the Divine Will; reliance on a higher power; belief in the efficacy of prayer in bringing one into closer communion with God; affirmation of God's benevolence in the face of suffering; and recognition of an ironic contrast between human pretense and Divine omniscience.[52] Bearing witness to God's justice, Lincoln faithfully trusts in the Divine Will even though its ultimate workings are inscrutable.

The private expressions of humility and biblical faith in the above speeches correspond remarkably with Lincoln's public articulation of this faith in his Second Inaugural Address. Commenting on the profundity and sincerity of Lincoln's faith, the theologian Reinhold Niebuhr observed that "an analysis of Abraham Lincoln's religion in the context of the prevailing religion of his time and place and in light of the polemical use of the slavery issue, which corrupted religious life in the days before and during the Civil War, must lead to the conclusion that Lincoln's religious convictions were superior in depth and purity to those held by the religious as well as by the political leaders of his day."[53]

Magnanimity does not shrink from great deeds. In his discussion of the presidency in the *Federalist Papers*, Alexander Hamilton articulates a vision of magnanimity that speaks to the unique tasks and challenges of the chief executive in a democratic republic. He maintains that the vitality and security of republican government requires an independent executive to act for the PUBLIC GOOD. According to Hamilton, the "Executive should be in a situation to dare to act his own opinion with vigor and decision." Hamilton capitalizes each letter of the term *PUBLIC GOOD* to emphasize its importance. The PUBLIC GOOD is not simply the will of the majority at any given moment. Such a simple equation would convert republican government into rule of the mob, a danger feared by Hamilton, and one that an independent and vigorous executive is intended to counteract. In sum, Hamilton views the magnanimous man in a republic as one who defends the PUBLIC GOOD against the momentary impulses of the people. He reserves his highest praise for those statesmen who "saved the people from the very fatal consequences of their own mistakes"—that is, to those "who had the courage and magnanimity enough to serve them at the peril of their displeasure."[54]

As chief executive during this nation's greatest crisis, Lincoln epitomized Hamilton's description of magnanimity. He "took the heat" and faced public pressure without capitulating to the public demands of a dishonorable peace that would return to the status quo antebellum. As mentioned in the previous chapter on duty, two deeds in particular speak to Lincoln's greatness of soul in the face of intense political pressure to compromise his core principles: (1) his moral fortitude in sustaining the Emancipation Proclamation; and (2) his corresponding demand that the abolition of slavery serve as a precondition of peace and reunion with the seceded states.

Lincoln's manly determination to preserve the Union stands in stark contrast to James Buchanan's cowardice in allowing the Union to be dismembered. In his Farewell Address to Springfield on February 11, 1861, Lincoln humbly acknowledged the great task before him while also publicly acknowledging his reliance Divine Providence to sustain and guide him through the impending national ordeal:

> I now leave, not knowing when, or whether ever, I may return, with a task before me greater than that which rested upon Washington. Without the assistance of that Divine Being, who ever attended him, I cannot succeed. With that assistance I cannot fail. Trusting in Him, who can go with me, and remain with you and be every where for good, let us confidently hope that all will yet be well. To His care commending you, as I hope in your prayers you will commend me, I bid you an affectionate farewell.[55]

Characteristically, Lincoln compares his task to that of Washington—his model of magnanimity.

With the first shots fired, secession completed, the Confederacy formed, and federal property seized, Lincoln girded the nation for war in his special message to Congress on July 4, 1861: "And having thus chosen our course, without guile, and with pure purpose, let us renew our trust in God, and go forward without fear, and with manly hearts."[56] Historian Douglas L. Wilson reveals that in the original draft of this message, Lincoln wrote, "let us renew our trust in the justice of God." This was deleted in the final draft, however, which was changed to, "let us renew our trust in God." Wilson correctly infers that Lincoln did this to avoid self-righteousness. He states that Lincoln's "apparent reluctance here to claim the justice of God for his cause, which he emphatically believes is just, is a telling discrimination."[57] Put another way, this telling discrimination perfectly illustrates Aquinas's view of the reconciliation between humility and magnanimity.

The Union's preservation, however, required a concerted effort between its leaders, its army, and the public. The city of Baltimore, Maryland, was a hotbed of Copperhead insurgency. Before the outbreak of war, agents uncovered a plot to assassinate Lincoln en route to his inauguration in Washington. After first blood was spilled at Fort Sumter, Baltimore insurgents obstructed the government's efforts to suppress the rebellion, destroying bridges and railroads that would carry reinforcements to Washington. In a statement that captures the justifiable contempt that a magnanimous leader has for the pusillanimous, Lincoln chided the leaders of Baltimore for their failure to perform their duty in saving the Union:

> You, gentlemen, come here to me and ask for peace on any terms, and yet have no word of condemnation for those who are making war on us. You express great horror of bloodshed, and yet would not lay a straw in the way of those who are organizing in Virginia and elsewhere to capture this city. The rebels attack Fort Sumter, and your citizens attack troops sent to the defense of the Government, and the lives and property in Washington, and yet you would have me break my oath and surrender the Government without a blow. There is no Washington in that—no Jackson in that—no manhood or honor in that.[58]

While Lincoln was conscious of his intellectual superiority over others who failed in their duty, he also was capable of great humility in putting his ego aside when it came to serving the common good of the nation. His decision as president to appoint a cabinet of talented and ambitious competitors—a "team of rivals"—further testifies to his magnanimous self-assurance.[59] In contrast to tyrants who are notorious for surrounding themselves with sycophants and "yes-men," Lincoln was not threatened by talented competitors. A mediocre leader would likely have been dominated by such men. One need only consider how Buchanan was dominated by the southern members of his administration. On the contrary, Lincoln set the tone right from the beginning of his administration as the new chief executive by checking Seward's attempts to supplant him as a cabinet puppet master. And he subsequently checked Chase's ambition when it undermined the administration. As Doris Kearns Goodwin has shown, Lincoln was able to manage and maintain the important public services of these ambitious and talented individuals while mitigating their potential for mischief. Indeed, his magnanimity or greatness of soul was displayed in his ability to harness the talents of these ambitious and great men and to direct them toward the common good.

Lincoln's willingness to put aside his ego in the service of the common good was also vividly revealed through his forbearance of the continual slights and insults that he received from General George B. McClellan, who contemptuously referred to the president as "nothing more than a well meaning baboon" and "the *original gorilla*."[60] Just as Lincoln placed the good of the country above his ego in terms of his cabinet selection, so he swallowed his pride when dealing with McClellan whose self-serving megalomania is vividly seen in a letter he wrote to his wife after becoming commander of the Army of the Potomac on July 27, 1861: "I find myself in a new & strange position here—Presdt, Cabinet, Genl Scott & all deferring to me—by some strange operation of magic I seem to have become *the* power of the land. I almost think that were I to win some small success now I could become Dictator or anything else that might please me—but nothing of that kind would please me—*therefore* I *won't* be Dictator. Admirable self denial!"[61]

In one telling episode, the president, his personal secretary, John Hay, and the secretary of state, William Seward, called on McClellan at his home. They had waited for some time. When the general finally arrived, he rebuffed his guests by refusing to acknowledge their presence. He then went upstairs to his bed chamber. After letting Lincoln wait for another half an hour, he sent his servant down with a note to inform the presidential entourage that he had retired for the evening. In his diary, Hay reported, "I merely record this unparalleled insolence of epaulettes without comment. . . . Coming home I spoke to the President about the matter but he seemed not to have noticed it specially, saying it was better at this time not to be making points of etiquette and personal dignity."[62] On another occasion, "when the general failed to keep an appointment with the president": "After a long wait, Lincoln said: 'Never mind; I will hold McClellan's horse if he will only bring us success.'"[63] McClellan's arrogance, his incessant whining, his failure to take responsibility, his treachery in undermining the administration (he actually considered a coup at one point), and his smallness of soul in ridiculing the president, may be contrasted to Lincoln's magnanimity and his rare combination of both humility and greatness of soul.

Lincoln's humility enabled him to assess honestly his own strengths and weaknesses, allowing him to grow from mistakes. Lincoln was able to take responsibility for his errors, as when he wrote to Grant about a previous disagreement over war strategy: "I now wish to make the personal acknowledgment that you were right, and I was wrong."[64] It prevented the kind of arrogance that blinds a person to his own flaws and insufficiencies, as was the case with McClellan. Humility in politics is also opposed to self-righteousness. It eschews an ideological rigidity and a Manichean dualism that divides the world into competing camps of absolute good and absolute evil. As will be seen in the case of his Second Inaugural Address, Lincoln's humility prevented him from demonizing the South, thereby promoting national reconciliation.

Lincoln's biblical magnanimity culminates in his Second Inaugural Address—what some have called his "greatest speech."[65] The circumstances of Lincoln's reelection are noteworthy. He had won a second term, a feat that had not been accomplished since Andrew Jackson. He had triumphed over his political opponents in the North and on the battlefield. After four years of carnage, the end of the war was near. With this context in mind, one would have expected a strong statement of personal vindication by Lincoln, rebuking his critics and proclaiming the righteousness of the Union's cause. Instead, his Second Inaugural shifted the entire drama of the war toward the inscrutable workings of God, the complicity of both sides, and the charitable admonition to bind up the nation's wounds. Noting the irony of each side invoking God's aid against the other, he states:

> Both read the same Bible, and pray to the same God; and each invokes His aid against the other. It may seem strange that any men should dare to ask a just God's assistance in wringing their bread from the sweat of other men's faces; but let us judge not that we be not judged. The prayers of both could not be answered; that of neither has been answered fully. The Almighty has His own purposes.[66]

Then, paraphrasing Genesis 3:19, Lincoln points to the manifest incompatibility between God's justice and slavery. Yet he consciously guards against self-righteousness in forbearing ultimate judgment on the motives of the southern people. Such judgment must be left to God.

Moreover, in what clearly shocked some in his audience, Lincoln humbly acknowledged the complicity of both North and South in the sin of "American Slavery." Neither side can claim perfect rectitude: the "prayers of both could not be answered."

> If we shall suppose that American Slavery is one of those offences which, in the providence of God, must needs come, but which, having continued through His appointed time, He now wills to remove, and that He gives to both North and South, this terrible war, as the woe due to those by whom the offence came, shall we discern therein any departure from those divine attributes which the believers in a Living God always ascribe to Him?[67]

The distinguished religious historian Mark Noll contrasts the humility and charity of Lincoln's remarks with the self-righteousness and vindictiveness of northern clergy members. Around the same time as Lincoln's Second Inaugural, with the end of the war imminent, renowned preacher Henry Ward Beecher let loose the following anathema:

> I charge the whole guilt of this war upon the ambitious, educated, plotting, political leaders of the South. They have shed this ocean of blood. . . . A day will come when God will reveal judgment, and arraign at his bar these mighty miscreants. . . . Blood shall cry out for vengeance, and tears shall plead for justice. . . . And, then, the guiltiest and most remorseless traitors . . . these most accursed and detested of criminals, that have drenched in needless blood, and moved the foundations of their times with hideous crimes and cruelty, caught up in black clouds full of voices of vengeance and lurid with punishment, shall be whirled aloft and plunged downward forever and forever in an endless retribution; while God shall say, "Thus shall it be to all who betray their country"; and all in heaven and upon the earth will say, "Amen."[68]

Indeed, Lincoln's generous plan for Reconstruction may be contrasted to the more punitive plan proffered by the radical Republicans. Recognizing that his message would not be popular with all, Lincoln defended his posture of reconciliation and humility in a letter to Thurlow Weed on March 15, 1865:

> I believe it is not immediately popular. Men are not flattered by being shown that there has been a difference of purpose between the Almighty and them. To deny it, however, in this case, is to deny that there is a God governing the world. It is a truth which I thought needed to be told; and as whatever of humiliation there is in it, falls most directly on myself, I thought others might afford for me to tell it.[69]

Lincoln's letter to Weed illustrates the potential reconciliation between humility and magnanimity as understood by Aquinas. On the one hand, the sixteenth president's scorn for those who self-righteously confuse their own will with the Divine Will reflects the contempt that magnanimity has for those who are deficient in God's gifts. On the other hand, his affirmation of the ultimate inscrutability of the Divine Will reflects a humility that acknowledges the distance between human deficiency and Divine perfection. Lincoln's courage to proclaim this message in the face of vengeance against a defeated and prostrate South is yet further consistent with Hamilton's vision of magnanimity, which affirms the PUBLIC GOOD against the momentary passions of the people.

Lincoln ends his Second Inaugural Address with a plea to the Christian virtue of charity—perhaps the only force powerful enough to overcome hatred and revenge: "With malice toward none; with charity for all; with firmness in the right, as God gives us to see the right, let us strive on to finish the work we are in; to bind up the nation's wounds; to care for him who shall have borne the battle, and for his widow, and his orphan—to do all which may achieve and cherish a just, and a lasting peace, among ourselves, and with all nations."[70]

In conclusion, the coexistence of both greatness and humility in the character of Abraham Lincoln reveals the potential compatibility between magnanimity and Christianity as described by Aquinas. Our admiration for Lincoln's greatness today, however, should not obscure us to the fact that he was denigrated by many in his own time. When it was revealed that en route to his inauguration he had entered Washington, D.C., in disguise to avoid an assassination plot, he was lampooned mercilessly by the press as a coward and a buffoon. For many, the uncouth, joke-telling, country bumpkin from Illinois paled in comparison to his Confederate counterpart—the dashing, polished, war hero Jefferson Davis. Indeed, many considered Davis to be the very embodiment of southern honor, of spirited, manly self-assertion. As a leader, however, Davis lacked both Lincoln's political skill and his humility.[71] Indeed, the presence of this latter virtue in Abraham Lincoln did not make him less of a man; it made him more of one.

Lincoln, the budding statesman in 1858, at the time of the Lincoln-Douglas Debates. Library of Congress.

Perhaps the most memorable seated image of Lincoln the Statesman as president, February 9, 1864—three days before his fifty-fifth birthday. Library of Congress.

Daniel Webster, Lincoln's Whig predecessor, whose national vision of "Liberty and Union, now and for ever, one and inseparable" defined the ends of Lincoln's statesmanship. Library of Congress.

Henry Clay, Lincoln's "beau ideal of a statesman." Lincoln's eulogy to Clay, June 6, 1852, provides a window into the sixteenth president's philosophical patriotism: "He loved his country partly because it was his own country, but mostly because it was a free country; and he burned with a zeal for its advancement, prosperity and glory, because he saw in such, the advancement, prosperity and glory, of human liberty, human right, and human nature." Library of Congress.

Stephen A. Douglas, Lincoln's rival from Illinois and champion of the doctrine of popular sovereignty, whose demagogic appeals to race were a formidable obstacle during the Great Debates of 1858 for the Illinois Senate. Library of Congress.

Roger B. Taney, chief justice of the Supreme Court and author of *Dred Scott v. Sanford*, 1857, whose opinion undermined the core plank of the Republican Party by prohibiting the federal restriction of slavery in the territories and affirming a federal right to property in a slave. Library of Congress.

John C. Calhoun, mastermind of the South, whose doctrines of states' rights and slavery as a "positive good" disposed southern public opinion toward secession. Lincoln referred to Calhoun's teaching as an "ingenious sophism" and "sugar-coated rebellion." Library of Congress.

James H. Hammond, senator from South Carolina and author of the "mudsill" theory of labor, which provoked some of Lincoln's most eloquent writings on free labor. Library of Congress.

Alexander Stephens of Georgia, a Whig colleague of Lincoln's in the U.S. House of Representatives before the war. Though he voted against Georgia's secession, Stephens would become vice president of the Confederacy. His speech on slavery as the cornerstone of the Confederacy, March 21, 1861, provides a revealing contrast with Lincoln's "Fragment on the Constitution and Union" circa 1861. In this fragment, which was likely a reply to an earlier letter by Stephens, Lincoln describes the Union in terms of the Declaration as the apple of gold, its moral centerpiece, framed by the Constitution as its picture of silver. Library of Congress.

Frederick Douglass, black abolitionist from Rochester, New York, who, not without criticisms of the president, also came to appreciate the distinct character of statesmanship, how it differed from the political leadership of a radical reformer, and how the two kinds of leadership might work together in common cause. Library of Congress.

Wendell Phillips, radical abolitionist from Massachusetts, whom historian Michael Burlingame aptly describes as "the national scold" for his self-righteousness and uncompromising political immoderation. Library of Congress.

William Lloyd Garrison, radical abolitionist and founder of the *Liberator*, who burned a copy of the Constitution, calling it "a covenant with death" and "an agreement with hell" for its concessions to slavery. Garrison ultimately supported Lincoln in the 1864 election. Library of Congress.

William H. Seward, Lincoln's secretary of state from Auburn, New York, who advised a war with British Canada to reunite America during the secession crisis. An early antagonist of the president, Seward and Lincoln would become friends and confidantes. Library of Congress.

George B. McClellan. Though a good administrator, McClellan was slow to act, personally opposed emancipation, and failed to recognize that the ultimate strategic objective was to destroy the Confederate army. Lincoln's duties as commander in chief involved managing his generals, including the egotistical McClellan. Library of Congress.

Ulysses S. Grant, a tenacious general Lincoln could rely on. Their political-military collaboration brought success to the Union cause. Library of Congress.

Sojourner Truth, the abolitionist who recognized the greatness and goodness of Lincoln's character. Library of Congress.

William Tecumseh Sherman, who captured the essence of Lincoln's magnanimity when he said, "Of all the men I ever met, he seemed to possess more of the elements of greatness, combined with goodness, than any other." Library of Congress.

The author's favorite photo of Lincoln, taken in 1865, shortly before his assassination. The expression captures the suffering, wisdom, and mirth of the president. Library of Congress.

Created after Lincoln's assassination, this illustration reveals the continuity in the public mind between the nation's political Founder and its Savior. Library of Congress.

5

RHETORIC

*O*n its own accord, philosophical wisdom rarely, if ever, prevails in politics. It is all too easily silenced through the shouts of demagogues or distorted through the wiles of sophists. The voice of wisdom in politics is made audible through the art of public persuasion or what the ancients called rhetoric. Particularly in democracies, the statesman's success depends not only on a clear and profound understanding of human nature and politics but also on the ability to communicate his or her vision through a philosophic rhetoric that ennobles the public.

Speaking of the statesman's rhetorical task in a democracy, Lincoln explained: "In this and like communities, public sentiment is everything. With public sentiment, nothing can fail; without it nothing can succeed. Consequently he who moulds public sentiment, goes deeper than he who enacts statutes or pronounces decisions. He makes statutes and decisions possible or impossible to be executed."[1] Nonetheless, as Lincoln well recognized, public opinion was fallible. It was susceptible to manipulation by demagogues and sophists whose false doctrines sought to dehumanize an entire race or stir rebellion against the government. Thus, Lincoln further emphasized that although "public opinion settles every question . . . [it must be in] accordance with the philosophy of the human mind as it is."[2] In other words, legitimate policies must correspond to the truth of reality and human nature, rather than the selfish interests, distortions, or delusions of the persuaders. The following chapter thus reveals both the substance and style of Lincoln's philosophic rhetoric as a crucial dimension of his statesmanship.

Aristotle defines rhetoric as "the faculty of observing in any given case the available means or modes of persuasion."[3] He describes three modes "furnished by the spoken word": (1) the character of the speaker; (2) the reaction of the audience; (3) the speech itself.[4] Lincoln's rhetoric excelled in each of these three modes. In regard to the first mode, character, his reputation as "Honest Abe" was no mere myth, but a political asset that helped him secure the Republican nomination in 1860, as Michael Burlingame has shown in his encyclopedic biography.[5] In regard to the second mode, the audience, Lincoln's emotional intelligence and familiarity with the common people attuned him to the sentiments and thoughts of his listeners. His stock of stories, jokes, and folksy yarns conveyed political teachings in a simple and forceful manner. Finally, in regard to third mode, the speech itself, Lincoln's written word was enhanced by a simple and clear style infused by his command of logic, the Bible, and the English language. The late great historian Donald E. Fehrenbacher correctly noted that "Lincoln's words have acquired transcendent meaning as contributions to the permanent literary treasure of the nation."[6]

Indeed, Lincoln's rhetorical prowess has been widely recognized by scholars of both history and literature. As seen, Garry Wills goes so far as to claim that Lincoln's rhetorical feat at Gettysburg "remade America" by redefining the founding in more egalitarian terms. In a more recent work, Fred Kaplan describes Lincoln as a "genius with language."[7] Ronald C. White Jr. likewise praises him as "our most eloquent president" and concludes that his "rhetoric embodies the principles" of Aristotle.[8] In *Lincoln's Sword*, a work that "approaches Lincoln's presidency from the aspect of his writing," Douglas Wilson reveals the "degree to which his pen, to alter the proverb, became his sword."[9] Speaking of the president's uncanny ability to communicate in simple yet forceful terms, James M. McPherson argues that the sixteenth president "won the war with metaphors"—as when he described slavery as a casualty of war in terms of "broken eggs" that could not be mended, or secession doctrines as "sugar-coated rebellion."[10]

In addition to the foregoing scholars of history and literature, the political philosopher Ralph Lerner offers a profound treatment of Lincoln's statesmanship in terms of *Kalam*—a philosophic rhetoric that is protective and defensive of a religious or political founding.[11] As taught by the great medieval Arab political philosopher Alfarabi, the art of Kalam enables one to "argue in the defense of the specific opinions and actions stated explicitly by the founder of the religion, and against everything that opposes these opinions and actions."[12] The Kalam thus refers back to some original intent. Addressed to the public, a political Kalam provides "a place for reflexion and meditation, and hence for reason, in the elucidation and defense of the content of the faith."[13] Elucidating this teaching, Ken Deutsch explains that "the leader provides all of the arguments in defense of the religious or political founding; the arguments of the Kalam use a defensive and protective rhetoric of the founding and a criticism of its opponents."[14] Consistent with the Kalam's rhetorical function, Lincoln similarly recurred to the principles of the founding and defended the "ancient faith" of the American regime against politically heretical doctrines of popular sovereignty and proslavery theology that undermined it. He reserved his harshest criticism for the intellectual and political elite of his time who exercised a prominent influence on the moral climate of public opinion, or what he also referred to as "the public mind." Thus, referring to popular sovereignty as a political heresy, Lincoln warned that his nemesis Stephen Douglas "is in every possible way preparing the public mind, by his vast influence, for making the institution of slavery perpetual and national."[15]

Wielded in defense of the "ancient faith," Lincoln's philosophical rhetoric appealed to reasoned argument and logic against two alternative forms of persuasion that debauched the public mind in his own era—sophistry and demagoguery.[16] Indeed, Lincoln used the term *sophistry* in its ancient sense to describe the twisting of the truth for unjust and harmful purposes. In particular, he repudiated the moral relativism of popular sovereignty as a deceptive sophistry that dehumanized the African American. Its feigned moral indifference was a clever ruse to make the institution perpetual and national. In sophistic fashion, popular sovereignty evaded the question of slavery's inherent evil or goodness. Lincoln thus warned: "Let us be diverted by none of those *sophistical contrivances* wherewith we are so industriously plied and belabored—contrivances such as grouping for some middle ground between the right and wrong: vain as the search for a man who should be neither a living man nor a dead man; such as a policy of 'don't care' on a question about which all men do care" (emphasis added).[17] The distinction between sophistry and philosophy was not lost on Lincoln's generation as it has become obscured for us today. Carl Schurz, a Republican ally of Lincoln, likewise noted that Douglas's "sophisms [were] skillfully woven so as to throw the desired flood of darkness upon the subject and thus beguile the untutored mind."[18] Whereas sophistry darkens and debases public opinion, philosophical rhetoric elucidates and ennobles it.

In a revealing passage cited at the beginning of this work, Lincoln explicitly contrasted his philosophical statesmanship to the "false philosophy" and "false statesmanship" of popular sovereignty: "Yet this is the policy here in the North that Douglas is advocating—that we are to care nothing about it! I ask you if it is not a false philosophy? Is it not a false statesmanship that undertakes to build up a system of policy upon the basis of caring nothing about *the very thing that every body does care the most about?*—a thing which all experience has shown we care a very great deal about?"[19] To be sure, the terms "false philosophy" and "false statesmanship" are comparable expressions for sophistry.

Richard Hofstadter regarded Lincoln as one of "the world's great political propagandists."[20] The statement is true insofar as it acknowledges
the sixteenth president's ability to communicate his vision. It is problematic, however, insofar as the moral ambiguity of the term "propaganda"
fails to distinguish between noble and base forms of persuasion. It fails
to distinguish between the statesman's philosophical rhetoric based on
reasoned argument and the sophist's distortions or a demagogue's pandering. Trotsky may have been a great propagandist, but he was not a
statesman. In contrast to Hofstadter's morally ambiguous use of the term
"propaganda," Fred Kaplan describes Lincoln as a president "whose character and standards in the use of language avoided the distortions and
other dishonest uses of language that have done so much to undermine
the credibility of national leaders." Kaplan goes so far as to say that "the
ability and commitment to use language honestly and consistently have
largely disappeared from our political discourse."[21]

Lincoln's philosophic rhetoric was predicated on the ancient teaching
that "statecraft is soulcraft"—the belief that public opinion necessarily
shaped, for better or worse, the moral character of citizens. He sought
to mold public opinion in accordance with the truth of reality—that is
to say, "in accordance with the philosophy of the human mind as it is."
His philosophical rhetoric was indispensable to his role as both party
leader and president, which he supremely fulfilled by providing a clear
moral alternative on the issues of the day to the public: "The Republicans
inculcate, with whatever of ability they can, that the negro is a man;
that his bondage is cruelly wrong, and that the field of his oppression
ought not to be enlarged. The Democrats deny his manhood; deny, or
dwarf to insignificance, the wrong of his bondage; so far as possible,
crush all sympathy for him, and cultivate and excite hatred and disgust against him; compliment themselves as Union-savers for doing
so; and call the indefinite outspreading of his bondage 'a sacred right
of self-government.'"[22]

Lincoln's philosophical rhetoric was particularly adept at the use of
metaphor to convey public policies in a forceful and simple manner. His
comparison of slavery to a venomous snake that should be treated differently depending on whether it was in a child's bed or in an open field
merits particular attention. The respective location of the snake in either
the bed or the field corresponded to the Republican Party's policy of non-
interference with the existing institution of slavery in the states and its
lawful restriction in the territories. The rhetorical power of the passage
is worth quoting in full:

If, then, we of the Republican party who think slavery is a wrong, and would mould public opinion to the fact that it is wrong, should get the control of the general government, I do not say we would or should meddle with it where it exists; but we could inaugurate a policy which would treat it as a wrong, and prevent its extension.

For instance, out in the street, or in the field, or on the prairie I find a rattlesnake. I take a stake and kill him. Everybody would applaud the act and say I did right. But suppose the snake was in a bed where children were sleeping. Would I do right to strike him there? I might hurt the children; or I might not kill, but only arouse and exasperate the snake , and he might bite the children. Thus, by meddling with him here, I would do more hurt than good. Slavery is like this. We dare not strike at it where it is. The manner in which our constitution is framed constrains us from making war upon it where it already exists. The question that we now have to deal with is, "Shall we be acting right to take this snake and carry it to a bed where there are children?" The Republican party insists upon keeping it out of the bed.[23]

Lincoln's snake metaphor was perhaps inspired by the classical wisdom of Aesop, whom he had read, and who likewise used animals in his fables. The metaphor conveys the difficult challenge of balancing moral and legal obligation. While it rejects the moral relativism of popular sovereignty by likening slavery to a snake, a symbol of evil in the Bible, it also conveys the need for prudence in how to handle this evil in different circumstances. While the snake itself is inherently harmful, it may be more or less dangerous depending on where it is found: in the child's bed or in the field. The Union is stuck with the evil of slavery just as the people in Lincoln's fable are stuck with the snake. As Lincoln points out, though one's first moral inclination may be to kill the snake in the bed, doing so would "do more hurt than good," just as actions against state slavery in defiance of the Constitution would do more harm to the Union than good. In this case, Lincoln's philosophic rhetoric teaches the public an important lesson in political moderation and prudence.

The snake in the field or prairie (territorial slavery), however, is a different matter. Here it can be killed in the open without harming the children, just as the restriction of slavery in the territories would not harm the Union. Finally, so as to leave no doubt about the moral and legal right of the Republican Party to restrict territorial slavery, Lincoln adds that the person who kills the snake in the prairie should be congratulated for doing a great service. In sum, the metaphor treats the South's demand to extend slavery into the virgin territories as comparable to introducing a snake into a child's bed where none existed before. It is one thing to exercise caution if a snake is already present in the bed, it is quite another to bring forth one where none before existed. A genuine concern for the happiness and safety of the children (the Union) thus obligates the Republican Party to prevent this from happening as much as they can within their power and consonant with the rule of law.

The sophistry of popular sovereignty aimed at dehumanizing the African American by "deal[ing] with him everywhere as with a brute."[24] The argument from definition, discussed in Chapter 1, is worth revisiting in this context, since it was also a key element of Lincoln's philosophic rhetoric in response to sophistic efforts to dehumanize the African American. As seen, the argument was based on a corresponding philosophical understanding of the Nature of man and its relationship to self-government. "But if the Negro is a man," Lincoln rhetorically asked, "is it not to that extent a total destruction of self government to say he too shall not govern himself. When the white man governs himself, that is self-government; but when he governs himself and also governs another man, that is more than self-government—that is despotism. If the Negro is a man, why then my ancient faith teaches me that "all men are created equal," and that there can be no moral right in connection with one man's making a slave of another."[25] As Weaver correctly notes "Lincoln's principal charge was that his opponents, by straddling issues and through deviousness, were breaking down the essential definition of man."[26]

The Peoria address clearly demonstrates Lincoln's rhetorical prowess through its appeal to the slaveholder's intuitive recognition of the slave's common humanity.[27] Rather than attacking the cruelty and injustice of the institution directly, Lincoln allowed his audience to draw their own conclusion by presenting several examples of how the actions of slaveholders themselves provide the greatest indictment against slavery. His argument thus embodies Aristotle's second mode of persuasion, pertaining to the speaker's understanding of the thoughts and emotions of his audience.

Lincoln invokes "the moral sense" against slaveholders whose actions betray their own proslavery principles. The rhetorical design of the argument presumes that his listeners intuitively recognize the wrong of slavery. Much like one's innate sensibility to pain, the "moral sense" persists despite sophistic arguments to the contrary. Its voice cannot be silenced completely. Thus, Lincoln explains: "The great majority, south as well as north, have human sympathies, of which they can no more divest themselves than they can of their sensibility to physical pain. These sympathies in the bosom of southern people, manifest in many ways, their sense of the wrong of slavery, and their consciousness that, after all, there is humanity in the negro."[28]

In making his case, Lincoln uses a rhetorical device known to classical scholars as *prosopopoeia*. "Taken from the Greek word for 'masked person,' *prosopopoiia*, it defines personification, an argument directed against an absent person."[29] Though Lincoln was actually speaking to northerners in the state of Illinois, his speech nonetheless gave the impression that he was addressing southerners and slaveholders as if they were present in the audience. Knowing full well who his audience was, he directs his question to southerners: "But while you thus require me to deny the humanity of the negro, I wish to ask whether you of the south yourselves, have ever been willing to do as much?"[30]

In Socratic fashion, he then poses a series of rhetorical questions and observations that reveal the glaring contradiction between the slaveholder's speech and deed. Repeatedly using the second person for rhetorical effect, as if southerners were present, he asks: "In 1820 you joined the north, almost unanimously, in declaring the African slave trade piracy, and in annexing to it the punishment of death. Why did you do this? If you did not feel that it was wrong, why did you join in providing that men should be hung for it?"[31] In regard to southerner's treatment of "SLAVE-DEALER," he likewise observes: "You despise him utterly. You do not recognize him as a friend, or even as an honest man. Your children must not play with his; they may rollick freely with the little negroes, but not with the 'slave-dealers' children. If you are obliged to deal with him, you try to get through the job without so much as touching him. It is common with you to join hands with the men you meet; but with the slave dealer you avoid the ceremony—instinctively shrinking from the snaky contact. . . . Now why is this? You do not so treat the man who deals in corn, cattle or tobacco."[32] Pointing to the humanitarian sentiments that led some southerners to free their human "property," Lincoln again asks: "Why have they manumitted their slaves at great cost? How comes this vast amount of property to be running about without owners? We do not see free horses or free cattle running at large. How is this? All these free blacks are the descendants of slaves, or have been slaves themselves, and they would be slaves now, but for SOMETHING which has operated on their white owners, inducing them, at vast pecuniary sacrifices, to liberate them."[33]

Lincoln then draws his audience's attention to the "SOMETHING" that has operated on the minds and hearts of southern people in tacitly recognizing the humanity of the slave. He poses the question in a way that allows the audience to reach the conclusion for itself: "What is that SOMETHING?" Leaving no doubt, he answers, "Is there any mistaking it? In all these cases it is your sense of justice, and human sympathy, continually telling you, that the poor negro has some natural right to himself—that those who deny it, and make mere merchandise of him, deserve kickings, contempt and death."[34] Notably, Lincoln capitalizes each letter of the word *something* for rhetorical emphasis. He concludes with a final question: "And now, why will you ask us to deny the humanity of the slave? and estimate him only as the equal of the hog? Why ask us to do what you will not do yourselves?" The concluding question divides the audience between "you" of the South and "us" of the North.

Lincoln's rhetoric at Peoria can also be analyzed in terms of what David Zarefsky has described as his "triangulation of argumentation," in which he "makes an offer to speak to the South, knowing that Southern newspapers do not print what he says, and immediately going above the heads of Southern audiences to direct his message to the North."[35] In sum, Lincoln's rhetoric is a perfect illustration of how to make a righteous argument against without being self-righteous.

Popular sovereignty was not the only sophistry that Lincoln inveighed against. He also repudiated secession doctrines for corrupting the public mind. The erroneous teachings of states' rights and nullification, relentlessly preached by southern leaders like John C. Calhoun, severed the bonds of Union, undermined the legitimate authority of the federal government, and persuaded law-abiding citizens to take up arms against their country in defense of slavery. In a particularly telling passage, Lincoln blamed the "movers of secession" for commencing "an insidious debauching of the public mind. They invented *an ingenious sophism*, which, if conceded, was followed by perfectly logical steps, through all the incidents, to the complete destruction of the Union. The sophism itself is, that any state of the Union may, *consistently* with the national Constitution, and therefore *lawfully*, and *peacefully*, withdraw from the Union, without the consent of the Union, or of any other state" (emphasis added).[36] If the point was not made clear enough by stigmatizing such doctrines as sophistry, Lincoln further reinforced it through inventive metaphor: "With rebellion thus sugar-coated, they have been drugging the public mind of their section for more than thirty years; and, until at length, they have brought many good men to a willingness to take up arms against the government."[37]

Lincoln also used the argument from definition as a rhetorical weapon against states' rights doctrines. Secession was "the very essence of anarchy."

Based on the Nature of majority rule, he likewise argued that if "a minority, in such case, will secede rather than acquiesce, they make a precedent which, in turn will divide and ruin them; for a minority of their own will secede from them whenever a majority refuses to be controlled by such a minority."[38] And based on the Nature of every government's right to self-preservation, he argued: "Perpetuity is implied, if not expressed, in the fundamental law of all national governments."[39]

As a type of persuasion, Lincoln's philosophic rhetoric is revealed further in contrast to demagoguery—pandering to the people by arousing the base emotions of fear, envy, and hatred for political gain. James Ceaser explains, "Demagoguery always functions in the realm of appealing to a public; its distinguishing characteristic is the practice of enhancing popular standing. . . . Demagoguery is more at home in the mass assembly, or on the street before a crowd, as in Marc Anthony's famous address following Caesar's assassination, or in modern times, in election campaigns."[40] To be sure, the Founders were deeply concerned about the danger that demagogues posed to popular government. With the turbulent history of Rome and Greece in mind, Hamilton warns in *Federalist 1* that "of those men who have overturned the liberties of republics, the greatest number have begun their career by playing an obsequious court to the people, commencing demagogues and ending tyrants."[41]

Lincoln confronted the dangers of demagoguery and mob rule early in his career in the Lyceum address of 1838, where he warned of a "towering genius" who would pose as the people's savior while exploiting sectional passions and divisions to satisfy his own ambition. His often cited appeal to "cold, calculating, unimpassioned reason" occurs in the context of the "wild and furious passions" of mob rule and of the demagogues who incite it.

Douglas's racial pandering and jingoistic appeals to Manifest Destiny provide clear examples of demagoguery. In his biography of the sixteenth president, Burlingame refers to Douglas as "a drunken demagogue" who "raved like a mad bull."[42] The *Cincinnati Commercial*, an independent journal, forthrightly exposed Douglas's demagogic appeal to "the prejudices of the white people against the African race, to the political self-righteousness of American citizens, or to the love of Conquest and Dominion, the passion of the extension of Territory and National self-aggrandizement."[43]

Indeed, Douglas began his remarks at the first debate, at Ottawa, Illinois, August 21, 1858, by racial pandering to his audience. Playing on the base emotions of fear and hatred, he warned that the antislavery policies of the Republican Party would encourage an influx of blacks, making the state of Illinois "a negro colony." Knowing full well that the Illinois state constitution prohibited free blacks from even entering the state, he asked: "Do you desire to strike out of our State Constitution that clause which keeps slaves and free negroes out of the State, and allow the free negroes to flow in, and cover your prairies with black settlements? Do you desire to turn this beautiful State into a free negro colony, in order that when Missouri abolishes slavery she can send one hundred thousand emancipated slaves into Illinois, to become citizens and voters, on an equality with yourselves?"[44]

In the second debate, at Freeport, Illinois, August 27, 1858, Douglas descended even further into demagoguery by arousing the taboo of miscegenation and insulting white male pride. He claimed to have witnessed the "dishonorable" spectacle of a black man (the abolitionist Frederick Douglass) in a carriage with a fawning white woman: "The last time I came here to make a speech, while talking from the stand to you, people of Freeport, as I am doing to-day, I saw a carriage and a magnificent one it was, drive up and take a position on the outside of the crowd; a beautiful young lady was sitting on the box seat, whilst Fred. Douglass and her mother reclined inside, and the owner of the carriage acted as driver. I saw this in your own town."[45] Douglas predicted that the carriage episode was just a taste of what would happen if the Republicans were elected: the entire racial hierarchy would be turned upside down with blacks on top and whites on the bottom. If the interracial sexual suggestion was not enough to inflame passions, he further aroused the manly pride of his audience by providing a future spectacle of white men who would act as servants for predatorial black men who were stealing their women: "All I have to say of it is this, that if you, Black Republicans, think that the negro ought to be on a social equality with your wives and daughters, and ride in a carriage with your wife, whilst you drive the team, you have a perfect right to do so." Indeed, as Burlingame candidly notes, "such crude race-baiting further diminished Douglas's claim to statesmanship."[46]

In understanding Lincoln's response to this racial demagoguery, it must be kept in mind that the issue of slavery and racial equality were quite separate in the minds of most Americans at the time of the Lincoln-Douglas debates in 1858. Many opposed slavery while still harboring racist sentiments against black people, including some of the most prominent abolitionists themselves.[47] As seen, the Illinois constitution prohibited both slavery and racial equality by forbidding free blacks from entering the state and by stripping those already there of the rights of citizenship. African Americans were prohibited from voting, holding office, and serving on juries. Indeed, Burlingame explains that appeals "to race prejudice resonated in Illinois, one of the most Negrophobic of the Free States."[48] Douglas's racial pandering distracted the northern public from uniting in opposition to slavery by focusing their fears and passions on racial equality rather than the injustice of slavery and its threat to the nation's republican institutions. As Fehrenbacher notably observed, opposition to slavery united the Republican Party while support for full racial equality divided it.[49]

This historical context explains the extent to which Lincoln walked a rhetorical tightrope between his opposition to slavery and full civic equality for blacks. He disavowed miscegenation while at the same time making it clear that his opponent was exploiting the volatile issue for crass partisan purposes: "There is a natural disgust in the minds of nearly all white people, to the idea of an indiscriminate amalgamation of the white and black races and Judge Douglas evidently is basing his chief hope, upon the chances of being able to appropriate the benefit of this disgust to himself."[50] Lincoln's evasive language in this context is noteworthy. He describes the "natural disgust in the minds of nearly all white people" but does not reveal whether or not he personally shares this revulsion or whether or not it is even warranted, thereby leaving some doubt in the mind of the careful reader.

The fact that Lincoln consistently drew attention to Douglas's racial pandering provides a further caveat to the careful reader about taking his statements about race completely at "face value." What he subsequently says provides an important qualification to the careful reader: "Now I protest against that counterfeit logic which concludes that, because I do not want a black woman for a *slave* I must necessarily want her for a *wife*. I need not have her for either, I can just leave her alone. In some respects she certainly is not my equal; but in her natural right to eat the bread she earns with her own hands without asking leave of any one else, she is my equal, and the equal of all others."[51]

Part of Lincoln's rhetorical brilliance involved deflecting his opponents' demagogic charge that the Republicans supported full social and political equality for black people, a politically suicidal policy at the time in Illinois. Refusing to take this bait, Lincoln's strategy was to keep the North's attention focused on the inherent evil of slavery and its threat to the Union. The belief in the common humanity of the African American had to be publicly recognized before any real progress could me made toward full equality. Keeping the "central idea" of equality before the public mind, Lincoln thus proclaimed: "let us discard all this quibbling about this man and the other man—this race and that race and the other race being inferior, and therefore they must be placed in an inferior position—discarding our standard that we have left us. Let us discard all these things, and unite as one people throughout this land, until we shall once more stand up declaring that all men are created equal."[52]

Lincoln's rhetoric was also shaped through his lifelong reading of the Bible. The pervasive influence of the Bible on public opinion during the Civil War cannot be overstated. To be sure, Lincoln regarded proslavery theology as a sophistry that had to be combated through an appeal to both reason and revelation. As seen in chapter 1, the sixteenth president compared proslavery theology to how Satan twisted the words of scripture in an effort to deceive Christ. Indeed, he claimed that the devil's attempt "was no more false, and far less hypocritical."

With reference to the aforementioned Presbyterian minister Frederick Ross, author of *Slavery Ordained of God*, Lincoln revealed the sophistry of proslavery theology in these terms:

> The sum of pro-slavery theology seems to be this: Slavery is not universally right, nor yet universally wrong; it is better for some people to be slaves; and, in such cases it is the Will of God that they be such. Certainly there is no contending against the Will of God; but still there is some difficulty in ascertaining, and applying it to particular cases. For instance we will suppose the Rev. Dr. Ross has a slave named Sambo, and the question is "Is it the will of God that Sambo shall remain a slave, or be set free?"[53]

Appealing to the Golden Rule, he then observed, "But, slavery is good for some people!!! As a good thing, slavery is strikingly peculiar, in this, that it is the only good thing which no man ever seeks the good of, for himself."[54]

Lincoln humorously concluded his reflection on Ross's proslavery theology with an allusion to Aesop's memorable fable about the "wolf in sheep's clothing," a story that is also mentioned in Matthew 7:15. Proslavery theology is just like the clever wolf in the fable who claims to be a protector of the sheep. In fact, the wolf's claim is a thinly disguised ruse that masks greedy self-interest. In sum, paternalistic justifications of proslavery theology are a wolf in sheep's clothing. Lincoln dismisses Ross's argument: "Nonsense! Wolves devouring lambs, not because it is good for their own greedy maws, but because it [is] good for the lambs!!!!"[55] The characterization of proslavery as a "wolf in sheep's clothing" must have resonated with the sixteenth president since he also appealed to it in a speech to Sanitary Fair on April 18, 1864: "The shepherd drives the wolf from the sheep's throat, for which the sheep thanks the shepherd as a *liberator*, while the wolf denounces him for the same act as the destroyer of liberty, especially as the sheep was a black one."[56]

More specifically, Lincoln used biblical rhetoric in at least four different ways to address the Bible reading public of his time: (1) theologically when he was speaking about God himself and his purposes; (2) civil theologically in applying a particular moral precept of the Bible like the Golden Rule to the antislavery politics of his time; (3) evocatively for stylistic purposes in borrowing the motifs, cadences, images, and symbolism of the King James Bible, as in the "four score and seven years" of the Gettysburg Address; (4) allegorically or didactically as a means to convey a political teaching to the audience through the use of a biblical illustration or example. These four different ways are not mutually exclusive. Rather, they are interrelated parts that display the rhetorical richness of Lincoln's use of the Bible in American public life. It is worth providing an example of each.

Lincoln's Second Inaugural Address is perhaps the most notable example of his theological use of biblical language:

> The Almighty has His own purposes. "Woe unto the world because of offences! for it must needs be that offences come; but woe to that man by whom the offence cometh!" If we shall suppose that American Slavery is one of those offences which, in the providence of God, must needs come, but which, having continued through His appointed time, He now wills to remove, and that He gives to both North and South, this terrible war, as the woe due to those by whom the offence came, shall we discern therein any departure from those divine attributes which the believers in a Living God always ascribe to Him?[57]

The biblical language in this passage may be described as theological insofar as it raises ultimate questions about the Divine Will and justice. Political questions are situated in the context of this more comprehensive view of the Divinity. While affirming the ultimate inscrutability of the Divine Will, Lincoln suggests that *if* the war was indeed a punishment for the national sin of slavery, then it was merited. Instead of a self-righteous argument against the South as might be expected of a two-term president who was on the brink of winning the bloodiest war in American history, Lincoln remarkably suggested that both sides were culpable before God: "Both read the same Bible, and pray to the same God; and each invokes His aid against the other. . . . The prayers of both could not be answered; that of neither has been answered fully."[58] The speech displays Lincoln's magnanimity in calling for national reconciliation rather than vengeance: "With malice toward none; with charity for all; with firmness in the right, as God gives us to see the right, let us strive on to finish the work we are in; to bind up the nation's wounds."[59]

If theological language focuses on Divine agency and God's will, civil theological language makes reference to a particular teaching or precept of the Bible as a standard to judge political practices of the time. Despite sophistic claims to the contrary, Lincoln believed that, rightly understood, the teachings of Christianity were antislavery, as when he remarked: "Indeed it is difficult to conceive how it could be otherwise with any one professing christianity, or even having ordinary perceptions of right and wrong."[60] Moreover, consistent with his view of the mutual relationship between faith and reason, Lincoln notes that the moral teachings of Christianity are confirmed by "ordinary perceptions of right and wrong."[61] He thus applies the precept of Genesis 3:19 against slavery: "To read in the Bible, as the word of God himself, that 'In the sweat of *thy* face shalt thou eat bread,['] and to preach there-from that, 'In the sweat of *other mans* faces shalt thou eat bread,' to my mind can scarcely be reconciled with honest sincerity. When brought to my final reckoning, may I have to answer for robbing no man of his goods; yet more tolerable even this, than for robbing one of himself, and all that was his."[62]

Lincoln also used biblical rhetoric in an allegorical sense when he applied the metaphor of "the apple of gold and picture of silver" from Proverbs 25:1 to explain the complementary roles of the Declaration and Constitution to the Union. Perhaps the most memorable example of Lincoln's allegorical use of biblical rhetoric is his "House Divided" metaphor from Matthew 12: "'A house divided against itself cannot stand.' I believe this government cannot endure, permanently half *slave* and half *free*." The original biblical context reveals Christ's Divine authority to perform miracles. As used by Lincoln, however, the primary purpose of the metaphor is didactic. It helps Lincoln explain the extent to which slavery and freedom are utterly incompatible and the corresponding need for a national moral consensus on this truth.

Lincoln appealed to evocative biblical rhetoric for stylistic purposes. When used evocatively, biblical language borrows the cadences and rhythm, literary images, and motifs and symbols from the King James Bible, including its monosyllabic Anglo-Saxon words like "score," "birth," and "forth." As many scholars of Lincoln's writing have pointed out, the sixteenth president "wrote for the ear." The sound as well as the symbolism of the language thus mattered to him. The use of biblical style solemnized the occasion by clothing the secular event in sacred language.

The Gettysburg Address provides several vivid examples of evocative biblical rhetoric: "Four score and seven years ago our fathers brought forth, upon this continent, a new nation, conceived in liberty, and dedicated to the proposition that 'all men are created equal.'" Its beginning of "four score and seven years ago" recalls the language of the King James Bible in measuring time. In biblical terms, a "score" is a span of twenty years. Significantly, Lincoln's narrative places the birth of the nation at 1776, the date of the Declaration, not 1787, the date of the Constitution. This is in accord with his belief that a Union preceded the Constitution and that its "philosophical cause," the principle of equal consent, culminated with the Declaration. Of course, "our fathers" is a reference to the Lord's Prayer. The speech applies the biblical narrative of birth, sin, sacrifice, death, rebirth and redemption to the American regime. The Founders "brought forth" or gave birth to the nation conceived in liberty, which was tainted by the original sin of slavery. The sacrificial death of the soldiers who consecrate the field with their blood is symbolic of the atonement. The suffering and death, the passion, of the nation leads to "a new birth of freedom"—that is, a country redeemed from the sin of slavery. Through the use of biblical language, Lincoln distills the essence of the American creed. He defined the Civil War as a test of the regime's fidelity to its ancient faith in the Declaration that had worldwide significance. It would secure the perpetuity of popular government "of the people, by the people, for the people." The immediate political context asks the country to ratify the Emancipation Proclamation that had been issued in January of the same year in view of these higher ends.

Lincoln's letter to Erastus Corning of June 12, 1863, provides a final example of how his philosophical rhetoric sought to balance liberty and security in wartime. The letter was written in response to Democrats who had criticized Lincoln's record on civil liberties, including his suspension of habeas corpus and the use of military tribunals. The protest was sparked by the controversial arrest of Clement Vallandigham, a Copperhead (peace Democrat) and a member of the U.S. House of Representatives from Ohio. In April 1863, "without Lincoln's knowledge of approval," General Burnside decreed martial law and issued General Order 38, which "punished treasonable expression in the Department of the Ohio during the war."[63] About a month later, Vallandigham delivered a speech before fifteen to twenty thousand people repudiating General Order 38 and the war as one "for freedom of the blacks and enslavement of the whites." Vallandigham was subsequently arrested.

Democrats assailed Lincoln for the arrest and held protests meetings throughout the country. One of the most important of these meetings was held in Albany, New York, on May 16, 1863, and led by Erastus Corning. Though Lincoln's letter was addressed to Corning, the president fully knew that its subsequent publication and distribution would provide a rhetorical opportunity to justify his policies before the nation. Like the letter to Greeley anticipating emancipation, the letter to Corning was part of Lincoln's public relations campaign.

Lincoln began by distinguishing between the Constitution in times of peace and times of war: "I was slow to adopt the strong measures, which by degrees I have been forced to regard as being within the exceptions of the constitution, and as indispensable to the public Safety. Nothing is better known to history than that courts of justice are utterly incompetent to such cases. Civil courts are organized chiefly for trials of individuals, or, at most, a few individuals acting in concert; and this in quiet times, and on charges of crimes well defined in the law."[64] To illustrate rhetorically the difference between the Constitution in times of peace and war, he used the homely metaphor of emetics—medicines used to purge the body of disease. He explains: "The constitution itself makes the distinction; and I can no more be persuaded that the government can constitutionally take no strong measure in time of rebellion, because it can be shown that the same could not be lawfully taken in time of peace, than I can be persuaded that a particular drug is not good medicine for a sick man, because it can be shown to not be good food for a well one."[65]

In sum, Lincoln explains that the military arrests, suspension of habeas corpus, and other abridgements of civil liberties were temporary measures done in the extreme circumstances of war. When the crisis passes, the measures, that Lincoln likens to emetics or purgatives will be ended. In a clear and shocking example to Victorian sensibilities, Lincoln states that the likelihood of their persistence as permanent measures cannot be seriously entertained "any more than I am able to believe that a man could contract so strong an appetite for emetics during temporary illness, as to persist in feeding upon them through the remainder of his healthful life."[66]

Lincoln then addressed the Vallandigham arrest, which had garnered national attention. As commander in chief, he was placed in the untenable position of defending General Burnside. Civil libertarian Geoff Stone explains that Lincoln sought to stake out a "middle ground" that would provide some guidance in terms of distinguishing between protected and unprotected speech. He thus conceded that the arrest would have been wrong if Vallandigham were indeed arrested because of the political content of his speech. According to Stone, however, Lincoln made an important distinction between political speech that is protected under the First Amendment and illegal incitement against the draft that was not. This distinction anticipated the Court's subsequent First Amendment jurisprudence. Vallandigham was arrested not because his speech opposed the policies of the government, but because his speech crossed over the line into action, by fomenting open resistance to the draft. Lincoln thus explained:

> But the arrest, as I understand, was made for a very different reason. Mr. Vallandigham avows his hostility to the war on the part of the Union; and his arrest was made because he was laboring, with some effect, to prevent the raising of troops, to encourage desertions from the army, and to leave the rebellion without an adequate military force to suppress it. He was not arrested because he was damaging the political prospects of the administration, or the personal interests of the commanding general; but because he was damaging the army, upon the existence, and vigor of which, the life of the nation depends. He was warring upon the military; and this gave the military constitutional jurisdiction to lay hands upon him.[67]

Just as Lincoln made his constitutional argument accessible to the public through the use of the emetics metaphor, in the case of Vallandigham, he frames the issue to the public through a vivid contrast between a wily agitator and the simpleminded soldier boy: "Must I shoot a simple-minded soldier boy who deserts, while I must not touch a hair of a wiley agitator who induces him to desert? This is none the less injurious when effected by getting a father, or brother, or friend, into a public meeting, and there working upon his feeling, till he is persuaded to write the soldier boy, that he is fighting in a bad cause, for a wicked administration of a contemptable government, too weak to and punish him if he shall desert. I think that in such a case, to silence the agitator, and save the boy, is not only constitutional, but, withal, a great mercy."[68] Lincoln's rhetoric had transformed Vallandigham from a martyr of civil liberty into a wily agitator responsible for inducing simpleminded soldier boys to desert upon pain of death.

In sum, Lincoln's philosophic rhetoric sought to persuade, elevate, and ennoble the public mind through reasoned argument about the common good. Informed by knowledge and wisdom about human nature and politics, this philosophic rhetoric comes to light in response to both sophistry and demagoguery and in defense of the ancient faith of the regime. In crafting a philosophical rhetoric, the statesman serves as a civic educator to both his party and the nation. To be sure, Lincoln's rhetorical sword not only helped the Union win the war, it has defined us a people ever since.

6

PATRIOTISM

$\mathscr{A}$ true statesman is imbued with a love of country that stirs service and sacrifice to the common good.[1] Patriotism is a potent force that grips statesmen and unites them with their fellow countrymen in a common moral enterprise. Indeed, Alexander Stephens went so far as to say that Lincoln's devotion to "the Union rose to the sublimity of religious mysticism." Though as former vice president of the Confederacy, he meant this as a criticism, Stephens can at least be given credit for appreciating the patriotic motives of the sixteenth president.

Much has been said about Lincoln's ambition, and even his melancholy, as a spur to his greatness.[2] Scholars often point to William Herndon's statement that his law partner's ambition was a "little engine that knew no rest." Yet Herndon also bore witness to his law partner's patriotism, as when he recollected him saying in 1851: "How hard—oh how more than hard it is to die and leave one's Country no better for the life of him that lived and died her child."[3] Such expressions of gratitude and service are characteristics of the true patriot. Unfortunately, modern efforts to uncover the subconscious springs of Lincoln's political motivations have too often overlooked love of country. While Lincoln's honorable ambition has already been made clear, this chapter considers the role that love of country or patriotism likewise played in inspiring the sixteenth president and in rallying support for the Union cause during the war.

Because Lincoln's love of country involved a critical self-reflection on the success, failures, and promise of the American regime, it may be described as a reflective or philosophical patriotism. As will be seen, this philosophical patriotism was compatible with reason and principles of universal justice. It viewed American national identity primarily, though not exclusively, in terms of allegiance to the ideals of the Declaration and therefore held out the promise of a multiracial society.

Historically, Lincoln's philosophical or reflective patriotism was articulated as a concrete response to rival forms of allegiance that he opposed as both unreasonable and unjust during the Civil War era: (a) Manifest Destiny, (b) sectionalism, (c) nativism, and (d) secession. Each of these rival forms of allegiance was based on an inordinate racial, ethnic, sectional, or imperial pride that transgressed moral and legal norms and harmed the common good. By violating the principles of the Declaration and/or the rule of law in the Constitution, each broke the moral and fraternal bonds of liberty and Union that Lincoln sought to perpetuate through an ordinate love of country guided by wisdom under God's Providence.

Finally, though Lincoln's reflective patriotism viewed American identity primarily in terms of devotion to the universal principles of the Declaration rather than race or ethnicity, it also appealed to a common history and heritage—that is, to what Lincoln poetically described as the "mystic chords of memory" in his First Inaugural Address. Lincoln reflective patriotism thus involved a cultural as well as a creedal element. In tracing this cultural element to the Puritan origins of American patriotism, George McKenna correctly emphasizes that love of country is more than "deducing conclusions from the Declaration of Independence and other documents."[4] Since patriotism is "an affection rather than a syllogistic process, it is a highly evocative word, recalling all kinds of memories stored up in images from George Washington crossing the icy Delaware to the Marines hoisting the flag at Iowa Jima."[5] Notably, Lincoln would appeal to these common memories in rallying support of the Union. To be sure, his philosophical patriotism appealed to both the heads and hearts of his fellow countrymen.

In sum, Lincoln's philosophical patriotism was constituted by his appeal to the natural law teaching in the Declaration, the republican legacy of the Founders, and biblical faith as mediated by the Puritan understanding of a city on an hill (Matthew 5:14) under God's Providence.[6] As seen, his ultimate moral justification for American public life drew on three broad sources of political order, the three R's of his political faith: (1) reason; (2) revelation; (3) republicanism.[7] His reflective patriotism similarly integrated these sources to inspire devotion to the Union, as vividly seen in his First Inaugural Address, March 4, 1861, where he invoked: "Intelligence, patriotism, Christianity, and a firm reliance on Him, who has never yet forsaken this favored land, are still competent to adjust, in the best way, all our present difficulty."[8] In *Patriotic Fires*, Melinda Lawson correctly notes that "it was the extraordinary accomplishment of Abraham Lincoln to construct a composite national loyalty—one which drew from nearly all the elements in the Union's patriotic repertoire."[9]

Much of the criticism of patriotism as chauvinistic, imperial, and racist is misguided since it stems from critics' confusion of patriotism with romantic and/or ethnic nationalism.[10] *In Imagined Communities: Reflections on the Origin and Spread of Nationalism*, Benedict Anderson states: "In an age when it is so common for progressive and cosmopolitan intellectuals . . . to insist on the near-pathological character of nationalism, its roots of fear and hatred of the Other, and its affinities with racism, it is useful to remind ourselves that nation's inspire love. The cultural projects of nationalism—poetry, prose fiction, music, plastic arts—show this love very clearly in thousands of different forms and styles."[11] In a more recent work, *Lincoln and the Triumph of the Nation*, Mark E. Neely, distinguishes between a "pathological nationalism" and the more benign "role of nationalism in the constitutional history of the Civil War."[12] In response to those who see patriotism as inherently vicious, Neely approvingly quotes Benedict Anderson's assessment above. Seward's jingoistic scheme to provoke a war with Great Britain in order to restore national unity during the secession crisis, a plan Lincoln rejected on both principled and practical grounds, was much more consistent with the pathological nationalism referred to by Neely.

Neely's and Anderson's distinction between a salutary nationalism and a "pathological nationalism" has a sound lineage in the historical and philosophical distinction between patriotism and nationalism. To avoid analytical confusion, I use the term patriotism to describe this salutary nationalism in contrast to its pathological variety. An appreciation of Lincoln's reflective patriotism thus requires a basic familiarity with the historical and philosophical distinction between patriotism and nationalism.

For example, George Orwell explains the distinction in a seminal essay, *Notes on Nationalism*:

> By "nationalism" I mean first of all the habit of assuming that human beings can be classified like insects and that whole blocks of millions or tens of millions of people can be confidently labelled "good" or "bad." But secondly—and this is much more important—I mean the habit of identifying oneself with a single nation or other unit, placing it beyond good and evil and recognising no other duty than that of advancing its interests. *Nationalism is not to be confused with patriotism.* Both words are normally used in so vague a way that any definition is liable to be challenged, but one must draw a distinction between them, since two different and even opposing ideas are involved . . . ; by "patriotism" I mean devotion to a particular place and a particular way of life, which one believes to be the best

in the world but has no wish to force on other people. Patriotism is
of its nature defensive, both militarily and culturally. Nationalism,
on the other hand, is inseparable from the desire for power. The
abiding purpose of every nationalist is to secure more power and
more prestige, *not* for himself but for the nation or other unit in
which he has chosen to sink his own individuality. . . . Nationalism
is power-hunger tempered by self-deception.[13]

Political philosopher Maurizio Viroli likewise traces the republican
roots of patriotism from antiquity to modernity and distinguishes them
both historically and theoretically from nationalist beliefs in racial purity,
ethnic homogeneity, and imperial domination.[14] Throughout, he copiously
cites ancient, medieval, and modern republican sources from Cicero to
Leonardi Bruni, a fifteenth-century medieval Florentine patriot, to Milton, Montesquieu, and Mazzini. In the republican tradition to which Lincoln and the Founders belonged, love of patria was understood primarily
in political terms. It involved gratitude, duty (*officiis*), care (*pietas*), and
sacrifice for the common good.[15] Indeed, the elements of classical republican patriotism are tersely expressed in Cicero's motto from *Tusculan
Disputations 4. 43 "pro legibus, pro libertate, pro patria"* (in behalf of laws,
liberty, and country). Unlike nineteenth century nationalism, classical
republican patriotism was allied to liberty and the rule of law and inimical
to despotism and tyranny. It is epitomized by Cato of Utica's resistance
to Caesar. Given its republican and patriotic motifs, it is no coincidence
that Joseph Addison's *Cato* was one of Washington's favorite plays and
that he had it performed at Valley Forge.[16]

According to Viroli, the "love of patria—which is the basis of political
virtue (*Politicam virtutem*)—is a rational love because it is a love for a
good (the free city) that is rational for each citizen to want to preserve."[17]
By contrast, nineteenth-century romantic nationalism tended to distrust
reason. It exalted feeling and passion as a more reliable source of achieving
mystical communion with a tribe or ethnic group.

Medieval Christians interpreted patriotism as a species of charity or
love of neighbor. In a passage that has been attributed to Thomas Aquinas
from *On Princely Government*, but was most likely written by Ptolemy
of Luca, patriotism is described as being "founded in the root of charity
[*Amor patriae in radice caritatis fundatur*] which puts not private things
before those held in common, but the things held in common before the
private as the Blessed Augustine says."[18] Patriotism was thus understood
as a kind of sacrificial love and selfless duty that serves the common good.

In *Lincoln and the Politics of Christian Love*, Grant N. Havers reveals the extent to which Lincoln's politics applied the principle of "love of neighbor" and "the golden rule to politics."[19] Havers argues that Lincoln's charity was displayed as a "moral force opposed to hypocrisy in public life as well as an inspiration to heal the conflicts of a divided nation."[20] Lincoln's opposition to the hypocritical mistreatment of others in the case of slavery and Manifest Destiny, his willingness to consider and appreciate the dilemma of slaveholders in ridding themselves of the institution, his recognition of the North's culpability in the sin of slavery, and his teaching that "the victors of the civil War must place themselves in the position of the vanquished" are just a few examples of how charity imbued his political outlook.[21]

To summarize: whereas republican patriotism had classical and medieval roots, nationalism was primarily a nineteenth-century movement whose origins can be traced to the French Revolution and in the romantic response to Enlightenment universalism. Whereas republican patriotism was primarily understood as a political virtue, nationalism emphasizes racial, ethnic, and linguistic homogeneity as the basis of Union-Fatherland. And whereas romantic nationalism was seen as mystical and even irrational, republican love of country was seen as rational.

The core elements of the classical and medieval tradition of patriotism would be transmitted to modern republican thinkers like Bolingbroke, Milton, Addison, and Montesquieu. These modern thinkers exercised a direct influence on the Founders, who, in turn, influenced Lincoln. Montesquieu, for example, identifies patriotism as the affective disposition to place the common good over private interest and ambition. "Love of the homeland," he states, "leads to goodness in mores, and goodness in mores leads to the love of the homeland. The less we can satisfy our particular passions, the more we give ourselves up to the passions for the general order."[22]

Because Lincoln's reflective patriotism combines devotion to both the universal and the particular, it is imbued with a reverence and filial piety for the deeds and actions of the Founders who sought to realize the principles of the Revolution through the concrete rule of law in the Constitution. As a young man, Lincoln read Parson Mason Locke Weems's *Life of Washington* as well as Pericles' "Funeral Oration" in Plutarch's *Lives*.[23] The patriotic themes of these works would have been unmistakable to him. Not surprisingly, Lincoln saw Washington, the *pater patriae*, as a patriotic role model. Indeed, Washington's Farewell Address, which Lincoln had read, defines patriotism in terms of subordinating sectional interest to the common good of the country. In language that anticipates Lincoln's reflective patriotism, Washington states: "The name of American which belongs to you, in your national capacity, must always exalt the just pride of Patriotism, more than any appellation derived from local discriminations."[24]

The essence of Lincoln's reflective patriotism is found in his eulogy to Henry Clay, which will be considered at greater length later in this chapter: "He loved his country partly because it was his own country, but mostly because it was a free country."[25] Following both Washington and Clay's example, Lincoln defined patriotism in terms of devotion to the country as whole against mere sectional interests or passions, whether northern or southern, that broke the inseparable bonds of liberty and an inclusive Union dedicated to the principles of the Declaration. Melinda Lawson correctly describes Lincoln's patriotic vision in these terms: "The nation he described offered Americans a meaningful history and was a vehicle for realization of self and freedom. His national state was strong but beneficent, bestowing economic well-being and guaranteeing liberty to his people. His patriotism served self-interest but demanded sacrifice; was partisan while seemingly above party; required vigilant citizenship yet commanded obedience."[26]

In the Lyceum address of 1838, what many consider to be his first great speech, a young Lincoln forthrightly declared his patriotic aim to perpetuate the Founders' legacy of ordered liberty. Unfortunately, the overt patriotic motives of the speech have been eclipsed by psychoanalytic accounts of Lincoln's subconscious ambition. As seen, psycho-historians claim that Lincoln actually projected himself into the figure of "the towering genius."[27] They see, as self-referential, his warning against ambitious tyrants like Alexander, Caesar, and Napoleon who crave distinction at any cost, "whether at the expense of emancipating the slaves, or enslaving freemen."[28] On the contrary, Lincoln's self-described task in the Lyceum address springs from "gratitude to our fathers, justice to ourselves, duty to posterity and love for our species in general."[29] Indeed, this statement nicely encapsulates the key components of his reflective patriotism.

Lincoln's love of republican liberty stirred him to oppose plebiscitarian impulses implicit to democracy itself—namely, the passions of mob rule. In the Lyceum address, he emphasizes that the preservation of ordered liberty in a democratic republic requires that it be exercised within lawful boundaries. Exhorting his fellow citizens to revere both the liberty promised by the Declaration and the particular rule of law established by the Constitution to safeguard it, Lincoln proclaims: "As the patriots of seventy-six did to the support of the Declaration of Independence, so to the support of the Constitution and Laws, let every American pledge his life, his property, and his sacred honor;—let every man remember that to violate the law, is to trample on the blood of his father, and to tear the character [charter?] of his own, and his children's liberty."[30]

In the same speech it will also be recalled that Lincoln famously invoked "a political religion," based on "reverence for the laws,"[31] as a solution to the problem of mob rule. If unbounded by the restraining force of law, passion will turn against itself and jeopardize the very liberty the patriots fought so hard to secure during the Revolution. Significantly, Lincoln demands that reverence be guided by reason, intelligence, and sound morality. "Passion has helped us," he states, "but can do so no more. It will in future be our enemy. Reason, cold, calculating, unimpassioned reason, must furnish all the materials for our future support and defence.—Let those [materials] be moulded into *general intelligence*, [sound] *morality*, and, in particular, *a reverence for the constitution and laws*."[32] Thus, as early as the Lyceum address of 1838, Lincoln distinguished between a blind allegiance based on a passion, and a thoughtful reverence based on reason and in accord with sound morality. Put another way, he called for a reflective patriotism.

Consonant with the potential harmony between love of one's own and the good of humanity, Lincoln's reflective patriotism envisioned America as an exemplar of free government to the world. Thus in the Lyceum address he describes America as "the fondest hope, of the lovers of freedom, throughout the world." Lincoln would consistently articulate this view of America's mission to uphold the torch of democracy for the rest of the world.

In the decade that followed the Lyceum address, from 1840 to 1850, consistent with his earlier call for reverence based on reason, intelligence, and sound morality, whenever Lincoln mentioned patriotism he did so in connection with wisdom. Moreover, he repeatedly qualified this type of patriotism as being thoughtful rather than impulsive. A close textual analysis shows that the words "intelligence" and "wisdom" consistently precede the word "patriotism" in his speeches and writings from this time. For example, on February 26, 1841, he stated that the efforts of the Whig Party "required our utmost wisdom and patriotism."[33] And in his eulogy to Zachary Taylor on July 25, 1850, he declares, "I will not pretend to believe that all the wisdom, or all the patriotism of the country, died with Gen. Taylor. But we know that *wisdom* and *patriotism*, in a public office, under institutions like ours, are wholly inefficient and worthless, unless they are sustained by the confidence and devotion of the people."[34] In sum, the connection in Lincoln's mind between patriotism and wisdom was part of a pattern that can be traced from the Lyceum address in the 1830s to his presidency. In each case, Lincoln, who carefully chose words, places wisdom and intelligence before patriotism.

As will be shown, Lincoln did not believe that all forms of love of country are wise and intelligent. For this reason, he opposed nativism and Manifest Destiny as disordered forms of love that were contrary to a more reflective or philosophical patriotism based on wisdom and justice. Lincoln's reflective patriotism demanded that he challenge his government when it betrayed itself. In speech and deed, his actions coincide with Edmund Burke's dictum that "to be loved a country must be lovely." Like the patriotic statesmanship of Burke, who believed that Great Britain had betrayed herself in flawed policies toward the American colonies, Ireland, and India, Lincoln's reflective patriotism demanded a critical engagement with his country when it pursued unjust and imprudent policies.[35]

This critical engagement is vividly seen in his opposition to the Mexican war and in response to allegations about his own allegiance to the American regime. Such accusations were likely to have deepened his subsequent reflections on patriotism. As a first-term congressman from Illinois, Lincoln refused to support a resolution that called members of Congress to vindicate President Polk's aggression during the Mexican war. In response, he accused Polk of initiating hostilities on Mexican soil, and, on December 22, 1847, he proposed his controversial "Spot Resolutions" demanding to know the exact spot where American blood was shed. Less than a month later, Lincoln made another speech in the House of Representatives condemning President Polk for abusing executive power, claiming that "the blood of this war, like the blood of Abel, is crying to Heaven against him [Polk]."[36]

William Herndon warned his law partner that he was committing political suicide. His opponents were already questioning his patriotism, derisively calling him "spotty Lincoln." Indeed, a decade later, in 1858, during the Great Debates, Stephen A. Douglas would relentlessly attack Lincoln's patriotism for his stance during the Mexican war. For example, at Springfield on October 20, 1858, playing the demagogue, Douglas accused Lincoln of treason, alleging that he was a member of the "Mexican Party in the congress of the United States." "Lincoln's vote," according to Douglas, "did more to encourage the Mexicans and the Mexican army than all of the soldiers that were brought into the field; they induced the Mexicans to hold out the longer, and the guerrillas to keep up their warfare on the roadside, and to poison our men, and to take the lives of our soldiers wherever and whenever they could."[37]

Just as Lincoln opposed the nationalistic impulses of Manifest Destiny during the Mexican war, so he likewise opposed Douglas's imperial ambitions a decade later. In a *Speech of Discoveries and Inventions 1859*, he satirized "Young America," the pro-Douglas, expansionist wing of the Democratic Party committed to Manifest Destiny.[38] He further opposed Douglas's efforts to annex Cuba under the principle of popular sovereignty. The Little Giant forthrightly proclaimed: "When we get Cuba we must take it as we find it, and leave the people of Cuba to decide the question of slavery for themselves without the interference of the federal government, or of any other State in the Union." As Harry V. Jaffa has aptly noted, Douglas saw slavery as a mere distraction that impeded the more important work of nationalist expansion and empire building. By contrast, Lincoln opposed both slavery and imperialism as twin evils that were rooted in the same lust for power.[39]

In sum, Lincoln's criticism of American nationalist aggression and imperialism, whether it be the Mexican war or the annexation of Cuba ten years later by proslavery expansionists, displays further the potential compatibility between his reflective patriotism and legitimate dissent. Whether or not the factual basis of his claim was true, that Polk had initiated hostilities, the larger point is that Lincoln did not exploit patriotism as an excuse to shield leaders from public scrutiny or to quell debate. On the contrary, his love of liberty demanded that he speak out against his government when it betrayed its own principles and abused power in a way that was more consistent with monarchical despotism than republican freedom. Ironically, Lincoln's own actions as president in exercising broad power to crush the rebellion would test whether or not he would extend this same principle to political dissenters during the Civil War, especially in his letter to Erastus Corning where he raises questions about the Democrats loyalty in opposing the war effort.

Less than a decade after the Mexican war, in his "Resolutions in Behalf of Hungarian Freedom," 1852, Lincoln further articulated a vision of reflective patriotism based on a common love of liberty shared in solidarity with other peoples. The resolutions were drafted in response to a freedom tour made by Louis Kossuth, the hero of Hungarian independence movement, which recently had been crushed by the combined imperial forces of Austria and Russia. The Illinois legislature was summoned to deliberate on whether or not the United States should intervene to aid the Hungarians.

Lincoln began the resolutions by affirming the general principle of nonintervention. He then noted that the circumstance of Russian aggression could potentially justify foreign assistance. Such intervention, however, depended on the prudential weighing and balancing of circumstances. Regardless of whether or not the United States ultimately intervened, Lincoln believed that as the exemplar of democracy to the world, at the very least, America was called upon to affirm, in principle, moral solidarity with the Hungarian people. "We, the American people" he declares "cannot remain silent, without justifying an inference against our continued devotion to the principles of our free institutions."[40]

Lincoln's tribute to Kossuth shows that the love of liberty is not chauvinistic per se. Kossuth embodied the same principles that Americans hold dear. Lincoln thus praised him as "the most worthy and distinguished representative of the cause of civil and religious liberty on the continent of Europe. A cause for which he and his nation struggled until they were overwhelmed by the armed intervention of a foreign despot, in violation of the more sacred principles of the laws of Nature and of nations—principles held dear by the friends of freedom everywhere, and more especially by the people of these United States."[41]

Lincoln often used the term "friends of freedom" to describe common love of liberty between different peoples and nations. Consistent with his devotion to the natural law principles of justice in the Declaration, this love of liberty must observe the "sacred principles of the laws of nature and nations." Such principles are "especially" "held dear" by the people of the United States given its Puritan heritage and self-understanding as "a city upon a hill," dedicated to the cause of civil and religious liberty. In sum, the Hungarian resolutions show that a reflective patriotism is not tantamount to armed intervention, but may involve flying the American flag alongside countries who share a common love of liberty.

Lincoln's eulogy to Henry Clay, June 6, 1852 (the same year as the Hungarian resolutions), is perhaps the most vivid and profound expression of his reflective patriotism. Indeed, Lincoln admired Clay as his "beau ideal of a statesman, the man for whom I fought all my humble life."[42] While much attention has been given to Lyceum address as a window into Lincoln's soul, too little attention has been given to his eulogy to Henry Clay as a clearer window. In praising Clay, Lincoln affirms those qualities that he admires most in the man and his country. Not surprisingly, foremost among these are: "wisdom, experience and patriotism." Lincoln extols Clay's patriotism in these powerful terms:

Mr. Clay's predominant sentiment, from first to last, was a deep devotion to the cause of human liberty—a strong sympathy with the oppressed every where, and an ardent wish for their elevation. With him, this was a primary and all controlling passion. Subsidiary to this was the conduct of his whole life. He loved his country partly because it was his own country, but mostly because it was a free country; and he burned with a zeal for its advancement, prosperity and glory, because he saw in such, the advancement, prosperity and glory, of human liberty, human right and human nature. He desired the prosperity of his countrymen partly because they were his countrymen, but chiefly to show to the world that freemen could be prosperous.[43]

To be sure, in praising Clay, Lincoln was describing those virtues he sought to develop in himself as a young statesman.

Lincoln applauds Clay for envisioning national glory as something altogether different from military might and the projection of power throughout the globe. Rather Clay and Lincoln both envision glory in terms of America's moral worth at home and its moral influence abroad. The true glory of America is measured by the extent to which it advances the cause of liberty as a "city upon a hill" and "a light unto other nations." Following the Founders, Lincoln's reflective patriotism applies these Puritan symbols to the American experiment in self-government. The republican critics of democracy said that it was prone to the extremes of tyranny and anarchy. In reply to these critics, Lincoln would subsequently characterize the Civil War as an ordeal that tested the viability of democracy. The success or failure of the American experiment would reverberate throughout the globe, providing hope or despair for the friends of freedom everywhere.

Because Clay's legacy belonged to the world as much as America, Lincoln proclaims him as, "freedom's champion." As we may recall, Clay's American System promised moral support for the fledgling democracies in Latin America who were struggling against Spain's colonial domination. Lincoln also followed Clay and the Whigs in opposing the Democratic policies of Manifest Destiny and imperial expansion.

Further consistent with what we have seen, Lincoln associates patriotism with the qualities of wisdom and intelligence. He admires Clay's "wisdom and patriotism." And he extols his undeniable legacy "amongst intelligent and Patriotic Americans."[44] The implication being that those who place sectional interest above devotion to the Union, whether they are northerners or southerners, are both unreasonable and unpatriotic.

Clay's statesmanship was exemplary because it placed the common good of the Union above sectional interest. Lincoln explains: "As a politician or statesman, no one was so habitually careful to avoid all sectional ground. Whatever he did, he did for the whole country. In the construction of his measures he ever carefully surveyed every part of the field and duly weighed every conflicting interest. Feeling as he did, and as the truth is, that the world's best hope depended upon the continued Union of these States, he was ever jealous of and watchful for, whatever might have the slightest tendency to separate them."[45] Moreover, preserving the Union advanced a humanitarian end since the American experiment was the "world's best hope." It inspired freedom at home and abroad through one's right to rise or a foreign patriot's resistance to tyranny.

The Whig devotion to the inseparability of liberty and Union that Lincoln so admired in Henry Clay and that fueled his reflective patriotism would be challenged by threats of sectionalism over slavery, nativism, and secession in defense of slavery. Each will be considered in turn.

The essence of Lincoln's antislavery convictions and the most vivid expression of political faith to date, are found in the Peoria address of October 16, 1854. As Lew Lehrman has shown, Peoria was a turning point for both Lincoln and the nation. Indeed, this pivotal speech deserves its proper place alongside the Gettysburg Address and Second Inaugural as one of Lincoln's greatest. It was occasioned by the repeal of the Missouri Compromise, which opened up the virgin territories to slavery under the doctrine of popular sovereignty. Lincoln used the strong language of hate in exposing popular sovereignty as a smoke screen for the spread of slavery, which he condemns in equally visceral terms as a monstrous injustice: "This *declared* indifference, but as I must think, covert *real* zeal for the spread of slavery, I can not but hate. I hate it because of the monstrous injustice of slavery itself. I hate it because it deprives our republican example of its just influence in the world—enables the enemies of free institutions, with plausibility, to taunt us as hypocrites—[and] causes the real friends of freedom to doubt our sincerity."[46]

Lincoln's righteous indignation at Peoria is the other side of his love for the Union. Slavery was a twin threat that violated both the moral and national integrity of the Union. It undermined America's moral credibility abroad and its survival at home. Havers notes, "Charity, as Lincoln understood it, is the only viable faith for a democracy because it puts an end to egregious double standards (like the inequality of slavery) that make a mockery of self-government. Charity also presupposes knowledge of the Christian commitment to duty, which transcends mere self-interest."[47]

Because it preserved the Union on just terms that placed slavery on a path to ultimate extinction, the Missouri Compromise was rightfully praised as a "great patriotic measure."[48] Although Clay was its principal champion, Lincoln quotes approvingly the general view that "the honor was equally due to others as well as to him. . . . it had its origin in the hearts of all patriotic men, who desired to preserve and perpetuate the blessings of our glorious Union—an origin akin to that of the constitution of the United States, conceived in the same spirit of fraternal affection, and calculated to remove forever, the only danger, which seemed to threaten, at some distant day, to sever the social bond of union."[49]

Following the example of Clay, at Peoria, Lincoln denounced the extremes of both southern and northern sectionalism as threats to the inseparable bonds of liberty and Union: "Stand with anybody that stands RIGHT," Lincoln intoned. "Stand with him while he is right and PART with him when he goes wrong. Stand WITH the abolitionist in restoring the Missouri Compromise; and stand AGAINST him when he attempts to repeal the fugitive slave law. In the latter case you stand with the southern disunionist. What of that? you are still right. In both cases you are right. In both cases you oppose [expose?] the dangerous extremes. In both you stand on middle ground and hold the ship level and steady. In both you are national and nothing less than national. This is good old whig ground. To desert such ground, because of any company, is to be less than a whig—less than a man—less than an American."[50] Significantly, following Washington's example, the Peoria address contrasts patriotism to sectionalism. Northern and southern extremists are "less than . . . American" in placing factional interest above the common good.

The Declaration comes to the fore as the inspirational source of Lincoln's leadership at Peoria. He exhorts patriots to join hands in striving to make the Union worthy of preserving. The Union, however, is worthy of preserving in light of the principles for which it stands—namely, the ideals of liberty, equality, and consent in the Declaration, what Lincoln described as the nation's "ancient faith" or "political faith." Lincoln's patriotism thus involves a critical reflection over the meaning of the first principles of natural law and right. It was part of his political genius to demonstrate so cogently how slavery, nativism, and imperialism violated the moral principles of America's "ancient faith."

The poetry of Lincoln's reflective patriotism crescendos in the following passage, where he calls on his country to live up to its moral promise: "Let us re-adopt the Declaration of Independence, and with it, the practices, and policy, which harmonize with it. Let north and south—let all Americans—*let all lovers of liberty everywhere*—join in the great and good work. If we do this, we shall not only have saved the Union; but we shall have so saved it, as to make, and to keep it, forever worthy of the saving. We shall have so saved it, that the succeeding millions of free happy people, the world over, shall rise up, and call us blessed, to the latest generations" (emphasis added).[51] In this last sentence, Lincoln applies the biblical symbolism of the Magnificat in Luke's Gospel to the American experiment. Just as Christ's birth holds significance for the entire world, gentile and Jew, the blessings of liberty promised by the American experiment holds a universal promise for all people who yearn to be free.

Based on such rhetoric, political philosopher Walter Berns views Lincoln as America greatest patriotic poet.[52] While Berns rightly notes that Lincoln's love of country was based on devotion to universal principles, his understanding of these principles as derived exclusively from modern secular rationalism is inconsistent with Lincoln's natural law understanding of the Declaration and the potential harmony between faith and reason.[53] According to Berns, "the very idea of natural rights is incompatible with Christian doctrine and, by its formulators, was understood to be incompatible."[54]

Contrary to Berns, James Wilson, one of the foremost legal theorists of founding era, whose works Lincoln had read, explained that "the law of nature . . . and the law of revelation are both divine: they flow, though in different channels, from the adorable source. The object of both is—to discover the will of God—and both are necessary for the accomplishment of that end. . . . The moral precepts delivered in the sacred oracles form a part of the law of nature, are of the same origin, and of the same obligation, operating universally and perpetually."[55] Moreover, as noted, the full range of Lincoln's patriotism embraces more than the love of an abstract idea or principle. It also includes a cultural component—that is, common memories, religion, a shared political heritage, and history. It thus embraces a love of the particular places, people, institutions and the role of Divine Providence in preserving and perpetuating these ideals.

A year after the Peoria address, in 1855, in what would surely be considered blasphemous to an "unreflective patriot," Lincoln denounced the hypocrisy of Fourth of July celebrations in view of the new found militancy of slavery extension. The failure of Henry Clay to achieve gradual emancipation in Kentucky along with "a thousand other signs" convinced Lincoln that the nation was "off track." In a private letter, on the most patriotic occasion of the year, Lincoln indicted his country for its moral failures in characteristically republican terms: "On the question of liberty, as a principle, we are not what we have been. When we were the political slaves of King George, and wanted to be free, we called the maxim that 'all men are created equal' a self evident truth; but now when we have grown fat, and have lost all dread of being slaves ourselves, we have become so greedy to be *masters* that we call the same maxim 'a self-evident lie.' The fourth of July has not quite dwindled away; it is still a great day—*for burning fire-crackers!!!*"[56] Thus, like Frederick Douglass, Lincoln inveighed against the hollowness of America's pretensions to freedom in the face of slavery.[57] As with his dissent during the Mexican war, Lincoln's reflective patriotism calls for critical engagement and even denunciation when the nation betrays itself.

Nativism was yet another threat to the moral credibility of the Union and therefore incompatible with Lincoln's reflective patriotism. In a letter to Joshua Speed in 1855, he repudiated the nativist Know-Nothing Party, rhetorically claiming that if they ever took power he would rather live in Russia where the principle of despotism could be taken pure, without the base alloy of hypocrisy: "I am not a Know-Nothing. That is certain. How could I be? How can any one who abhors the oppression of negroes, be in favor of degrading classes of white people? Our progress in degeneracy appears to me to be pretty rapid. As a nation, we began by declaring that *'all men are created equal.'* We now practically read it 'all men are created equal, *except negroes.'* When the Know-Nothings get control, it will read "all men are created equal, except negroes, *and foreigners, and catholics.'* When it comes to this I should prefer emigrating to some country where they make no pretence of loving liberty—to Russia, for instance, where despotism can be taken pure, and without the base alloy of hypocracy [*sic*]."[58]

Lincoln's opposition to nativist racial and ethnic chauvinism is illustrated by the following poignant story. A leader of the Know-Nothing-American Party and Springfield lawyer, Richard H. Ballinger, stopped by Lincoln's office and asked him if he would consent to being on the nativist ticket for state assembly. Lincoln declined, saying that "he was not in sentiment with this new party." He then pointed to the irony of the Know-Nothings' pretensions in claiming to be native by noting America's unjust treatment of indigenous peoples—the real Native Americans. "Do [the real Native Americans]," he rhetorically asked, "not wear breech-clout and carry the tomahawk? We pushed them from their homes and now turn upon others not fortunate enough to come over as early as we our forefathers. Gentlemen of the committee your party is wrong in principle." Lincoln ended his scolding by using humor to convey a moral message about ethnic and racial pride: "When this Know-nothing party first came up, I had an Irishman, Patrick by name, hoeing in my garden. One morning I was there with him, and he said, 'Mr. Lincoln, what about the Know nothings?' I explained that they would possibly carry a few elections and disappear and I asked Pat why he was not born in this country. 'Faith, Mr. Lincoln,' he replied, 'I wanted to be, but my mother wouldn't let me.'"[59]

An appreciation of America's moral failures, however, did not blind Lincoln to its promise and progress. In a speech at Chicago in 1858, around the time of the Fourth of July, Lincoln provided a compelling vision of the unity that underlies American pluralism and its "melting pot." In this speech, he borrowed a biblical metaphor from St. Paul to convey the potential harmony between national unity and diversity. Just as St. Paul in Corinthians 12 spoke of diverse spiritual gifts that are made one in spirit to serve the larger spiritual community through the mystical body of Christ, so in America, diverse ethnic, racial, and religious groups are united by a common devotion to the principles of the Declaration and its moral promise. Though American immigrants cannot trace their ancestry back to the glory of the Revolution, they nonetheless can claim that equality is their birthright. This equality, Lincoln proclaims, is "the father of all moral principle in them, and that they have a right to claim it as though they were blood of the blood, and flesh of the flesh of the men who wrote that Declaration, and so they are. That is the electric cord in that Declaration that links *the hearts of patriotic and liberty-loving men* together, that will link those patriotic hearts as long as the love of freedom exists in the minds of men throughout the world" (emphasis added).[60]

Unlike nationalism, which is exclusive, Lincoln's vision of the Union was inclusive.[61] Membership in the American Union was political. Regardless of race, creed, or color, Lincoln extended the principle of equality to include national citizenship for former slaves and immigrants.[62] The many in our national motto *e pluribus unum* are not abolished into a forced unison, but harmonized through their dedication to the shared political faith in the Declaration. This faith constitutes the minimal core convictions that make possible a shared public life in a pluralistic society.

The maintenance of American liberty depends on upholding liberty at home, and abroad when necessary, Lincoln thus asks, "What constitutes the bulwark of our own liberty and independence. . . . Our reliance is in the *love of liberty* which God has planted in our bosoms. Our defense is in the preservation of the spirit which prizes liberty as the heritage of all men, in all lands, every where. Destroy this spirit, and you have planted the seeds of despotism around your own doors."[63]

In *Notes on the State of Virginia* Jefferson famously warned not only of Divine judgment over slavery, but also its corrosive effect on the slaves' *"amor patriae"* and the formation of habits that are inimical to liberty.[64] As with his eulogy to Clay, Lincoln's statement above reaffirms that national greatness is measured not in terms of the regime's military prowess, but in terms of its love of liberty and willingness to sacrifice for it.

The preservation of the Union and its promise of liberty to all would depend on Lincoln's success in articulating a patriotic vision that could unite and mobilize preservation of the Union and its principles. His speech at Trenton on February 21, 1861, is exemplary in combining the various aspects of his reflective patriotism—devotion to abstract principles, reverence for the Founders, republican love of ordered liberty, and a belief in Providence under God.

At Trenton, Lincoln appealed not only to the principles of the Revolution as the moral foundation of the Union, but to the concrete places, people, and history who have struggled to sustain liberty for others. He invokes the common memories of George Washington and the Revolution as sources of fraternal affection that bind patriotic hearts.

> "May I be pardoned," he asks, "if, upon this occasion, I mention that away back in my childhood, the earliest days of my being able to read, I got hold of a small book, such a one as few of the younger members have ever seen, 'Weem's Life of Washington.' I remember all the accounts there given of the battle fields and struggles for the liberties of the country, and none fixed themselves upon my imagination so deeply as the struggle here at Trenton, New-Jersey. The crossing of the river; the contest with the Hessians; the great hardships endured at that time, all fixed themselves on my memory more than any single revolutionary event; and you all know, for you have all been boys, how these early impressions last longer than any others. I recollect thinking then, boy even though I was, that there must have been something more than common that those men struggled for. I am exceedingly anxious that that thing which they struggled for; that something even more than National Independence; that something that held out a great promise to all the people of the world to all time to come."[65]

Consonant with the three R's (reason, revelation, and republicanism) of his political faith, Lincoln's reflective patriotism is further informed by a biblical faith, the Puritan legacy of a Divine calling under God's

Providence. In the same speech, he regards himself as a "humble instrument" called to serve the purposes of the Almighty and the American people: "I shall be most happy indeed if I shall be an humble instrument in the hands of the Almighty, and of this, his almost chosen people, for perpetuating the object of that great struggle."[66] In referring to the Americans as an "almost chosen people" Lincoln acknowledges that his country must serve a higher moral purpose while, at the same time, consciously guarding against self-righteousness that equates the perfection of the heavenly city with any earthly city.

A day later at Independence Hall, Lincoln characteristically appealed to "the wisdom, the patriotism, the devotion to principle, from which sprang the institutions under which we live."[67] Not surprisingly then, the reflective patriotism in Lincoln's First Inaugural on March 4, 1861, is further consistent with his earlier tendency to connect intelligence and patriotism. Thus, on the eve of the Civil War, Lincoln appealed to "Intelligence, patriotism and Christianity" as the common social bonds and traditions that unite the country.[68]

Lincoln ended his First Inaugural with an appeal to patriotism based on the fraternal ties and common memories of the nation: "I am loth to close. We are not enemies, but friends. We must not be enemies. Though passion may have strained, it must not break our bonds of affection. The mystic chords of memory, streching from every battle-field, and patriot grave, to every living heart and hearthstone, all over this broad land, will yet swell the chorus of the Union, when again touched, as surely they will be, by the better angels of our nature."[69]

Lincoln viewed secession as a kind of infidelity. He viewed sectional pride as inordinate, unreasonable, unlawful, and unjust. Secession in defense of slavery broke the fraternal bonds of Union, thereby jeopardizing the American experiment in ordered liberty. In his message to Congress in special session, July 4, 1861, he once again invoked Washington's legacy by appealing to "the patriotic instinct of the plain people. They understand, without an argument, that destroying the government, which was made by Washington, means no good to them."[70]

The sacrifice of black soldiers on the battlefield contrasted sharply with the treason of white southerners. The contrast and its implications for an interracial democracy was not lost on the sixteenth president who recognized that military service was a traditional avenue of citizenship: "there will be some black men who can remember that, with silent tongue, and clenched teeth, and steady eye, and well-poised bayonet, they have helped mankind on to this great consummation; while, I fear, there will be some white ones, unable to forget that, with malignant heart, and deceitful speech, they have strove to hinder it."[71]

On July 12, 1862, Lincoln appealed to both patriotism and statesmanship in persuading the border state representatives to accept his compensated emancipation proposal: "You are patriots and statesmen; and, as such, I pray you, consider this proposition; and, at the least, commend it to the consideration of your states and people. As you would perpetuate popular government for the best people in the world, I beseech you that you do in no wise omit this. Our common country is in great peril, demanding the loftiest views, and boldest action to bring it speedy relief."[72]

Notably, in this speech, Lincoln explicitly makes the connection between patriotism and statesmanship. The "loftiest views" and "boldest action" are hallmarks of a patriotic statesman who is capable of rising above particular interests for the greater good of the "common country," particularly when it is in "great peril." The border states would remain unmoved, which reveals the extent to which they still believed that slavery could coexist within the Union. Ten days later Lincoln revealed a preliminary draft of the Emancipation Proclamation to his cabinet.

Lincoln's reflective patriotism would be further tested during the war in dealing with dissent. Did his patriotism allow legitimate dissent in times of war? In his public letter to Corning, he chided the delegation for designating themselves as Democrats instead of American citizens. He explained that "in time of national peril I would have preferred to meet you upon a level one step higher than any party platform. . . . I am sure that from such more elevated position, we could do better battle for the country we all love, than we possibly can from those lower ones, where from the force of habit, the prejudices of the past, and selfish hopes of the future, we are sure to expend much of our ingenuity and strength, in finding fault with, and aiming blows at each other."[73] Lincoln called on the members to put aside petty partisanship for the sake of the country. In the same letter, however, he made the more problematic assertion that true patriots are called to break silence in the face of subversive efforts to undermine the government: "The man who stands by and says nothing, when the peril of his government is discussed cannot be misunderstood. If not hindered, he is sure to help the enemy. Much more, if he talks ambiguously—talks for his country with 'buts' and 'ifs' and 'ands.'" Here we see some of the limits of Lincoln's reflective patriotism in times of war.

Nonetheless, contrary to those who claim that the sixteenth president stifled dissent through military tribunals, Melinda Lawson, citing Mark Neely's work on the subject, notes that "the majority of Northern civilians arrested under Lincoln's suspension of the writ of habeas corpus were suspected deserters or draft evaders."[74] Moreover, as seen in chapter 4, on duty, Lincoln distinguished in the Vallandigham case between constitutionally protected speech that criticized the government and speech that incited resistance to the draft.

While compatible with universal norms, Lincoln's reflective patriotism appreciates our limits and duties as citizens who are encumbered within a particular time and place. It recognizes that the love of one's own is not only natural, but it may also be reasonable, honorable, and just. And that gratitude and care of one's own inspires us to serve a greater good than our own self-interest. The abstract love of humanity implicit to cosmopolitan belief is a seductive yet illusory charm that disengages citizens from fulfilling their duties to fellow citizens and from loving concretely their neighbors. Cato may have loved humanity, but still he sacrificed his life for Rome and died as a Roman. Lincoln's example remains a gift for the world, yet he sacrificed himself for America.

In conclusion, Lincoln's reflective patriotism appreciates both the success and the failures of the American experiment. It invites national self-examination and critical reflection on the first principles of our "ancient faith." While appealing to American exceptionalism to inspire the "better angels" of the nation, it also checks against its possible triumphalism. Indeed, "Lincoln's universalism was tempered with a biblical realism about humanity's frailties."[75] That is to say, it self-consciously guards against the temptation to regard "the city on the hill" as something that has already been realized in its moral purity here on earth rather than as a normative standard that is struggling to be realized, but never fully reached given the limits of human nature. In view of this tension between the ideal and real, Lincoln ironically referred to Americans as God's "almost chosen people." Contrary to the self-righteous assertion of the North's victory in the Civil War, he humbly observed in his Second Inaugural Address that prayers of neither side could be answered fully.

On the other hand, Lincoln's reflective patriotism may also be viewed as an antidote to self-loathing political correctness and deconstructionist accounts of American history that see only what is destructive and despicable in our past. It defends the rule of law as the best means to preserve the principles of the ancient faith and the legacy of those who sought to realize ordered liberty for others at home and abroad. In sum, Lincoln the philosophical statesman observed a dynamic tension between appealing to the loftier aspects of patriotism while self-reflectively guarding against its potential perversion.

CONCLUSION

$\mathcal{T}$he conclusion of this work returns to the questions posed in the preface: What makes Lincoln great, and how do we measure his greatness? Though statesmanship is still vaguely recognized today as the pinnacle of political greatness, its precise character has been obscured. It is all too often confused with other kinds of leadership, dismissed as unscientific, or reduced to a set of skills without regard to its Nature, task, or end. Yet as both Aristotle and Aquinas recognized, statesmanship is a moral enterprise that proceeds from deep-seated habits of mind and character—that is, from virtue. Among the virtues that make for this political greatness are wisdom, prudence, magnanimity, humility, and patriotic sacrifice. Lincoln's life testifies that these virtues may be combined in the same person. As General Sherman and Sojourner Truth both perceived, the sixteenth president was both a great and a good man. Though certainly ambitious, Lincoln, like Washington, also sought to be *worthy* of this recognition through noble deeds. His reputation as "Honest Abe" was no myth; rather, it helped carry him to the presidency. Indeed, humility was part and parcel of his greatness of soul or magnanimity. His humble recognition of the vast difference between the Divine Will and the human will enabled him to place politics and human affairs in their proper perspective. It shielded him from hubristic excesses and overreach of which so many great leaders, conscious of their superiority over others, are prone. It enabled him to respect the limits of politics, to learn from his mistakes, and to empathize with others. His humility also explains his rare ability to make a righteous argument in politics without being self-righteous.

Lincoln was inspired not only by an honorable ambition, but also by a sacrificial love of country that placed the common good above calculations of fame and self-interest. His political vocation was a calling, a servant leadership involving a willingness to suffer in behalf of core convictions for the greater good. This explains his humble self-description as an "instrument of God." His public life may be viewed as a struggle to make the Union "worthy of the saving." The Union was worth saving, however, in view of its moral and constitutional ends—namely, the principles of the Declaration (the apple of gold) as framed by the Constitution (the picture of silver). In sum, Lincoln was guided by a normative vision of the Union as it "ought to be." His statesmanship helped to complete the unfinished work of the Founders and can be seen in terms of affirming, defending, and extending their legacy of ordered liberty.

This work has identified and evaluated statesmanship in terms of six dimensions: (1) wisdom; (2) prudence; (3) duty; (4) magnanimity; (5) rhetoric; and (6) patriotism. Lincoln excelled in each of these respects and is properly regarded as an exemplary statesman. Thus, an understanding of statesmanship points to Lincoln as its concrete embodiment. The ancient Greek Plutarch believed that the task of the historian was to present models of virtue to inspire greatness: "For as that colour is most suitable to the eye whose freshness and pleasantness stimulates and strengthens the sight, so a man ought to apply his intellectual perception to such objects as, with the senses of delight, are apt to call it forth, and allure it to its own proper good and advantage. Such objects we find in the acts of virtue, which also prudence in the minds of mere readers about them an emulation and eagerness that may lead them on to imitation."[1] One wonders if these words stirred the young Lincoln who read Plutarch as part of his self-education.

This work has also characterized Lincoln more specifically as a philosopher statesman. True, Lincoln wrote no systematic treatise on government, but neither did Socrates, the first and perhaps greatest political philosopher in Western civilization. In addition to his practical wisdom, Lincoln's greatness as a statesman also consisted in his knowledge of human nature and politics and his ability to provide a comprehensive moral justification for popular government. Lincoln is rightly considered a philosopher of democracy, and anyone who wishes to understand the Nature of democracy would do well to consult him along with the likes of Aristotle, Plato, Rousseau, Locke, and Tocqueville.

Borrowing from the insights of various fields, I hope to have made accessible the contributions of political philosophy and to show how it can further our understanding of the sixteenth president. Because Lincoln was a man of both ideas and action, his philosophical statesmanship has been presented in contrast to the theological, philosophical, and political alternatives and challenges of his time. As seen, his prudent statesmanship was neither pragmatic in its moral obtuseness nor idealistic in its moral abstractness. His success as a philosopher statesman likewise depended on a philosophic rhetoric that was neither sophistic in its disregard for truth and justice nor demagogic in pandering to the base emotions of the crowd. His love of country was neither chauvinistic nor imperialistic, but self-reflective and philosophical. In defending universal principles under the rule of law and God's Providence, it recognized the sometimes competing demands of what it means to be both a good citizen and a good human being.

The study of Lincoln's philosophical statesmanship is not merely academic but part of an effort to revive in some small way the older understanding of political greatness. Indeed, reviving the distinction between sophistry and statesmanship, a distinction made by Lincoln himself, would greatly enrich our public discourse and civic awareness in an age of ubiquitous spin and verbal manipulation. It might provide a clearer standard for us to identify future leaders, to judge them, and to hold them accountable. The older vision helps us to make important moral distinctions that have been increasingly blurred or lost in our time.

The great historian Allan Nevins once described Lincoln as "more than a statesman."[2] He meant this favorably in comparison to the real-politik of Bismarck and Talleyrand. Nevins is correct insofar as Lincoln was qualitatively different from these "great" nation builders. However, the term *statesmanship* should not be abandoned to its Machiavellian usage. The more traditional understanding of statesmanship as moral greatness still lingers. To be sure, it accounts, in part, for our enduring public fascination with Abraham Lincoln. It is my hope that this public fascination will inspire political greatness and civic virtue "to the latest generation."[3]

NOTES
SELECTED BIBLIOGRAPHY
INDEX

NOTES

The epigraph for this book is quoted from the NIV Bible (New International Version). Unless otherwise noted, all biblical citations quote this version.

PREFACE

1. Doris Kearns Goodwin, *Team of Rivals: The Political Genius of Abraham Lincoln* (New York: Simon and Schuster, 2005), xvii.

2. Lincoln, "Seventh and Last Debate with Stephen A. Douglas," Alton, Illinois, October 15, 1858, in *The Collected Works of Abraham Lincoln*, 8 vols., ed. Roy P. Basler (New Brunswick, N.J.: Rutgers University Press, 1953), 8:101.

INTRODUCTION

1. John Adams, "Thoughts on Government," *The Plan—The Works of John Adams, Second President of the United States* (Boston: Little, Brown, 1856), 4:136.

2. Lincoln, "Seventh and Last Debate with Stephen A. Douglas," Alton, Illinois, October 15, 1858, in *The Collected Works of Abraham Lincoln*, 8 vols., ed. Roy P. Basler (New Brunswick, N.J.: Rutgers University Press, 1953), 3:311.

3. Marc Landy and Sidney Milkis, *Presidential Greatness* (Lawrence: University Press of Kansas, 2001).

4. *Four Texts on Socrates: Plato's Euthyphro, Apology and Crito and Aristophanes' Clouds.* Trans. with notes by Thomas G. West and Grace Starry West (Ithaca: Cornell University Press, 1992), 82. *Apology*, 30e–31b.

5. Lincoln, "Speech at New Haven, Connecticut," March 6, 1860, in *Collected Works*, 4:17.

6. John Burt, *Lincoln's Tragic Pragmatism: Lincoln, Douglas and Moral Conflict* (Cambridge, Mass.: Belknap Press of Harvard University, 2013), 1.

7. These six dimensions are hardly novel. They are attributes of great political leadership recognized from antiquity to today. For example, in *Federalist No. 10* Publius identifies "wisdom," "patriotism," and "love of justice" as statesmanlike qualities that enable representatives to refine and enlarge the public. In addition to checks and balances, ordered liberty in an extended republic likewise depends upon those "whose wisdom may best discern the true interest of their country and whose patriotism and love of justice will be least likely to sacrifice it to temporary or partial considerations." Alexander Hamilton, James Madison, and John Jay, *The Federalist Papers*, ed. Clinton Rossiter with

a new introduction by Charles R. Kessler (New York: Mentor Books, 1999), 50. A more recent example is Fred Greenstein's criteria for evaluating the modern presidency, which includes a similar list of statesmanlike qualities: (1) public communication; (2) organizational capacity; (3) political skill; (4) policy vision; (5) cognitive style; and (6) emotional intelligence. Much of Greenstein's description of public communication is consistent with my discussion of rhetoric; his discussion of policy vision, cognitive style, and emotional intelligence with my discussion of theoretical and practical wisdom; see Fred I. Greenstein, *The Presidential Difference: Leadership Style from FDR to Barack Obama*, 3rd ed. (Princeton: Princeton University Press, 2009); and *Inventing the Job of President: Leadership Style from George Washington to Andrew Jackson* (Princeton: Princeton University, 2009).

8. Harry V. Jaffa, *Crisis of the Strauss Divided: Essays on Leo Strauss and Straussianism East and West* (Lanham: Rowman and Littlefield, 2012) 10.

9. Jaffa, *Crisis of the Strauss Divided*, 1.

10. Jaffa, *Crisis of the Strauss Divided*, 6.

11. Jaffa, *Crisis of the Strauss Divided*, 12.

12. Richard Striner, *Lincoln and Race* (Carbondale: Southern Illinois University Press, 2012). Striner goes so far as to say "that in all probability Lincoln had no racial bias," 2.

13. Howard Zinn, *A People's History of the United States* (New York: Harper Collins E-books, 2009), 461.

14. *Federalist 1*: Hamilton, speaking as Publius states: "It has been frequently remarked that it seems to have been reserved to the people of this country, by their conduct and example, to decide the important question, whether societies of men are really capable or not of establishing good government from reflection and choice, or whether they are forever destined to depend for their political constitutions on accident and force," *The Federalist Papers*, ed. Clinton Rossiter, with a new introduction by Charles R. Kessler (New York: Mentor Books, 1999).

15. Lerone Bennett Jr. *Forced into Glory: Abraham Lincoln's White Dream* (Chicago: Johnson, 2000). Also see Robin Blackburn, *An Unfinished Revolution: Karl Marx and Abraham Lincoln* (New York: Verso, 2011).

16. Richard Hofstadter, *The American Political Tradition and the Men Who Made It* (New York: Vintage, 1976), 169.

17. Friedrich Nietzsche, *Beyond Good and Evil: Prelude to a Philosophy of the Future*, translated, with a commentary by Walter Kaufman (New York: Vintage Books, 1966), 85.

18. Aristotle in *Nicomachean Ethics* (New York: Macmillan Punishing, 1989) 5. Aristotle states: "For a well-schooled man is one who searches for the degree of precision in each kind of study which the nature of the subject at hand admits: it is obviously just as foolish to accept arguments of probability

from a mathematician as to demand strict demonstrations from an orator." (1094b25).

19. Ceaser, *Designing a Polity*, 77.

20. Leo Strauss, *What Is Political Philosophy?*, 18; and Strauss, "Natural Rights and the Distinction between Facts and Values," chap. 2 in *Natural Rights and History*, 35–80.

21. Strauss, *What Is Political Philosophy*, 19–27.

22. Some excellent programs throughout the country are dedicated to the study and revival of statesmanship. This work may be considered, in part, an invitation for the concerned reader to discover them. Often a simple Web search of the word "statesmanship" will bring up those programs genuinely dedicated to its preservation.

23. Donald T. Phillips, *Lincoln on Leadership: Executive Strategies for Tough Times* (New York: Warner Books, 1993).

24. For an outstanding study of statesmanship and how the Founders, consistent with Aristotle's teaching, sought to balance oligarchical and democratic elements in a polity or democratic republic, see Paul Eidelberg, *A Discourse on Statesmanship: The Design and Transformation of the American Polity* (Urbana: University of Illinois Press, 1974). Notably, Eidelberg concludes his work with an appendix entitled "Toward the Establishment of a National University and an Institute of Statesmanship" that outlines an educational vision for reviving the theory and practice of statesmanship.

25. For Tocqueville and Lincoln, see "Lincoln and Tocqueville on Democratic Leadership and Self-Interest Properly Understood," in Brian Danoff, *Educating Democracy: Alexis de Tocqueville and Leadership in America* (Albany: State University of New York Press, 2010, 67–101; "Tocqueville and Lincoln on Religion and Democracy in America Lincoln's America," in *Lincoln's America 1809–1865*, ed. Joseph R. Fornieri and Sara Vaughn Gabbard (Carbondale: Southern Illinois University Press, 2008), 28–54.

26. John Adams, letters to John Taylor of Caroline, April 15, 1814, *The Works of John Adams*, 6:303.

27. The fact that the word "politician" is viewed as pejorative today does not mean that politics itself is inherently a base or ignoble profession. As Thomas Schneider admirably shows, politics can be an honorable vocation. Yet, even in this positive sense, the statesman is still regarded as the pinnacle of political excellence—that is to say, the politician par excellence. See Thomas E. Schneider, *Lincoln's Defense of Politics: The Public Man and His Opponents in the Crisis over Slavery* (Columbia: University of Missouri Press, 2006).

28. See Hannah Arendt, *Eichmann in Jerusalem: A Report on the Banality of Evil* (New York: Penguin Books, 1992).

29. Augustine, *City of God*, Introduction by Thomas Merton, bk. 19, chap. xxiii–xxiv, 176. Trans. by Marcus Dods (Modern Library. New York: Random

House, 1950). See Grant N. Havers, *Lincoln and the Politics of Christian Love* (Columbia: University of Missouri Press, 2009). Havers argues that charity is at the center of Lincoln's political religion.

30. *The Memoirs of General William T. Sherman*, Civil War Centennial Series (New York: D. Appleton, 1875), 2:328.

31. Lincoln, "Speech at Peoria, Illinois," October 16, 1854, in *Collected Works*, 2:276. Lincoln emphasized that the moral worthiness of the Union is measured in terms of its conformity to the principles of the Declaration: "Let us re-adopt the Declaration of Independence, and with it, the practices, and policy, which harmonize with it. Let north and south—let all Americans—let all lovers of liberty everywhere—join in the great and good work. If we do this, we shall not only have saved the Union; but we shall have so saved it, as to make, and to keep it, forever *worthy* of the saving" (emphasis added).

32. Professor Eric Foner has claimed that this author has done a "disservice" to Lincoln by "simply anointing" him as a model of statesmanship and for failing to appreciate the contribution of the radicals and abolitionists to antislavery politics. Nonetheless Professor Foner likewise acknowledges Lincoln's greatness in the preface to this same work. The "hallmark of Lincoln's greatness," he claims, was "his capacity for growth." "If Lincoln achieved greatness, he grew into it. Not every individual possesses the capacity for growth; some, like Lincoln's successor, seem to shrink, not grow in the face of crisis. But to rise to the occasion requires not only an inner compass, but also a willingness to listen to criticism, to seek out new ideas. Lincoln's career was a process of moral and political education and deepening antislavery conviction." *The Fiery Trial*, xvii–xx. At issue then is a disagreement over the Nature of Lincoln's greatness. Did Lincoln's greatness consist in some vague capacity to evolve and progress toward the more advanced vision, judgment, and, or historical consciousness of the radical abolitionists? Rather, does not his true greatness consist in deep-seated virtues like wisdom, prudence, moderation, magnanimity, patriotism, humility, and sacrificial service to the common good? Without claiming that Lincoln was either static or perfect as a leader, do not these deep-seated qualities make possible "the capacity for growth" in the right direction? Change implies something better or worse, as measured by a fixed standard. Indeed, the disposition to grow or shrink ultimately depends upon virtue or vice. As Shakespeare notes, the true, inner character of a leader is most fully revealed when holding power, "Hence shall we see, If power change purpose, what our seemers be" (*Measure for Measure*, act 1, scene 3). Moreover, Lincoln's greatness further involved theoretical wisdom and the ability to provide an ultimate moral justification for democracy based on the timeless truths of the Declaration as safeguarded by the rule of law in the Constitution. Notwithstanding the historian's aversion to "contra-factual" history and the abolitionists' contribution to antislavery politics, are we not fortunate as a nation that Lincoln the prudent statesman, despite his flaws, was at the helm during the Civil War rather than men like John Brown, Salmon Chase, or Wendell Phillips?

33. Jaffa, *Crisis of the Strauss Divided*, 18.

34. Lincoln, "Speech at Chicago, Illinois," July 10, 1858, in *Collected Works*, 2:492.

35. Frederick Douglass, "Oration in Memory of Abraham Lincoln, Delivered at the Unveiling of the Freedmen's Monument in Memory of Abraham Lincoln in Lincoln Park, Washington D.C., April 14, 1876," in *Frederick Douglass: Selected Speeches and Writings*, ed. Philip S. Foner, abridged and adapted by Yuval Taylor (Lawrence Hill Books, 1999), 621.

36. Oakes, *The Radical and the Republican*, xix.

37. Burt, *Lincoln, Douglas, and Moral Conflict*, 6–7. Burt describes Lincoln's tragic pragmatism "as the art of the possible in realizing" "demands" that are "imperative and absolute." Though his analysis is indebted to John Rawls, Burt identifies this tragic pragmatism with Aristotle's virtue of *phronesis*—that is, the same virtue of practical wisdom or prudence described in this work.

38. James MacGregor Burns, *Leadership*, 390–91 (HarperCollins, New York, 2010).

39. Burns, *Leadership*, 390–91.

40. Lincoln, "Fragment on Sectionalism," July 23, 1856, in *Collected Works*, 2:352.

41. Michael Burlingame, *Abraham Lincoln: A Life*, 1:684 (Baltimore: Johns Hopkins University Press, 2008).

42. For a clear contrast between astuzia and prudence see, Joseph Pieper, *The Four Cardinal Virtues* (Notre Dame: University of Notre Dame Press, 1966), 19.

43. Joseph R. Fornieri, *Lincoln's View of the Declaration*.

44. Lincoln, "Speech at Springfield, Illinois," October 4, 1854, in *Collected Works*, 2:245.

45. Lincoln, "Speech at a Republican Banquet, Chicago, Illinois," December 10, 1856, in *Collected Works*, 2:386.

46. Lincoln, "Fragment on the Constitution and the Union," January 1861, in *Collected Works*, 4:168–69.

47. Guelzo, "Apples of Gold in a Picture of Silver," in *Abraham Lincoln as a Man of Ideas* (Carbondale: Southern Illinois University Press, 2009), 106.

48. Phillip Shaw Paludan correctly explains that, "the political-constitutional system, conceived of and operated at its best, inescapably leads to equality. Lincoln operated on that premise and through his presidency tried to achieve that goal." *The Presidency of Abraham Lincoln* (Lawrence: University Press of Kansas, 1994), xv.

49. William Lee Miller, *The Duty of a Statesman* (New York: Knopf, 2008), 150–51.

50. Jividen, *Claiming Lincoln: Progressivism, Equality and the Battle for Lincoln's Legacy in Presidential Rhetoric* (DeKalb: Northern Illinois University Press, 2011).

51. Bradley C. S. Watson, *Living Constitution, Dying Faith: Progressivism and the New Science of Jurisprudence* (Wilmington, Del.: ISI Books, 2009). Also

see Ronald J. Pestritto, *Woodrow Wilson and the Roots of Modern Progressivism* (Lanham: Rowman Littlefield, 2005), 14–19.

52. Bradley C. S. Watson, *Living Constitution, Dying Faith* (Wilmington, Del.: ISA Books, 2009).

53. Lincoln, "Speech at Springfield, Illinois," October 4, 1854, in *Collected Works*, 2:407.

54. Jaffa, *Crisis of the Strauss Divided*, 18.

55. Quoted in Jividen, *Claiming Lincoln* (DeKalb: Northern Illinois University Press, 2011), 76–77.

56. Jividen, *Claiming Lincoln*, 76–77.

57. Franklin D. Roosevelt, "Commonwealth Club Speech," 1932, in *American Political Thought*, ed. Isaac Kramnick and Theodore J. Lowi (New York: Norton: 2009), 1170–79. Also quoted in Jividen, *Claiming Lincoln*, 118.

58. Herbert Croly, *The Promise of America* (Indianapolis: Bobbs-Merrill, 1965), 214.

59. Landy and Milkis, *Presidential Greatness* (Lawrence: University Press of Kansas, 2001), 149.

60. Thomas J. DiLorenzo, *The Real Lincoln* (Roseville, Calif.: Pima Publishing, 2002). Also see Thomas J. DiLorenzo, "The Great Centralizer: Abraham Lincoln and the War between the States," in *Lincoln's American Dream: Clashing Political Perspectives*, Kenneth L. Deutsch and Joseph R. Fornieri (Dulles: Potomac, 2005), 398–423.

61. Allen C. Guelzo, "Abraham Lincoln or the Progressives: Who Was the Real Father of Big Government?," in *First Principles*. B. Kenneth Simon Center for Principles and Politics: The Heritage Foundation. Special Report No. 100, February 8, 2012, 1–17.

62. James M. McPherson, *Abraham Lincoln and the Second American Revolution* (New York: Oxford University Press, 1988).

63. George P. Fletcher, Our *Secret Constitution: How Lincoln Redefined American Democracy* (Oxford: Oxford University Press, 2001), 2.

64. Willmoore Kendall and George Carey, *The Basic Symbols of the American Political Tradition* (Washington, D.C.: Catholic University Press, 1995), 75–95. Also see Kendall, "Equality: Commitment or Ideal," in *Lincoln's American Dream: Clashing Political Perspectives*, ed. Kenneth L. Deutsch and Joseph R. Fornieri (Washington, D.C.: Potomac Books, 2005), 60–71.

65. Friedrich Nietzsche, *Beyond Good and Evil*, 205.

66. Garry Wills, *Lincoln at Gettysburg: The Words That Remade America* (New York: Simon and Schuster, 1992), 38.

67. Wills, *Lincoln at Gettysburg*, 174–75.

68. Nietzsche, *Beyond Good and Evil*, 136.

69. Lincoln, "Speech at Columbus, Ohio," September 16, 1859, in *Collected Works*, 3:404.

70. In their seminal work on presidential greatness, Marc Landy and Sidney Milkis use the paradoxical term "revolutionary conservative" to characterize Lincoln's relationship to the Founders. See Landy and Milkis, *Presidential Greatness*, 114–52 (Lawrence: University Press of Kansas, 2001).

71. The Founders' Constitution.

72. Jaffa, *A New Birth of Freedom*, 20–27.

73. Thomas Jefferson, "The Particular Customs and Manners That May Happen to Be Received in the State," *Notes in the State of Virginia*, in *The Works of Thomas Jefferson*, vol. 4, federal edition (New York: G. P. Putnam's Sons, 1904–5).

74. Lincoln, "Address at Cooper Institute, New York City," February 27, 1860, in *Collected Works*, 3:535.

75. Madison, *The Writings of James Madison, comprising his Public Papers and his Private Correspondence, including his numerous letters and documents now for the first time printed*, ed. Gaillard Hunt (New York: G. P. Putnam's Sons, 1900) 2:363.

76. Lincoln, "Seventh and Last Debate with Stephen Douglas at Alton, Illinois," October 15, 1858, in *Collected Works*, 3:303–4.

77. Lincoln, "Annual Message to Congress," December 1, 1862, in *Collected Works*, 5:537. Also see David Zarefsky, "Lincoln's 1862 Annual Message: A Paradigm of Rhetorical Leadership," *Rhetoric and Public Affairs* 3 (2000): 5–14.

78. Jividen, *Claiming Lincoln*, 75.

1. WISDOM

1. For a fascinating study of Euclid's influence on Lincoln's reasoning and argumentation, see David Hirsch and Dan Van Haften, *Abraham Lincoln and the Structure of Reason* (New York: Savas Beatie, 2010). Hirsch and Van Haften suggest that Lincoln's greatness can be attributed to his powers of logical reasoning learned from Euclid. They analyze each of Lincoln's great speeches in terms of Euclid's method of demonstration, which is based on six elements of a proposition: (1) enunciation, (2) exposition, (3) specification, (4) construction, (5) proof, (6) conclusion. While I discuss Euclid's influence on Lincoln in terms of the argument from definition, a more detailed discussion is beyond the scope of this book. For our purposes, it suffices to say that Lincoln's Euclidean reasoning and logical rigor, ably broken down by Hirsch and Van Haften, was part of his theoretical and practical wisdom.

2. Mark E. Steiner, *An Honest Calling: The Law Practice of Abraham Lincoln* (DeKalb: Northern Illinois University Press, 2006); Brian Dirck, *Lincoln the Lawyer* (Urbana: University of Illinois Press, 2007), Frank J. Williams, *Judging Lincoln* (Carbondale: Southern Illinois University Press, 2002).

3. Burlingame, *Abraham Lincoln: A Life*, 37.

4. Plato's *Symposium* and *Phaedrus*.

5. Daniel Goleman, *Emotional Intelligence: Why It Can Matter More Than IQ* (New York: Bantam, 2005), xxiv. Goleman further defines emotional intelligence as "abilities such as being able to motivate oneself and persist in the face of frustration; to control impulse and delay gratification; to regulate one's moods and keep distress from swamping the ability to think; to empathize and hope" (34). Recognizing the extent to which new psychological discoveries may build upon timeless truth, Goleman begins his study of emotional intelligence with a nod to Aristotle. He states: "In the *Nicomachean Ethics*, Aristotle's philosophical enquiry into virtue, character, and the good life, his challenge is to manage our emotional life with intelligence. Our passions, when well exercised have wisdom; they guide our thinking, our values, our survival. But they can easily go awry, and do so all too often. As Aristotle saw, the problem is not with emotionality, but with the appropriateness of emotion and its expression" (xxiv).

6. Goleman, *Emotional Intelligence*, 34.

7. Goodwin, *Team of Rivals*, 11–12.

8. Goodwin, *Team of Rivals*, 12.

9. For a great resource on Lincoln's humor, see "Abraham Lincoln's Classroom: Abraham Lincoln's Humor and Stories," http://www.abrahamlincolnsclassroom.org/Library/newsletter.asp?ID=30&CRLI=110, accessed November 4, 2013. Also see *Abe Lincoln Laughing: Humorous Anecdotes from Original Sources by and about Abraham Lincoln* (Knoxville: University of Tennessee Press), 1995.

10. "Abraham Lincoln's Classroom," http://www.abrahamlincolnsclassroom.org/Library/newsletter.asp?ID=30&CRLI=110.

11. See Benjamin Thomas, "Lincoln's Humor: An Analysis," *Journal of the Abraham Lincoln Association* 3, no. 1 (1981).

12. Kearns Goodwin, *Team of Rivals* (New York: Simon and Schuster, 2005).

13. Lincoln to Joshua F. Speed, Springfield, August 24, 1855, in *Collected Works*, 2:320.

14. Miller, *President Lincoln: The Duty of a Statesman*, 318–26, 328–50, 459–64.

15. Lincoln, "Speech at New Haven, Connecticut," March 6, 1860, in *Collected Works*, 4:17. Lincoln stated: "Whenever this question shall be settled, it must be settled on some philosophical basis. No policy that does not rest upon some philosophical public opinion can be permanently maintained."

16. William Herndon, *Herndon's Lincoln* (Springfield, Ill., 1921), 3:594.

17. Richard Weaver, *The Ethics of Rhetoric*, 86 (Davis, Calif.: Hermagoras Press, 1985). Lincoln to James N. Brown, Oct. 18, 1858, in *Collected Works*, 3:327.

18. This term was borrowed from Allen C. Guelzo, whose work has traced Lincoln's intellectual influences and situated him within the context of the history of ideas. In particular, Guelzo emphasized the influence of nineteenth century liberalism on Lincoln's political thought. See *Abraham Lincoln as a Man of Ideas* (Carbondale: Southern Illinois University Press, 2009). Also see

Allen C. Guelzo, "A. Lincoln, Philosopher: Lincoln's Place in 19th Century Intellectual History," in *Lincoln's America*, ed. Joseph R. Fornieri and Sara Vaughn Gabbard (Carbondale: Southern Illinois University Press, 2008); Allen C. Guelzo, Redeemer President (Grand Rapids: Eerdmans, 1999).

19. Lincoln, "Address at Sanitary Fair, Baltimore, Maryland," April 18, 1864, in *Collected Works*, 7:301–2.

20. Aristotle, *Nicomachean Ethics*, book 6, section 5, 1140b8 (New York: Macmillan, 1989).

21. David Lowenthal likewise refers to Lincoln as a philosopher statesman in *The Mind and Art of Abraham Lincoln, Philosopher Statesman* (Lanham: Lexington Books), 2012. However, Lowenthal's conception of what this means differs from my own, particularly on the question of reason and revelation and the grounding of prudence and the moral virtues. I have already distinguished my position from this view in *Abraham Lincoln's Faith*, 95–97. Sean Wilentz rejects the notion of Lincoln as a philosopher and views him as the quintessential pragmatic politician. See "Who Lincoln Was and Was Not," *New Republic*, July 15, 2009. For a concise overview that explores Lincoln's contribution to Western civilization see Steven B. Smith's introduction in *The Writings of Abraham Lincoln* (New Haven, Conn.: Yale University Press, 2010), xi–xxiv.

22. John C. Calhoun, *Speeches of Mr. Calhoun of S. Carolina, on the Bill for the Admission of Michigan, Delivered in Senate of the United States, January 1837* (Washington, D.C.: Duff Green, 1837), "Remarks of Mr. Calhoun, on the Reception of Abolition Petitions, February 6, 1837,"148. Also online at http://teachingamericanhistory.org/library/index.asp?document=71, accessed on November 4, 2013.

23. See George Fitzhugh, *Cannibals All, or, Slavery without Masters*, ed. C. Vann Woodward (Cambridge, Mass.: Harvard University Press, 1988), 243–44; and *Sociology of the South; or, the Failure of Free Society* (1854; rpt., New York: B. Franklin, 1965).

24. J. H. Hammond, "Slavery in Light of Political Science," in *Cotton Is King, and Pro-Slavery Arguments Comprising the Writings of Hammond, Harper, Christy, Stringfellow, Hodge, Bledsoe, and Cartwright, on this Important Subject*, ed. E. N. Elliott (New York: Negro Universities Press, 1969), 637–38.

25. Lincoln, "Letter to George Robertson," August 15, 1855, in *Collected Works*, 2:318.

26. Douglas, *First Debate at Ottawa*, August 21, 1858, in *Collected Works*, 2:9.

27. "Seventh and Last Debate with Stephen A. Douglas at Alton, Illinois," October 15, 1858, in *Collected Works*, 3:301.

28. "Speech at Peoria, Illinois," October 16, 1854, in *Collected Works*, 2:275.

29. Alexander H. Stephens, "Cornerstone Speech," Savannah, Georgia, March 21, 1861. Available online at http://teachingamericanhistory.org/library/index.asp?document=76, accessed on November 4, 2013.

182   NOTES TO PAGES 35–38

30. Arthur Comte De Gobineau, *The Inequality of Human Races* (Burlington: Ostara Publications, 2011). Also see Richard Striner, *Lincoln and Race* (Carbondale: Southern Illinois University Press, 2012), 36.

31. George Fitzhugh, *Sociology for the South; or, The Failure of Free Society* (1854; rpt., New York: B. Franklin, 1965).

32. Lincoln, "Fragment: Notes for Speeches," October 1, 1858?, in *Collected Works*, 3:205.

33. See Harry V. Jaffa, *How to Think about the American Revolution: A Bicentennial Cerebration* (Durham, N.C.: Carolina Academic Press, 1978).

34. For a profound inquiry of the role of first principles in politics, see Hadley Arkes, *First Things: An Inquiry into the First Principles of Morals and Justice* (Princeton: Princeton University Press, 1986); and Hadley Arkes, *Beyond the Constitution* (Princeton: Princeton University Press, 1990).

35. Lincoln, "Speech at Chicago Illinois," July 10, 1858, in *Collected Works*, 2:499.

36. Lincoln, "To Henry L. Pierce and Others," April 6, 1859, in *Collected Works*, 3:375.

37. Lincoln to Henry L. Pierce and Others, Springfield, April 6, 1859, in *Collected Works*, 3:375.

38. Richard M. Weaver, *The Ethics of Rhetoric* (Davis, Calif.: Hermagoras Press, 1985), 86.

39. Lincoln, "Speech at Peoria, Illinois," October 16, 1854, in *Collected Works*, 2:265–66.

40. Lincoln, "Speech at Peoria, Illinois," October 16, 1854, in *Collected Works*, 2:265–66.

41. Jaffa states: "the perspective of the Declaration is in agreement with Thomas Aquinas's conception of the natural law as the rational creature's participation in the eternal law, the law by which God governs the universe. The Declaration also assumes the existence of an eternal law when it speaks of an appeal to 'the supreme judge of the world' and of 'the protection of divine providence.' The voice of right reason in the natural law, therefore, is as much the voice of God as is divine revelation. Also since every member of the human species has the potential to participate in the natural law, in this decisive respect, all men are created equal." *New Birth of Freedom*, 509.

42. Samuel Adams, "The Rights of the Colonist," November 20, 1772, quoted in *American Political Thought*, ed. Isaac Kramnick and Theodore J. Lowi (New York, W. W. Norton, 2009), 111.

43. Reinhold Niebuhr, *Theologian of Public Life*, ed. Rasmussen, 250–62; Arthur Melzer, *The Natural Goodness of Man* (Chicago: University of Chicago Press, 1990); Lincoln, *Collected Works*, 5:376.

44. Lincoln, "Speech at Peoria, Illinois," October 16, 1854, in *Collected Works*, 2:266.

45. Lincoln, "Speech at Peoria, Illinois," October 16, 1854, in *Collected Works*, 2:266–67.

46. "Seventh and Last Debate with Stephen A. Douglas," Alton, Illinois, October 15, 1858, in *Collected Works*, 3:311.

47. Lincoln, "Speech at Columbus, Ohio," September 16, 1859, in *Collected Works*, 3:425.

48. Lincoln, "Fragment on Slavery," April 1, 1854?, in *Collected Works*, 2:222–23.

49. Jefferson, "Letter to Henri Gregoire," February 25, 1809, in *The Works of Thomas Jefferson*, vol. 11, *Correspondence and Papers 1808–1816*.

50. Lincoln, "Definition of Democracy," August 1, 1858?, in *Collected Works*, 2:532.

51. Lincoln, "Letter to Henry L. Pierce and Others," April 6, 1859, in *Collected Works*, 3:375.

52. Lincoln, "Speech at Chicago, Illinois," July 10, 1858, in *Collected Works*, 2:500.

53. Lincoln, "Speech at Peoria, Illinois," October 16, 1854, in *Collected Works*, 2:278.

54. Lincoln, "Second Inaugural," March 4, 1865, *Collected Works*, 8:333.

55. For the biblical references in defense of proslavery theology see Elliott, *Cotton Is King*; and Fornieri, *Abraham Lincoln's Political Faith*, 70–91.

56. Davis quoted in Jaffa, *New Birth of Freedom*, 156.

57. Fornieri, *Abraham Lincoln's Political Faith*. For the mutual relationship between faith and reason in American founding and American public life, also see Ellis Sandoz, *A Government of Laws: Political Theory, Religion, and the American Founding* (Baton Rouge: Louisiana State University Press, 1990).

58. Joshua F. Speed, *Reminiscences of Abraham Lincoln and Notes of a Visit to California* (Louisville, Ky.: John P. Morton, 1884), 32–33.

59. Lincoln, "Speech at Lewistown, Illinois," August 17, 1859, in *Collected Works*, 2:546–47.

60. Lincoln, "Speech at Lewistown, Illinois," August 17, 1858, in *Collected Works*, 2:546.

61. Lincoln, "Fragment on Pro-Slavery Theology," October 1, 1858?, in *Collected Works*, 3:204.

62. Lincoln to Henry L. Pierce and Others, Springfield, April 6, 1859, in *Collected Works*, 3:376.

63. Lincoln, "Definition of Democracy," August 1, 1858, in *Collected Works*, 2:532.

64. Lincoln to George B. Ide, James R. Doolittle, and A. Hubbell, May 30, 1864, in *Collected Works*, 7:368.

65. Lincoln to George B. Ide, James R. Doolittle, and A. Hubbell, May 30, 1864, in *Collected Works*, 7:368.

66. Quoted in Sidney E. Ahlstrom, *A Religious History of the American People* (New Haven: Yale University Press, 1972), 671–72.

67. Lincoln, "Fragment on Government," July 1, 1854, in *Collected Works*, 2:186–87.

68. Lincoln, "Speech at New Haven, Connecticut," March 6, 1860, in *Collected Works*, 4:24.

69. Richard Carwardine, *Lincoln: Profiles in Power* (London: Pearson and Longman, 2003), 38.

70. Lincoln, "Fragments of a Tariff Discussion," December 1, 1847, in *Collected Works*, 1:411–12.

71. Lincoln, "Fragment on Free Labor," September 17, 1859, in *Collected Works*, 3:462.

72. Lincoln, "Speech at Hartford, Connecticut," March 5, 1860, in *Collected Works*, 4:3.

73. William Paley, *Natural Theology* (Oxford: Oxford University Press, 1999), 12.

74. Rufus Rockwell Wilson, *What Lincoln Read* (Washington, D.C.: Pioneer Publishing, February 12, 1932). Wilson states: "when asked to follow his wife's example and join the author's church [James Smith, who wrote *The Christian's Defense*], [Lincoln] declared that he 'could not quite see it.' Perhaps he found a stronger appeal to reason in Hitchcock's *Religious Truth*, Bailey's *Theology* and Paley's *Natural Theology*, which he procured and read in the years preceding his election to the Presidency." In a letter of December 6, 1866, Joshua Speed comments on Lincoln's reading habits and mentions that he read Paley, one of the few philosophers he mentions by name in the letter. See Douglas L. Wilson and Rodney O. Davis, eds., *Herndon's Informants: Letters, Interviews, and Statements about Abraham Lincoln* (Urbana: University of Illinois Press, 1998), 498–99. Allen C. Guelzo notes the influence of another work of Paley's, *Principles of Moral and Political Philosophy* (1785) on Lincoln. Also see Allen C. Guelzo, *Abraham Lincoln: Redeemer President* (Grand Rapids: William B. Eerdmans Publishing, 1999), 49.

75. Lincoln, "Address before the Wisconsin State Agricultural Society," Milwaukee, Wisconsin, September 30, 1859, in *Collected Works*, 3:479–80. Other references to natural theology are found in *Collected Works*, 2:222, 3:462, 4:9, 10:44–45.

76. Lincoln, "First Lecture on Discoveries and Inventions," April 6, 1858, in *Collected Works*, 2:437.

77. James Otis, *The Rights of the British Colonies Asserted and Proved*, 1764, quoted in *American Political Thought*, ed. Kramnick and Lowi (New York: W. W. Norton, 2009), 105.

78. Lincoln, "Emancipation Proclamation," January 1, 1863, in *Collected Works*, 6:30.

79. Gabor S. Boritt, *Abraham Lincoln and the Economics of the American Dream* (Urbana: University of Illinois Press, 1994).

80. Samuel Adams, "The Rights of the Colonist," November 20, 1772, quoted in *American Political Thought*, ed. Kramnick and Lowi (New York: W. W Norton, 2009), 111.

81. Jaffa, *How to Think about the American Revolution: A Bicentennial Celebration* (Durham, N.C.: Carolina Academic Press, 1978).

82. See Joseph R. Fornieri, "Abraham Lincoln and the Declaration of Independence: The Meaning of Equality," in *Abraham Lincoln: Sources and Style of Leadership*, ed. Frank J. Williams, William D. Pederson, and Vincent J. Marsala (Westport, Conn.: Greenwood Press, 1994), 45–69.

83. Lincoln, "Communication to the People of Sangamo County," March 9, 1832, in *Collected Works*, 1:8.

84. Lincoln, "Proclamation of Amnesty and Reconstruction," December 8, 1863, in *Collected Works*, 7:55.

85. Franklin quoted in *American Political Thought*.

86. Lew Lehrman has an instructive short essay comparing Lincoln and Franklin on the American Dream in *Lincoln by Littles*.

87. Franklin, quoted in *American Political Thought*.

88. Lincoln, "Fragment on Free Labor," September 17, 1859?, in *Collected Works*, 3:462.

89. Lincoln, "Annual Message to Congress," December 3, 1861, in *Collected Works*, 5:52.

90. Lincoln, "Fragment on Free Labor," September 17, 1859, in *Collected Works*, 3:462–63.

91. Carwardine, *Lincoln: Profiles in Power*, 118–19.

92. Lincoln, "Annual Message to Congress," December 3, 1861, in *Collected Works*, 5:51–52.

93. Lincoln, "Speech at Hartford, Connecticut," March 5, 1860, in *Collected Works*, 4:7.

94. Lewis E. Lehrman, *Lincoln "By Littles"* (New York: Lehrman Institute, 2013), 79.

95. Lincoln, "Speech at Hartford, Connecticut," March 5, 1860, in *Collected Works*, 4:8.

96. Lincoln, "Annual Message to Congress," December 3, 1861, in *Collected Works*, 5:51–52.

97. Lincoln, "Annual Message to Congress," December 3, 1861, in *Collected Works*, 5:51–52.

98. *Federalist* No. 9.

99. Lincoln, "First Inaugural Address—Final Text," March 3, 1861, in *Collected Works*, 4:268.

100. Lincoln, "First Inaugural Address—Final Text," March 3, 1861, in *Collected Works*, 4:264.

101. Republican Party platform, online at http://teachingamericanhistory. org/library/index.asp?document=149, accessed on November 4, 2013.

102. Lincoln, "Address to the New Jersey Senate," Trenton, New Jersey, February 21, 1861, in *Collected Works*, 4:236.

103. Lincoln, "Speech in Independence Hall," Philadelphia, Pennsylvania, February 22, 1861, in *Collected Works*, 4:240.

2. PRUDENCE

1. Joseph R. Fornieri, "Lincoln and the Emancipation Proclamation: A Model of Prudent Leadership," in *Tempered Strength: Studies in the Nature and Scope of Prudential Leadership* (Lanham, Md.: Lexington Books, 2002), 125–49; Allen C. Guelzo, "Prudence and the Proclamation," in *Lincoln as a Man of Ideas* (Carbondale: Southern Illinois University Press, 2009), 182–94; Ethan Fishman, "Under the Circumstances: Abraham Lincoln and Classical Prudence," in *Abraham Lincoln: Sources and Styles of Leadership.*

2. Jefferson, *Notes on Virginia, Query XVIII*, in *The Works of Thomas Jefferson*, vol. 4.

3. Lincoln, "Speech at Peoria, Illinois," October 16, 1854, in *Collected Works*, 2:255.

4. Lincoln, "Speech at Springfield," Illinois, June 26, 1857, in *Collected Works*, 2:406.

5. Jaffa states that Lincoln's "perspective of the Declaration is in agreement with Thomas Aquinas's conception of the natural law as the rational creature's participation in the eternal law, the law by which God governs the universe. The Declaration also assumes the existence of an eternal law when it speaks of an appeal to 'the supreme judge of the world' and of 'the protection of divine providence.' The voice of right reason in the natural law, therefore, is as much the voice of God as is divine revelation. Also, since every member of the human species has the potentiality to participate in the natural law, in this decisive respect, all men are created equal." Jaffa, *A New Birth of Freedom*, 509.

6. Lincoln, "Speech at Chicago, Illinois," July 10, 1858, in *Collected Works*, 2:501.

7. St. Thomas Aquinas, *Summa Theologica: Volume Three: II-II* (Westminster, Md.: Christian Classics, 1981), II-II, Q. 47–51, 1383–1406 (hereafter cited as Aquinas, S.T.).

8. Aquinas, S.T., II-II, Q. 49, Article 6, 1399.

9. Joseph R. Fornieri, "Lincoln, the Natural Law, and Prudence," in *The Language of Liberty: The Political Speeches and Writings of Abraham Lincoln* (Washington, D.C.: Regnery, 2008), xxvi–lxi.

10. Lincoln, "Protest in Illinois Legislature on Slaver," March 3, 1837, in *Collected Works*, 1:75.

11. Fornieri, "Lincoln, the Natural Law, and Prudence," xxvii–xxxviii.

12. Jaffa, *Crisis of the Strauss Divided*, 18.

13. William Lloyd Garrison, *Selections from the Writings and Speeches of William Lloyd* Garrison (New York: Wallcut, 1852), 118.

14. Gerrit Smith cited in James B. McPherson, *The Struggle for Equality: Abolitionists and the Negro in the Civil War and Reconstruction* (Princeton: Princeton University Press, 1995), 37.

15. Phillips quoted in McPherson, *The Struggle for Equality*, 62. I have borrowed Phillips's title of "national scold" from Michael Burlingame.

16. Burlingame.

17. Lerone Bennett Jr., *Forced into Glory: Abraham Lincoln's White Dream* (Chicago: Johnson Publishing, 2000), 277.

18. *Lincoln and the Border States* (Lawrence: University Press of Kansas, 2011).

19. Lincoln to Henry J. Raymond, Washington, March 9, 1862, in *Collected Works*, 5:153; Lincoln to James A. McDougall, March 14, 1962, in *Collected Works*, 5:160; Holzer, *Emancipating Lincoln* (Cambridge, Mass.: Harvard University Press, 2012), 20–21.

20. Stephen Douglas quoted in "Sixth Debate with Stephen A. Douglas, at Quincy, Illinois," October 13, 1858, in Lincoln, in *Collected Works*, 3:274.

21. Lincoln, "Seventh and Last Douglass Debate," in *Collected Works*, 3:303.

22. Lincoln, "Speech at Peoria, Illinois," March 14, 1960, in *Collected Works*, 2:270.

23. Lincoln, "Speech at the United States House of Representatives on Internal Improvements," June 20, 1848, in *Collected Works*, 1:484.

24. Lincoln, "Speech at Peoria, Illinois," March 14, 1960, in *Collected Works*, 2:273.

25. Lincoln to Elihu B. Washburne, Springfield, Illinois, December 13, 1860, in *Collected Works*, 4:151.

26. Taney, *Merryman*. For more information check: http://www.oyez.org/cases/1851-1900/1865/1865_0#sort=ideology, accessed on November 4, 2013. For a more recent detailed study of the *ex parte Merryman* case and habeas corpus during the war, see Jonathan W. White, *Abraham Lincoln and Treason in the Civil War: The Trials of John Merryman* (Baton Rouge: Louisiana State University, 2013).

27. Quoted in Harold Holzer, *Emancipating Lincoln*, 58.

28. Holzer, *Emancipating Lincoln*, 34.

29. Holzer, *Emancipating Lincoln*, 100–102.

30. Allen C. Guelzo, *Lincoln's Emancipation Proclamation: The End of Slavery in America* (New York: Simon and Schuster, 2004), 168.

31. Lincoln to Henry J, Raymond, March 9, 1862, in *Collected Works*, 5:153.

32. Lincoln to James A. McDougal, March 14, 1862, in *Collected Works*, 5:160.

33. Guelzo, *Lincoln's Emancipation*, 56.

34. Lincoln, "Appeal to Border State Representatives to Favor Compensated Emancipation," July 12, 1863, in *Collected Works*, 5:317.

35. Lincoln, "Appeal to Border State Representatives to Favor Compensated Emancipation," July 12, 1863, in *Collected Works*, 5:318.

36. Guelzo, *Lincoln's Emancipation*, 106; and Holzer, *Emancipating Lincoln*, 27.

37. Quoted in James M. McPherson, *Tried by War: Abraham Lincoln as Commander in Chief* (New York: Penguin Books, 2008), 76.

38. Guelzo, *Lincoln's Emancipation*, 106–9; McPherson, *Tried by War*, 106; Holzer, *Emancipating Lincoln*, 27–28.

39. Joshua Speed to Lincoln, quoted in Guelzo, *Lincoln's Emancipation*, 48.

40. Guelzo, *Lincoln's Emancipation*, 48.

41. Guelzo, *Lincoln's Emancipation*, 42.

42. Lincoln, "Annual Message to Congress," December 3, 1861, in *Collected Works*, 5:48–49; Simpson, 73.

43. James Oakes, *Freedom National: The Destruction of Slavery in the United States, 1861–1865* (New York: Norton, 2013), 213–14.

44. Lincoln, "Proclamation Revoking General Hunter's Order of Military Emancipation of May 9, 1862"; May 19, 1862, in *Collected Works* 5:222.

45. Lincoln, "Appeal to Border State Representatives to Favor Compensated Emancipation," July 12, 1863, in *Collected Works*, 5:318.

46. For the justification of the Emancipation Proclamation under the laws of war see Burrus M. Carnahan, *Act of Justice: Lincoln's Emancipation Proclamation and the Law of War* (Lexington: University of Kentucky Press 2007).

47. Guelzo, *Lincoln's Emancipation*, 80, 108.

48. Seward quoted in Guelzo, *Lincoln's Emancipation*, 35.

49. Lincoln, "Speech at Peoria, Illinois," October 16, 1854, in *Collected Works*, 2:256.

50. Epigram from Guelzo, *Lincoln's Emancipation*.

51. Harold Holzer, *Emancipating Lincoln*.

52. "Address on Colonization to a Deputation of Negroes," August 14, 1862, in *Collected Works*, 5:372.

53. Oakes, *Freedom National*, 310.

54. Holzer, *Emancipating Lincoln*, 121.

55. Holzer, *Emancipating Lincoln*, 67.

56. Holzer, *Emancipating Lincoln*, 71.

57. Oakes, *Freedom National*, 310.

58. Lincoln to Edwin M. Stanton, February 1, 1864, in *Collected Works*, 7:164.

59. Lincoln to Horace Greeley, August 22, 1862, in *Collected Works*, 5:388–89.

60. Lincoln, "Speech of Bloomington, Illinois," May 29 1856, in *Collected Works*, 2:341.

61. Lincoln, "Speech at Peoria, Illinois," March 14, 1960, in *Collected Works*, 2:276.

62. Quoted in Guelzo, *Lincoln's Emancipation*, 108.

63. Lincoln, "Annual Message to Congress," December 6, 1864, in *Collected Works*, 8:148.

64. Lincoln, "Reply to Emancipation Memorial Presented by Chicago Christians of All Denominations," September 13, 1862, in *Collected Works*, 5:420.

65. Holzer, *Emancipating Lincoln*, 64.

66. Lincoln, "Reply to Emancipation Memorial Presented by Chicago Christians of All Denominations," September 13, 1862, in *Collected Works*, 5:420.

67. Lincoln, "Reply to Emancipation Memorial Presented by Chicago Christians of All Denominations," September 13, 1862, in *Collected Works*, 5:421.

68. E&R, 14.

69. Lincoln to Salmon P. Chase, Washington, September 2, 1863, in *Collected Works*, 6:428–29.

70. Quoted in Holzer, *Emancipating Lincoln*, 81.

71. Holzer, *Emancipating Lincoln*, 104.

72. For a fuller treatment of how rights were extended to the freedmen, see Herman Belz, *A New Birth of Freedom: The Republican Party and Freedmen's Rights, 1861–1866* (New York: Fordham University Press, 2000), 21.

3. DUTY

1. Mark Blitz, *Duty Bound: Responsibility and American Public Life* (Lanham: Rowman and Littlefield), 2005.

2. William Lee Miller, *President Lincoln: The Duty of a Statesman* (New York: Knopf, 2008), 3.

3. Miller, *President Lincoln*, 3.

4. Lincoln, "Message to Congress in Special Session," July 4, 1861, in *Collected Works*, 4:426.

5. Lincoln, "Farewell Address at Springfield, Illinois B. Version," February 11, 1861, in *Collected Works*, 4:190.

6. Lincoln to Albert G. Hodges, Frankfurt, Kentucky, April 4, 1864, in *Collected Works*, 7:281.

7. William Lloyd Garrison, *William Lloyd Garrison, 1805–1879, The Story of His Life Told by His Children* (Boston: Houghton, Mifflin, 1894), 1:308. Also online at http://teachingamericanhistory.org/library/index.asp?document=570, accessed on http://teachingamericanhistory.org/library/index.asp?document=570, accessed on November 4, 2013.

8. Lincoln to Albert G. Hodges, Frankfurt, Kentucky, April 4, 1864, in *Collected Works*, 7:281.

9. Lincoln to Albert G. Hodges, Frankfurt, Kentucky, April 4, 1864, in *Collected Works*, 7:281.

10. James Buchanan "1860 Message to Congress," December 3, 1860, *The Works of James Buchanan* (Philadelphia: J. P. Lippincott, 1910) 9:7. Also available online at: http://teachingamericanhistory.org/library/index.asp?document=946, accessed on November 4, 2013.

11. James Buchanan, "1860 Message to Congress," December 3, 1860, 9:17.

12. Burlingame, *Abraham Lincoln: A Life*, 22.

13. Miller, *President Lincoln*, 12.

14. Lincoln, "First Inaugural Address—Final Text," March 4, 1861, in *Collected Works*, 4:263.

15. I have borrowed this helpful metaphor from Professor Allen C. Guelzo in his illuminating lectures on the Emancipation Proclamation.

16. Lincoln, "First Inaugural Address—Final Text," March 4, 1861, in *Collected Works*, 4:263.

17. McPherson, *Battle of Cry Freedom*, 227.

18. Lincoln, "Speech at Worcester, Massachusetts," September 12, 1848, in *Collected Works*, 2:3–4.

19. Lincoln, "Reply to Emancipation Memorial Presented by Christians of All Denominations," September 13, 1862, in *Collected Works*, 5:420.

20. Burlingame, *Abraham Lincoln: A Life*, 22.

21. Lincoln, "First Inaugural Address—Final Text," March 4, 1861, in *Collected Works*, 4:268.

22. Harold Holzer, "Lincoln President-Elect: Abraham Lincoln and the Great Secession Winter, 1860–61," *Journal of the Abraham Lincoln Association*, http://quod.lib.umich.edu/j/jala/2629860.0031.208?rgn=main;view=fulltext, accessed on November 4, 2013.

23. Lincoln, "Address at Cooper Institute, New York City," February 27, 1860, in *Collected Works*, 3:550.

24. Harold Holzer, *Lincoln President-Elect*.

25. Lincoln to Elihu B. Washburne, Springfield, Illinois, December 13, 1860, in *Collected Works*, 4:151.

26. See James Oakes, *Freedom National*.

27. Horace Greeley, *A Political Text Book for 1860* (New York: Tribune Association, 1860), 26.

28. James Madison, *Notes of the Debates in the Federal Convention of 1787* (New York: Norton, 1987), 532.

29. Madison, *Notes*, 648.

30. Lincoln, "Speech at Peoria, Illinois," October 16, 1864, in *Collected Works*, 2:274.

31. At Cooper Union, Lincoln referred to John Brown as an "enthusiast [who] broods over the oppression of a people till he fancies himself commissioned by Heaven to liberate them. He ventures the attempt, which ends in little else than his own execution." "Address at Cooper Institute," February 27, 1860, in *Collected Works* 3:541.

32. Lincoln, "Third Debate with Stephen A. Douglas at Jonesboro, Illinois," September 15, 1858, in *Collected Works*, 3:143.

33. Lincoln, "Speech at Springfield, Illinois," June 26, 1857, in *Collected Works*, 2:402.

34. Lincoln, "Speech at Springfield, Illinois," June 26, 1857, in *Collected Works*, 2:401.

35. Lincoln, "First Inaugural Address—Final Text," March 4, 1861, in *Collected Works*, 4:268.

36. Lincoln, "First Inaugural Address—Final Text," March 4, 1861, in *Collected Works*, 4:264.

37. Herman Belz, "Lincoln's Construction of the Executive Power in the Secession Crisis," *Journal of the Abraham Lincoln Association* 27, no. 1 (2006): 13–38. This official duty, he believed, both authorized and empowered him to use justifiable means of coercion to preserve the Union. Washington's example in suppressing the Whiskey rebellion in 1794 and Jackson's opposition to nullification in 1832 supplied two important precedents that buttressed the sixteenth president's use of force to preserve the Union. Making an argument from the Nature of the office of the chief executive, Lincoln stated, "His duty is to administer the present government as it came into his hands, and to transmit it unimpaired to his successor." Lincoln, "First Inaugural Address-Final Text," March 4, 1861, in *Collected Works*, 4:270.

38. Attorney General Bates, November 29, 1862.

39. Lincoln, "First Inaugural Address—Final Text," March 4, 1861, in *Collected Works*, 4:264–65.

40. Lincoln, "First Inaugural Address—Final Text," March 4, 1861, in *Collected Works*, 4:265.

41. Lincoln, "First Inaugural Address—Final Text," March 4, 1861, in *Collected Works*, 4:265.

42. Lincoln, "First Inaugural Address—Final Text," March 4, 1861, in *Collected Works*, 4:265.

43. Lincoln, "First Inaugural Address—Final Text," March 4, 1861, in *Collected Works*, 4:265.

44. Lincoln, "First Inaugural Address—Final Text," March 4, 1861, in *Collected Works*, 4:267.

45. Lincoln, "First Inaugural Address—Final Text," March 4, 1861, in *Collected Works*, 4:265–66.

46. Lincoln, "First Inaugural Address—Final Text," March 4, 1861, in *Collected Works*, 4:270.

47. Lincoln, "First Inaugural Address—Final Text," March 4, 1861, in *Collected* Works, 4:266.

48. Lincoln, "First Inaugural Address—Final Text," March 4, 1861, in *Collected Works*, 4:271.

49. William Lee Miller, *President Lincoln*, 109.

50. The classic study of civil liberties during the Civil War is Mark Neely, *The Fate of Liberty: Abraham Lincoln and Civil Liberties* (New York: Oxford University Press, 1991). Also see James G. Randall, *Constitutional Problems under Lincoln* (Urbana: University of Illinois Press, 1964); Geoffrey R. Stone,

Perilous Times: Free Speech in Wartime: From the Sedition Act of 1798 to the War on Terrorism (New York: Norton, 2004), 79–133. John Yoo, *War by Other Means: An Insider's Account of the War on Terror* (New York: Atlantic Monthly Press, 2006); William H. Rehnquist, *All the Laws but One: Civil Liberties in Wartime* (New York: Vintage, 2000).

51. Lincoln, "Message to Congress in Special Session," July 4, 1861, in *Collected Works*, 4:430.

52. John Locke, "Chapter XIV of Prerogative," in *Two Treatises of Government* (Cambridge: Cambridge University Press, 1991), 159–68, 374–80.

53. Clinton Rossiter, *Constitutional Dictatorship: Crisis in the Modern Democracies* (New Brunswick: Transaction, 2006), 222–45.

54. Herman Belz, "Lincoln and the Constitution: The Dictatorship Question Reconsidered," in *Lincoln's American Dream: Clashing Political Perspectives*, ed. Kenneth L. Deutsch and Joseph R. Fornieri (Washington, D.C.: Potomac), 289–303.

55. Mark E. Neely Jr., *Lincoln and the Triumph of the Nation: Constitutional Conflict in the American Civil War* (Chapel Hill: University of North Carolina Press, 2011), 9.

56. Neely, *Lincoln and the Triumph of the Nation*, 9.

57. Neely, *Lincoln and the Triumph of the Nation*, 9.

58. Lincoln, "Message to Congress in Special Session," July 4, 1861, in *Collected Works*, 4:423.

59. Farber, *Lincoln's Constitution* (Chicago: University of Chicago Press, 2003), 157.

60. White, *Abraham Lincoln and Treason in the Civil War*, 31–38.

61. Taney in *ex parte Merryman*, April 1861, online at: http://teachingamericanhistory.org/library/index.asp?document=442.

62. Lincoln, "Message to Congress in Special Session," July 4, 1861, in *Collected Works*, 4:429.

63. Lincoln, "Message to Congress in Special Session," July 4, 1861, in *Collected Works*, 4:429–30.

64. Frank J. Williams, *Judging Lincoln*.

65. Sidney M. Milkis and Michael Nelson, *The American Presidency: Origins and Development, 1776–2007*, 5th ed. (Washington, D.C.: Congressional Quarterly Press, 2008), 103.

66. Lincoln, "Message to Congress in Special Session," July 4, 1861, in *Collected Works*, 4:430.

67. Lincoln, "Message to Congress in Special Session," July 4, 1861, in *Collected Works*, 4:430.

68. Lincoln, "Message to Congress in Special Session," July 4, 1861, in *Collected Works*, 4:430.

69. See Dan Farber, *Lincoln's Constitution* (Chicago: University of Chicago Press, 2003), 158.

70. Lincoln, "Message to Congress in Special Session," July 4, 1861, in *Collected Works*, 4:430.

71. McPherson, *Tried by War*, 8.

72. Quoted in McPherson, *Tried by War*, 6; Clausewitz, I, I, 27, 121.

73. Lincoln to George B. McClellan, Washington, D.C., April 9, 1862, in *Collected Works*, 5:185.

74. Lincoln to George B. McClellan, Washington, D.C., September 15, 1862, in *Collected Works*, 5:426.

75. Lincoln to Don C. Buell, January 13, 1862, in *Collected Works*, 5:98.

76. Lincoln to Cuthbert Bullitt, New Orleans, Louisiana, July 28, 1862, in *Collected Works*, 5:346.

77. Lincoln, "Response to a Serenade," November 10, 1864, in *Collected Works*, 8:100–101.

78. Jennifer L. Weber, *Copperheads: The Rise and Fall of Lincoln's Opponents in the North* (Oxford: Oxford University Press, 2006), 10.

79. Weber, *Copperheads*, 120.

80. Weber, *Copperheads*, 77.

81. Henry Raymond, Letter to Abraham Lincoln, August 22, 1864, online at: http://teachingamericanhistory.org/library/index.asp?document=1475, accessed on November 4, 2013.

82. Lincoln to Charles D. Robinson, Washington, August 17, 1864, in *Collected Works*, 7:500.

83. "Annual Message to Congress," December 6, 1864, in *Collected Works*, 8:152.

84. William Lloyd Garrison, *William Lloyd Garrison* 103.

85. Geoffrey R. Stone, *Perilous Times: Free Speech in Wartime* (New York: Norton, 2004), 79–134.

86. Farber, *Lincoln's Constitution*, 163.

87. Mark E. Neely Jr., *The Fate of Liberty: Abraham Lincoln and Civil Liberties* (New York: Oxford, 1992); Stone, *Perilous Times*, 124.

88. Neely, *The Fate of Liberty*, 137–38.

89. Jennifer L. Weber, *The Rise and Fall of Lincoln's Opponents in the North* (Oxford: Oxford University Press), 2006.

90. Harvey C. Mansfield, *The Taming of the Prince: The Ambivalence of Modern Executive Power* (Baltimore: Johns Hopkins University Press, 1993).

91. Mansfield, *The Taming of the Prince*, xx.

4. MAGNANIMITY

1. Aristotle, *Nicomachean Ethics*, Book IV, Ch. 3, 1123a30–1125b; *Rhetoric*, Book I, Ch. 9, 1366b15–20. Portions of this chapter have been adapted from Joseph R. Fornieri, "Lincoln and Magnanimity," in *Magnanimity and Statesmanship*, ed. Carson Holloway (Lanham: Lexington Books, 2008), 171–96. Permission kindly granted from Lexington Books, A Member of the Rowman

and Littlefield Publishing Group. Also see Robert Faulkner, *The Case for Greatness: Honorable Ambition and Its Critics* (New Haven: Yale University Press, 2007), 16–57.

2. For an excellent analysis of Lincoln's humility, see David J. Bobb, *Humility: An Unlikely Biography of America's Greatest Virtue* (Nashville: Nelson Books, 2013), 127–55.

3. See Robert K. Greenleaf, *Servant Leadership: A Journey into the Nature of Legitimate Power and Greatness* (New York: Paulist Press, 202). Alexander Hamilton, James Madison, John Jay, *The Federalist Papers* with introduction and notes by Charles R. Kesler, ed. Clinton Rossiter (New York: Mentor, 1999), 399–403.

4. St. Thomas Aquinas, *Summa Theologica: Volume Three: II-II*, trans. Fathers of the English Dominican Province (Westminster, Md.: Christian Classics, 1981), II-II, Q. 129, A. 1–8, 1721–29.

5. Aquinas, *Summa*, II-II, q. 129, a. 2:1723.

6. Lincoln, "Communication to the People of Sangamo County," March 9, 1832, in *Collected Works*, 1:8.

7. Quoted in Allen C. Guelzo, "A. Lincoln, Philosopher: Lincoln's Place in 19th Century Intellectual History," in *Lincoln's America*, ed. Joseph R. Fornieri and Sara Vaughn Gabbard (Carbondale: Southern Illinois University Press, 2008) 16.

8. Ronald D. Rietveld, "Abraham Lincoln's George Washington," in *The Great Presidential Triumvirate at Home and Abroad: Washington, Jefferson, and Lincoln*, ed. William D. Pederson and Frank J. Williams (New York: Nova, 2006), 39–76.

9. Lincoln to Jesse W. Fell, Enclosing Autobiography, December 20, 1859, in *Collected Works*, 3:512.

10. I am indebted to Professor Gabor Boritt for pointing this out.

11. Lincoln, "Address before the Young Men's Lyceum of Springfield, Illinois," January 27, 1838, in *Collected Works*, 1:108–15.

12. Lincoln, "Address before the Young Men's Lyceum of Springfield, Illinois," January 27, 1838, *Collected Works*, 1:113–14. For a comparison between Washington's Farewell Address and Lincoln's Lyceum address see Fornieri, "Washington's Farewell Address and Lincoln's Lyceum Address," in *The Great Presidential Triumvirate at Home and Abroad: Washington, Jefferson, and Lincoln*, William D. Pederson and Frank J. Williams (New York: Nova, 2006), 77–94.

13. Edmund Wilson, *Patriotic Gore: Studies in the Literature of the American Civil War* (New York: Oxford University Press, 1962), 108; George B. Forgie, "Lincoln's Tyrants," in *The Historian's Lincoln: Pseudohistory, Psychohistory, and History*, ed. Gabor S. Boritt and Norman O. Forness (Urbana: University of Illinois Press, 1988), 296.

14. Lincoln, "Address before the Young Men's Lyceum of Springfield, Illinois," January 27, 1838, in *Collected Works*, 1:114.

15. Dwight Anderson, *Quest for Immortality: A Theory of Abraham Lincoln's Political Psychology* in *Historian's Lincoln*, ed. Boritt, 254.

16. Lincoln to James Hackett, in *Collected Works*, 6:392–93.

17. "Fragment on Stephen A. Douglas, December, 1856?" in *Collected Works*, 2:383.

18. David Herbert Donald, *Lincoln* (New York: Simon and Schuster, 1995), 333.

19. Aquinas, *Summa*, II-II, q. 131, a. 2:1732.

20. Aquinas, *Summa*, II-II, q. 131, a. 1:1731.

21. Aquinas, *Summa*, II-II, q. 131, a 1:1731.

22. Aquinas, *Summa*, II-II, q. 133, a. 1–2:1736–38.

23. Aquinas, *Summa*, II-II, q. 133, a. 1–2:1736–38.

24. Kenneth L. Deutsch, "Thomas Aquinas on Magnanimous and Prudent Statesmanship," in *Tempered Strength: Studies in the Nature and Scope of Prudential Leadership*, ed. Ethan Fishman (Lanham, Md.: Lexington Books, 2002), 41.

25. Aquinas, *Summa*, II-II, q. 161, a. 2:1843.

26. Aquinas, *Summa*, II-II, q. 129, a. 3:1724.

27. Aquinas, *Summa*, II-II, q. 161, a. 1:1842.

28. Deutsch, "Thomas Aquinas and Magnanimous Statesmanship," 40.

29. Aquinas, *Summa*, II-II, q. 129, a. 2:1722.

30. This has been demonstrated by William Lee Miller in his outstanding book *Lincoln's Virtues: An Ethical Biography* (New York: Alfred A. Knopf, 2002), 92–115.

31. Lincoln, "Last Speech of the Campaign at Springfield, Illinois, October 30, 1858," in *Collected Works*, 3:334.

32. Lincoln to Anson G. Henry, November 19, 1859, in *Collected Works*, 3:339.

33. Burlingame, *Abraham Lincoln: A Life*, 550.

34. Burlingame, *Abraham Lincoln: A Life*, 551.

35. Lincoln to Anson G. Henry, November 19, 1859, in *Collected Works*, 3:462, 2:240, 454, 1:112, 2 243, 272, 3 81.

36. Lincoln to Jesse W. Fell, December 20, 1859, in *Collected Works*, 3:511–12.

37. Lincoln, "Speech at Peoria, Illinois," October 16, 1854, in *Collected Works*, 2:276.

38. Lincoln, "Address at Cooper Institute, New York City," February 27, 1860, in *Collected Works*, 3:550.

39. Lincoln, "Address at Cooper Institute, New York City," February 27, 1860, in *Collected Works*, 3:240–41.

40. Lawrence M. Denton, *William Henry Seward and the Secession Crisis* (Jefferson, N.C.: McFarland, 2009), 93.

41. Wendell Phillips, *Speeches, Lectures, and Letters: Second Series* (New York: Arno Press, 1891), 155.

42. George Templeton Strong, *Diary of the Civil War, 1860–1865: George Templeton Strong*, ed. Allan Nevins (Macmillan, 1952), 256.

43. William T. Sherman, *Memoirs of General William T. Sherman* (New York: D. Appleton, 1875), 328.

44. *Sojourner Truth: Slave, Prophet, Legend* (New York: New York University Press, 1995), 121.

45. Joseph R. Fornieri, *Abraham Lincoln's Political Faith* (DeKalb: Northern Illinois University Press, 2003), 50–69; Lucas E. Morel, "Lincoln's Political Religion and Religious Politics," in *Lincoln Revisited*, ed. John Y. Simon, Harold Holzer, and Dawn Vogel (New York: Fordham University Press, 2007), 19–45; Allen C. Guelzo, *Abraham Lincoln: Redeemer President* (Grand Rapids, Mich.: William B. Eerdmans, 1999), 327; White, *Lincoln's Greatest Speech*, 128–48.

46. Lincoln to Joshua Speed, July 4, 1842, in *Collected Works*, 1: 289–90.

47. Lincoln, "Reply to Eliza Gurney," October 26, 1862, in *Collected Works* 5:478–79.

48. Lincoln to Eliza P. Gurney, in *Collected Works*, 7:535.

49. Lincoln, "Meditation on the Divine Will," September 2, 1862?, in *Collected Works*, 5:403–4.

50. John G. Nicolay and John Hay, *Abraham Lincoln: A History*, 10 vols. (New York: Century 1890), 6:340–42.

51. Lincoln, "Handbill Replying to Charges of Infidelity," July 31, 1846, in *Collected Works*, 1:382–83.

52. Fornieri, *Lincoln's Political Faith*, 50–69.

53. Reinhold Niebuhr, "The Religion of Abraham Lincoln," in *Lincoln's American Dream: Clashing Political Perspectives*, ed. Kenneth L. Deutsch and Joseph R. Fornieri (Washington, D.C.: Potomac Books, 2005), 378–92.

54. Hamilton, *Federalist No. 71*, 400.

55. Lincoln, "Farewell Address at Springfield, Illinois," February 11, 1861, in *Collected Works*, 4:190–91.

56. Lincoln, "Message to Congress in Special Session," July 4, 1861, in *Collected Works*, 4:441.

57. Douglas L. Wilson, *Lincoln's Sword: The Presidency and the Power of Words* (New York: Knopf, 2006), 100.

58. Lincoln, "Reply to Baltimore Committee," April 22, 1861, in *Collected Works*, 4:342.

59. Doris Kearns Goodwin, *Team of Rivals: The Political Genius of Abraham Lincoln* (New York: Simon and Schuster, 2005).

60. David Herbert Donald, *Lincoln* (New York: Simon and Schuster, 1995), 319.

61. *Encyclopedia of the American Civil War: A Political, Social, and Military History*, George B. McClellan to Mary Ellen McClellan, July 27, 1861 (New York: Norton, 2000), 2313.

62. Quoting from *Inside Lincoln's White House: The Complete Civil War Diary of John Hay*, ed. Michael Burlingame and John R. Turner Ettlinger (Carbondale: Southern Illinois University Press, 1999), 32.

63. F. A. Mitchel to John Hay, E. Orange, N.J., January 3, 1889, Nicolay-Hay MSS IHi.

64. Lincoln to Ulysses S. Grant, July 13, 1863, *Collected Works*, 326.

65. White, *Lincoln's Greatest Speech*.

66. Lincoln, "Second Inaugural Address," March 4, 1865, in *Collected Works*, 8:333.

67. Lincoln, "Second Inaugural Address," March 4, 1865, in *Collected Works*, 8:333.

68. Mark A. Beecher quoted in Noll, "'Both . . . Pray to the Same God': The Singularity of Lincoln's Faith in the Civil War," *Journal of the Abraham Lincoln Association* 18, no. 1 (1997): 1–26.

69. Lincoln to Thurlow Weed, March 15, 1865, in *Collected Works*, 8:356.

70. Lincoln to Thurlow Weed, March 15, 1865, in *Collected Works*, 8:332–33.

71. Bruce Chadwick, *Two American Presidents: A Dual Biography of Abraham Lincoln and Jefferson Davis* (Secaucus N.J.: Birch Lane Press, 1999); Brian R. Dirck, *Lincoln and Davis: Imagining America 1809–1865* (Lawrence: University Press of Kansas, 2001).

5. RHETORIC

1. Lincoln, "First Debate with Stephen A. Douglas at Ottawa, Illinois," August 21, 1858, in *Collected Works*, 2:27. Also see David Zarefsky, "'Public Sentiment Is Everything': Lincoln's View of Political Persuasion," *Journal of the Abraham Lincoln Association* 15 (1994): 23–40.

2. Lincoln, "Speech at Hartford, Connecticut," March 5, 1860, in *Collected Works*, 4:9.

3. Aristotle, *The Rhetoric and Poetics of Aristotle* (New York: Modern Library, 1984), 19 (1354a10).

4. Aristotle, *Rhetoric*, 25 (1356a).

5. See Burlingame, chap. 16, "I Have Been Elected Mainly on the Cry 'Honest Old Abe': The Presidential Campaign (May–November 1860)," in *Lincoln*, 1:627–84.

6. Douglas L. Wilson, *Lincoln's Sword: The Presidency and the Power of Words* (New York: Knopf, 2006), 7.

7. Fred Kaplan, *Lincoln: The Biography of a Writer* (New York: Harper, 2008), 1–2.

8. Ronald C. White Jr., *The Eloquent President: A Portrait of Lincoln through His Words* (New York: Random House, 2005), xxi.

9. Wilson, *Lincoln's Sword: The Presidency and the Power of Words*, 7.

10. James M. McPherson, *Abraham Lincoln and the Second American Revolution* (New York: Oxford University Press, 1991).

11. Ralph Lerner, "Lincoln's Revolution," chap. 6 in *Revolutions Revisited: Two Faces of the Politics of Enlightenment* (Chapel Hill: University of North Carolina Press, 1994), 88–111.

12. Quoted in Deutsch and Fornieri, *Lincoln's American Dream*, 22.

13. Deutsch and Fornieri, *Lincoln's American Dream*, 22.

14. Deutsch and Fornieri, *Lincoln's American Dream*, 22.

15. Lincoln, "Fifth Debate with Stephen A. Douglas, Galesburg, Illinois," October 7, 1858, in *Collected Works*, 3:234.

16. For the clash between sophistry and philosophy, see "Gorgias," chap. 2 in Eric Voegelin, *Order and History: Plato and Aristotle*, vol. 3 (Baton Rouge: Louisiana State University Press, 1990), 24–45.

17. Lincoln, "Address at Cooper Institute, New York City," February 27, 1860, in *Collected Works*, 3:550; "Speech at Hartford, Connecticut," March 5, 1860, in *Collected Works*, 4:29–30.

18. Carl Schurz, *The Reminiscences of Carl Schurz* (New York: McClure, 1907), 2:95.

19. Lincoln, "Seventh and Last Debate with Stephen A. Douglas, Alton, Illinois," October 15, 1858, in *Collected Works*, 3:311.

20. Hofstadter, *American Political Tradition*, 144.

21. Kaplan, *Lincoln: The Biography of a Writer*, 2.

22. Lincoln, "Speech at Springfield, Illinois," June 26, 1857, in *Collected Works*, 2:409.

23. Lincoln, "Speech at Hartford, Connecticut," March 5, 1860, in *Collected Works*, 4:5.

24. Lincoln, "Speech at Columbus, Ohio," September 16, 1859, in *Collected Works*, 3:424.

25. Lincoln, "Speech at Peoria, Illinois," October 16, 1854, in *Collected Works*, 2:266.

26. Weaver, *The Ethics of Rhetoric* (Davis, Calif.: Hermagoras Press, 1985), 94.

27. Lincoln's appeal in the Peoria address to the slaveholder's intuitive recognition of the humanity of the slave was perhaps influenced by his reading of the abolitionist minister William Ellery Channing, who argued similarly: "It is essential to rightful property in a thing, that the thing from its nature may be rightfully appropriated. If it cannot originally be made one's own without crime, it certainly cannot be continued as such without guilt. Now the ground, on which the seizure of the African on his own shore is condemned, is, that he is man, who has by his nature a right to be free. Ought not, then, the same condemnation to light on the continuance of his yoke?" *People's Edition of the Entire Works of W. E. Channing* (Belfast: Sims and McIntyre, 1843), 210. Lincoln then provides specific examples that prove Channing's point.

28. Lincoln, "Speech at Peoria, Illinois," October 16, 1854, in *Collected Works*, 2:264.

29. Holzer, *Lincoln at Cooper Union*, 131.

30. Lincoln, "Speech at Peoria, Illinois," October 16, 1854, in *Collected Works*, 2:264.

31. Lincoln, "Speech at Peoria, Illinois," October 16, 1854, in *Collected Works*, 2:264.

32. Lincoln, "Speech at Peoria, Illinois," October 16, 1854, in *Collected Works*, 2:264.

33. Lincoln, "Speech at Peoria, Illinois," October 16, 1854, in *Collected Works*, 2:265.

34. Lincoln, "Speech at Peoria, Illinois," October 16, 1854, in *Collected Works*, 2:265.

35. Holzer, *Cooper Union*, 132; David Zarefsky, "The Cooper Union Speech, 1860," Lecture no. 18 of *Abraham Lincoln: In his Own Words*, 24-lecture audio series (Springfield, Va.: Teaching Company, 1999).

36. Lincoln, "Message to Congress in Special Session," July 4, 1861, in *Collected Works*, 4:433.

37. Lincoln, "Message to Congress in Special Session," July 4, 1861, in *Collected Works*, 4:433.

38. Lincoln, "First Inaugural Address—Final Text," March 4, 1861, in *Collected Works*, 4:267.

39. Lincoln, "First Inaugural Address—Final Text," March 4, 1861, in *Collected Works*, 4:264.

40. Ceaser, *Designing a Polity*, 86–87.

41. Alexander Hamilton, *Federalist 1*.

42. Burlingame, *Lincoln*, 1:476–78, 488.

43. Burlingame, *Lincoln*, 1:508.

44. Stephen A. Douglas, in "First Debate with Stephen A. Douglas at Ottawa, Illinois," August 21, 1858, in *Collected Works*, 3:9.

45. Stephen A. Douglas, in "First Debate with Stephen A. Douglas at Ottawa, Illinois," August 21, 1858, in Lincoln, *Collected Works*, 3:9.

46. Burlingame, *Lincoln*, 1:507.

47. Burlingame, *Lincoln*, vol. 1.

48. Burlingame, *Lincoln*, 1:486.

49. Fehrenbacher, "Only His Stepchildren," in *Lincoln in Text and Context: Collected Essays* (Stanford: Stanford University Press, 1987).

50. Lincoln, "Speech at Springfield, Illinois," June 26, 1857, in *Collected Works*, 2:405.

51. Lincoln, "Speech at Springfield, Illinois," June 26, 1857, in *Collected Works*, 2:405.

52. Lincoln, "Speech at Chicago, Illinois," July 10, 1858, in *Collected Works*, 2:501; "Fifth Debate with Stephen A. Douglas, at Galesburg, Illinois," October

7, 1858, in *Collected Works*, 1:213–14; "Sixth Debate with Stephen A. Douglas, at Quincy, Illinois," October 13, 1858, in *Collected Works*, 3:263.

53. Lincoln, "Fragment on Pro-slavery Theology," October 1, 1858, in *Collected Works*, 3:204.

54. Lincoln, "Fragment on Pro-slavery Theology," October 1, 1858, in *Collected Works*, 3:205.

55. Lincoln, "Fragment on Pro-slavery Theology," October 1, 1858, in *Collected Works*, 3:205.

56. Lincoln, "Address at Sanitary Fair, Baltimore, Maryland," April 18, 1864, in *Collected Works*, 7:302.

57. Lincoln, "Second Inaugural Address," March 4, 1865, in *Collected Works*, 8:333.

58. Lincoln, "Second Inaugural Address," March 4, 1865, in *Collected Works*, 8:333.

59. Lincoln, "Second Inaugural Address," March 4, 1865, in *Collected Works*, 8:333.

60. Lincoln to George B. Ide, James R. Doolittle, and A. Hubbell, in *Collected Works*, 7:368.

61. Lincoln to George B. Ide, James R. Doolittle, and A. Hubbell, in *Collected Works*, vol. 7.

62. Lincoln to George B. Ide, James R. Doolittle, and A. Hubbell, in *Collected Works*, vol. 7.

63. Stone, *Perilous Times*, 96–105.

64. Lincoln to Erastus Corning and Others, Washington, D.C., June 12, 1863, in *Collected Works*, 6:264.

65. Lincoln to Erastus Corning and Others, Washington, D.C., June 12, 1863, in *Collected Works*, 6:267.

66. Lincoln to Erastus Corning and Others, Washington, D.C., June 12, 1863, in *Collected Works*, 6:267.

67. Lincoln to Erastus Corning and Others, Washington, D.C., June 12, 1863, in *Collected Works*, 6:266.

68. Lincoln to Erastus Corning and Others, Washington, D.C., June 12, 1863, in *Collected Works*, 6:266.

6. PATRIOTISM

1. Portions of this chapter have been adapted from Joseph R. Fornieri, "Lincoln's Reflective Patriotism," *Perspectives on Political Science* 39, no. 2 (April 2010): 108–17. Permission kindly granted by Taylor and Francis.

2. Joshua Wolf Shenk, *Lincoln's Melancholy: How Depression Challenged a President and Fueled His Greatness* (Boston: Houghton Mifflin, 2005); David Herbert Donald, *Lincoln* (New York: Simon and Schuster, 1995); Edmund Wilson, *Patriotic Gore: Studies in the Literature of the American Civil War*

(New York: Oxford University Press, 1962), 108; George B. Forgie, "Lincoln's Tyrants," in *The Historian's Lincoln: Pseudohistory, Psychohistory, and History*, eds. Gabor S. Boritt and Norman Forness (Urbana: University of Illinois Press, 1988), 296; Dwight G. Anderson, *Abraham Lincoln: The Quest for Immortality* (New York: Alfred A. Knopf, 1982).

3. Michael Burlingame, *Abraham Lincoln: A Life* (Baltimore: Johns Hopkins University Press, 2008), 1:358.

4. George McKenna, *The Puritan Origins of American Patriotism* (New Haven: Yale University Press, 2007), 8.

5. McKenna, *The Puritan Origins of American Patriotism*, 8.

6. McKenna, *The Puritan Origins of American Patriotism* 1–14, 128–63.

7. Joseph R. Fornieri, *Abraham Lincoln's Political Faith* (De Kalb: Northern Illinois University Press, 2003).

8. Lincoln, "First Inaugural Address," March 4, 1861, in *Collected Works*, 4:271.

9. Melinda Lawson, *Patriotic Fires: Forging a New Nationalism in the Civil War North* (Lawrence: University Press of Kansas, 2002), 161.

10. See Liah Greenfield, *Nationalism: Five Roads to Modernity* (Harvard University Press, 1993). Love of country is viewed with suspicion by many of today's postmodern and cosmopolitan intellectuals, who denounce it as a political vice that is practically indistinguishable from the sins of racial and ethnic nationalism, chauvinism, intolerance, jingoism, and imperialism. Patriotism, they contend, is synonymous with an irrational and overweening national pride that is contrary to critical reflection and universal norms of justice. Martha Nussbaum for example maintains that "patriotic pride is both morally dangerous and, ultimately, subversive of some of the worthy goals patriotism sets out to serve." *The Cosmopolitanism Reader* (Malden, Mass.: Polity Press, 2010), 154. Two recent works echo this opinion. In *Is Patriotism a Mistake?* George Kateb describes love of country as "a mistake twice over: it is typically a grave moral error and its source is typically a state of mental confusion." *Is Patriotism a Mistake? (Social Research*, vol. 67, no. 4, published by the New School, Winter 2000), 901–24. And in *The Truth about Patriotism* (Duke University Press, 2007), Steven Johnston goes so far as to argue that "democracy's future depends on its emergence from patriotism's self-obsessive grip" (13).

11. Benedict Anderson, *Imagined Communities: Reflections on the Origin and Spread of Nationalism*, rev. ed. (New York: Verso, 2006), 145–58.

12. Mark E. Neely Jr., *Lincoln and the Triumph of the Nation: Constitutional Conflict in the American Civil War* (Chapel Hill: University of North Carolina, 2011), 13–14.

13. Online at http://orwell.ru/library/essays/nationalism/english/e_nat, accessed June 19, 2013. Also see *George Orwell: As I Please, 1943–1946*, ed. Sonia Orwell and Ian Angus (Boston: Nonpareil Books, 2000), 362.

14. Maurizio Viroli, *For Love of Country: An Essay on Patriotism and Nationalism* (Oxford: Clarendon Press, 1995).

15. Viroli, *For Love of Country*, 19.

16. See Joseph Addison, *Cato: A Tragedy and Selected Essays*, ed. Christine Dunn Henderson and Mark E. Yelin (Indianapolis: Liberty Fund, 2004). For the influence of this play on the eighteenth century and the Founders, see Henderson and Yelin's fine introduction, xi–xxiii.

17. Viroli, *For Love of Country*, 25.

18. Viroli, *For Love of Country*, 22.

19. Havers, *Lincoln and the Politics of Christian Love* (Columbia: University of Missouri Press, 2009), 4.

20. Havers, *Lincoln and the Politics of Christian Love*, 5.

21. Havers, *Lincoln and the Politics of Christian Love*, 8.

22. Charles de Secondat, baron de Montesquieu, *The Spirit of the Laws*, ed. and trans. Anne M. Cohler, Basia Carolyn Miller, and Harold Samuel Stone (Cambridge: Cambridge University Press), 42–43.

23. Garry Wills, *Lincoln at Gettysburg: The Words that Remade America* (New York: Simon and Schuster, 1992), 41–42, 46, 49, 52, 56, 57, 65; Mason Locke Weems, *The Life of Washington* (New York: M. E. Sharpe, 1996).

24. Washington's Farewell Address. It may be found online through the Avalon Project, Yale Law School, http://avalon.law.yale.edu/18th_century/washing.asp, accessed November 4, 2013. Elsewhere I show the extent to which Lincoln's Lyceum address was modeled after Washington's Farewell Address.

25. Lincoln, "Eulogy on Henry Clay," July 6, 1852, in *Collected Works*, 2:126.

26. Melinda Lawson, *Patriotic Fires: Forging a New Nationalism in the Civil War North* (Lawrence: University Press of Kansas, 2002), 160–78.

27. Lincoln, "Address before the Young Men's Lyceum of Springfield, Illinois," January 27, 1838, in *Collected Works*, 1:114.

28. Lincoln, "Address before the Young Men's Lyceum of Springfield, Illinois," January 27, 1838, in *Collected Works*, 1:114.

29. Lincoln, "Address before the Young Men's Lyceum of Springfield, Illinois," January 27, 1838, in *Collected Works*, 1:108.

30. Lincoln, "Address before the Young Men's Lyceum of Springfield, Illinois," January 27, 1838, in *Collected Works*, 1:112.

31. Lincoln, "Address before the Young Men's Lyceum of Springfield, Illinois," January 27, 1838, in *Collected Works*, 1:112.

32. Lincoln, "Address before the Young Men's Lyceum of Springfield, Illinois," January 27, 1838, in *Collected Works*, 1:115.

33. Lincoln, "Address before the Young Men's Lyceum of Springfield, Illinois," January 27, 1838, in *Collected Works*, 1:246.

34. Lincoln, "Eulogy on Zachary Taylor," July 25, 1850, in *Collected Works*, 2:89.

35. Bruce P. Frohnen, "The Patriotism of a Conservative," *First Principles* 48, no. 2 (Spring 2006): 105–18.

36. Lincoln, "Speech in United States House of Representatives: The War with Mexico," January 12, 1848, in *Collected Works*, 1:439.

37. Burlingame, *Abraham Lincoln*, 526–27.

38. For Douglas and "Young America," see Stewart Winger, *Lincoln, Religion and Romantic Cultural Politics* (De Kalb: Northern Illinois University Press, 2003), 18–29, 43–44.

39. Harry V. Jaffa, *Crisis of the House Divided* (Chicago: University of Chicago Press, 1984).

40. Lincoln, "Resolutions in Behalf of Hungarian Freedom," January 9, 1852, in *Collected Works*, 2:115.

41. Lincoln, "Resolutions in Behalf of Hungarian Freedom," January 9, 1852, in *Collected Works*, 2:116.

42. Lincoln, "First Debate with Stephen A. Douglas at Ottawa, Illinois," August 21, 1858, in *Collected Works*, 3:29.

43. Lincoln, "Eulogy on Henry Clay," July 6, 1852, in *Collected Works*, 2:126.

44. Lincoln, "Eulogy on Henry Clay," July 6, 1852, in *Collected Works*, 2:127.

45. Lincoln, "Eulogy on Henry Clay," July 6, 1852, in *Collected Works*, 2:126.

46. Lincoln, "First Debate with Stephen A. Douglas at Ottawa, Illinois," August 21, 1858, in *Collected Works*, 3:14.

47. Havers, *Lincoln and the Politics of Christian Love*, 19–20.

48. Lincoln, "Speech at Peoria, Illinois," October 16, 1854, in *Collected Works*, 2:251.

49. Lincoln, "Speech at Peoria, Illinois," October 16, 1854, in *Collected Works*, 2:251–52.

50. Lincoln, "Speech at Peoria, Illinois," October 16, 1854, in *Collected Works*, 2:273–74.

51. Lincoln, "Speech at Peoria, Illinois," October 16, 1854, in *Collected Works*, 2:276.

52. Walter Berns, *Making Patriots* (Chicago: University of Chicago Press, 2001).

53. See the debate between Pangle and Jaffa in "Patriotism American Style" by Thomas L. Pangle and "Our Ancient Faith: A Reply to Thomas Pangle" by Harry V. Jaffa in *National Review*, November 20, 1985, 30–36. Bruce P. Frohnen offers a profound critique of Berns's conception of political religion and patriotism as "founded in total rejection of the western tradition of religion and morals." See Frohnen, "Patriotism," 105–18.

54. Frohnen, "Patriotism," 112.

55. James Wilson, *Collected Works of James Wilson* (Indianapolis: Liberty Fund, 2007), 2:509, 521.

56. Lincoln to George Robertson, August 15, 1855, in *Collected Works*, 2:318.

57. James Oakes, *The Radical and the Republican: Frederick Douglass, Abraham Lincoln and the Triumph of Antislavery Politics* (New York: Norton, 2007).

58. Lincoln to Joshua F. Speed, August 24, 1855, in *Collected Works*, 2:323.

59. Burlingame, *Abraham Lincoln*, 375.

60. "Speech at Chicago, Illinois," July 10, 1858, in *Collected Works*, 2:499–500.

61. Rogan Kersh, *Dreams of a More Perfect Union* (New York: Cornell University Press, 2001).

62. See Herman Belz, *A New Birth of Freedom: The Republican Party and Freedmen's Rights, 1861–1866* (New York: Fordham University Press, 2000), 17–34; and Christian G. Samito, *Becoming American under Fire: Irish Americans, African Americans, and the Politics of Citizenship during the Civil War Era* (New York: Cornell University Press, 2009).

63. Lincoln, "Speech at Edwardsville, Illinois," September 11, 1858, in *Collected Works*, 3:95.

64. Thomas Jefferson, *The Life and Selected Writings of Thomas Jefferson*, ed. Adriene Koch and William Peden (New York: Random House, 1993), 257–58.

65. Lincoln, "Address to the New Jersey Senate at Trenton, New Jersey," February 21, 1861, in *Collected Works*, 4:235–36.

66. Lincoln, "Address to the New Jersey Senate at Trenton, New Jersey," February 21, 1861, in *Collected Works*, 4:236.

67. Lincoln, "Speech in Independence Hall, Philadelphia, Pennsylvania," February 22, 1861, in *Collected Works*, 4:240.

68. Lincoln, "First Inaugural Address," March 4, 1861, in *Collected Works*, 4:271.

69. Lincoln, "First Inaugural Address," March 4, 1861, in *Collected Works*, 4:271.

70. Lincoln, "Message to Congress in Special Session," July 4, 1861, in *Collected Works*, 4:439.

71. Lincoln to James C. Conkling, August 26, 1863, in *Collected Works*, 6:410.

72. Lincoln, "Appeal to Border State Representatives to Favor Compensated Emancipation," July 12, 1862, *Collected Works*, 5:317–19.

73. Lincoln to Erastus Corning and others, June 12, 1863, in *Collected Works*, 6:260–69.

74. Lawson, *Patriotic Fires*, 164.

75. Havers, *Lincoln and the Politics of Christian Love*, 75.

CONCLUSION

1. *Lives of Ten Noble Greeks and Romans by Plutarch*, ed. Edmund Fuller (Grolier; Pennsylvania State University, 2011), 43.

2. Allan Nevins, *The Statesmanship of the Civil War* (Macmillan: University of Michigan, 1953), 57.

3. Lincoln, Lyceum Address at Springfield, *Collected Works*, 1:108.

SELECTED BIBLIOGRAPHY

Anastaplo, George. *Abraham Lincoln: A Constitutional Biography*. Lanham, Md.: Rowman and Littlefield, 1999.

———. "American Constitutionalism and the Virtue of Prudence: Philadelphia, Paris, Washington, Gettysburg." In *Abraham Lincoln: The Gettysburg Address and American Constitutionalism*, ed. Leo Paul S. de Alvarez, 77–170. Irving, Tex.: University of Dallas Press, 1976.

———. "Slavery and the Constitution: Explorations." *Texas Tech Law Review* 20 (1989): 677–786.

Aristotle. *Nicomachean Ethics*. New York: Macmillan Publishing, 1989.

———. *The Rhetoric and Poetics of Aristotle*. New York. Modern Library, 1984.

Arkes, Hadley. *Beyond the Constitution*. Princeton: Princeton University Press, 1990.

———. *First Things: An Inquiry into the First Principles of Morals and Justice*. Princeton: Princeton University Press, 1986.

Barton, William E. *The Soul of Abraham Lincoln*. New York: George H. Doran, 1920.

Belz, Herman. *Abraham Lincoln, Constitutionalism, and Equal Rights during the Civil War Era*. New York: Fordham University Press, 1997.

———. *A New Birth of Freedom: The Republican Party and Freedmen's Rights, 1861 to 1866*. New York: Fordham University Press, 2000.

Bennett, Lerone, Jr. *Forced into Glory: Abraham Lincoln's White Dream*. Chicago: Johnson, 2000.

———. "Was Abe Lincoln a White Supremacist?" *Ebony* 23 (February 1968).

Bobb, David J. *Humility: An Unlikely Biography of America's Greatest Virtue*. Nashville, Tenn.: Nelson Books, 2013.

Boritt, Gabor. *Abraham Lincoln and the Economics of the American Dream*. Urbana: University of Illinois Press, 1994.

———. *The Gettysburg Gospel: The Lincoln Speech That Nobody Knows*. New York: Simon and Schuster, 2006.

———, ed. *The Historian's Lincoln: Pseudohistory, Psychohistory and History*. Urbana: University of Illinois Press, 1988.

Bradford, M. E. *A Better Guide Than Reason: Studies in the American Revolution*. La Salle, Ill.: Sherwood Sugden, 1979.

———. "The Lincoln Legacy: A Long View." *Modern Age* 24 (1980): 355–63.

Burkhimer, Michael. *Lincoln's Christianity*. Yardley, Pa.: Westholme Publishing, 2007.

Burlingame, Michael. *Abraham Lincoln: A Life*. 2 vols. Baltimore: Johns Hopkins University Press, 2008.

———. *The Inner World of Abraham Lincoln*. Chicago: University of Illinois Press, 1994.

Burt, John. *Lincoln's Tragic Pragmatism: Lincoln, Douglas, and Moral Conflict*. Cambridge, Mass.: Belknap Press of Harvard University Press, 2013.

Carnahan, Burrus M. *Act of Justice: Lincoln's Emancipation Proclamation and the Law of War*. Lexington: University Press of Kentucky, 2007.

Carwardine, Richard J. *Lincoln: Profiles in Power*. London: Pearson Education, 2003.

Ceaser, James W. *Designing a Polity: America's Constitution in Theory and Practice*. Lanham, Md.: Rowman and Littlefield, 2011.

Charnwood, Lord. *Abraham Lincoln*. New York: Pocket, 1917.

Corlett, William. "The Availability of Lincoln's Political Religion." In *Political Theory*, 10: 520–40. 1982.

Cox, LaWanda. *Lincoln and Black Freedom: A Study in Presidential Leadership*. Columbia: University of South Carolina Press, 1994.

Current, Richard N. *The Lincoln Nobody Knows*. New York: Hill and Wang, 1984.

de Alvarez, Leo Paul S., ed. *Abraham Lincoln, the Gettysburg Address, and American Constitutionalism*. Irving, Tex.: University of Dallas Press, 1976.

Diggins, John P. *The Lost Soul of American Politics: Virtue, Self-Interest, and the Foundations of Liberalism*. Chicago: University of Chicago Press, 1986.

DiLorenzo, Thomas J. *The Real Lincoln*. Roseville, Calif.: Forum-Prima Publishing, 2002.

Deutsch, Kenneth L., and Joseph R. Fornieri, eds. *Lincoln's American Dream: Clashing Political Perspectives*. Dulles, Va.: Potomac, 2005.

Dirck, Brian. *Lincoln and Davis: Imagining America*. Lawrence: University Press of Kansas, 2001.

———. *Lincoln the Lawyer*. Urbana: University of Illinois Press, 2007.

Donald, David Herbert. *Lincoln*. New York: Simon and Schuster, 1995.

———. *Lincoln Reconsidered: Essays on the Civil War Era*. 2nd ed. New York: Vintage, Knopf, and Random House, 1961.

———. *Lincoln's Herndon*. New York: Knopf, 1948. Reprint, New York: Da Capo, 1989.

Douglass, Frederick. *Selected Speeches and Writings*. Ed. Philip S. Foner. Chicago: Lawrence Hill Books, 1999.

Ericson, David F. *The Shaping of American Liberalism: The Debates over Ratification, Nullification and Slavery*. Chicago: University of Chicago Press, 1993.

Farber, Daniel. *Lincoln's Constitution*. Chicago: University of Chicago Press, 2003.

Faulkner, Robert. *The Case for Greatness: Honorable Ambition and Its Critics*. New Haven: Yale University Press, 2007.

Fehrenbacher, Don E. *The Dred Scott Case: Its Significance in American Law and Politics*. New York: Oxford University Press, 1978.

———. *Lincoln in Text and Context: Collected Essays*. Stanford: Stanford University Press, 1987.

———. *Prelude to Greatness: Lincoln in the 1850's*. Stanford: Stanford University Press, 1962.

Fishman, Ethan M. "Under the Circumstances: Abraham Lincoln and Classical Prudence." In *Abraham Lincoln: Sources and Styles of Leadership*. Westport, Conn.: Greenwood Press, 1994.

———. *The Prudential Presidency: An Aristotelian Approach to Presidential Leadership*. Westport, Conn.: Praeger, 2001

Foner, Eric. *The Fiery Trial: Abraham Lincoln and American Slavery*. New York: Norton, 2010.

Forgie, George B. *Patricide in the House Divided*. New York: Norton, 1979.

Fornieri, Joseph R. *Abraham Lincoln's Political Faith*. DeKalb: Northern Illinois University Press, 2003.

Fornieri, Joseph R., and Sara Vaughn Gabbard. *Lincoln's America*. Carbondale: Southern Illinois University Press, 2008.

Genovese, Eugene D. *The Slaveholders' Dilemma: Freedom and Progress in Southern Conservative Thought, 1820–1860*. Columbia: University of South Carolina Press, 1992.

———. *The Southern Tradition: The Achievement and Limitations of an American Conservatism*. Cambridge, Mass.: Harvard University Press, 1994.

Goodwin, Doris Kearns. *Team of Rivals: The Political Genius of Abraham Lincoln*. New York: Simon and Schuster, 2005.

Greenstein, Fred I. *The Presidential Difference: Leadership Style from FDR to Barack Obama*. 3rd ed. Princeton: Princeton University Press, 2009.

———. *Inventing the Job of President: Leadership Style from George Washington to Andrew Jackson*. Princeton: Princeton University Press, 2009.

Greenstone, J. David. *The Lincoln Persuasion: Remaking American Liberalism*. Princeton: Princeton University Press, 1993.

Guelzo, Allen C. *Abraham Lincoln as a Man of Ideas*. Carbondale: Southern Illinois University Press, 2009.

———. "Abraham Lincoln or the Progressives: Who Was the Real Father of Big Government?" In *First Principles*, 1–17. B. Kenneth Simon Center for Principles and Politics: The Heritage Foundation. Special Report No. 100, February 8, 2012.

———. *Abraham Lincoln: Redeemer President*. Grand Rapids: Eerdmans Publishing, 1999.

———. *Lincoln and Douglas: The Debates That Defined America*. New York: Simon and Schuster, 2008.

———. *Lincoln's Emancipation Proclamation: The End of Slavery in America*. New York: Simon and Schuster, 2004.

Harris, William C. *Lincoln and the Border States: Preserving the Union*. Lawrence: University Press of Kansas, 2011.

———. *Lincoln's Rise to the Presidency*. Lawrence: University Press of Kansas, 2006.

Havers, Grant N. *Lincoln and the Politics of Christian Love*. Columbia: University of Missouri Press, 2009.

Hein, David. "Lincoln's Theology and Political Ethics." In *Essays on Lincoln's Faith and Politics*, ed. Kenneth W. Thompson, 105–79. Lanham, Md.: University Press of America, 1983.

Herndon, William H., and Jesse Weik. *Herndon's Life of Lincoln*. Cleveland: World, 1942. Reprint, New York: Da Capo, 1983.

Hirsch, David, and Dan Van Haften. *Abraham Lincoln and the Structure of Reason*. New York: Savas, 2010.

Holland, Matthew S. *Bonds of Affection: Civic Charity and the Making of America—Winthrop, Jefferson, and Lincoln*. Washington, D.C.: Georgetown University Press, 2007.

Holzer, Harold. *Emancipating Lincoln: The Proclamation in Text, Context, and Memory*. Cambridge: Harvard University Press, 2012.

———. *Lincoln at Cooper Union: The Speech That Made Abraham Lincoln President*. New York: Simon and Schuster, 2004.

Holzer, Harold, and Sara Vaughn Gabbard. *Lincoln and Freedom: Slavery, Emancipation, and the Thirteenth Amendment*. Carbondale: Southern Illinois University Press, 2007.

Jaffa, Harry V. *The Conditions of Freedom: Essays in Political Philosophy*. Baltimore: Johns Hopkins University Press, 1975.

———. *Crisis of the House Divided: An Interpretation of the Issues in the Lincoln-Douglas Debates*. Seattle: University of Washington Press/Washington Paperbacks, 1973. Reprint, Chicago: University of Chicago Press, 1982.

———. *Crisis of the Strauss Divided: Essays on Leo Strauss and Straussianism, East and West*. Lanham, Md.: Rowman and Littlefield, 2012.

———. *Equality and Liberty: Theory and Practice in American Politics*. New York: Oxford University Press, 1965.

———. *How to Think about the American Revolution: A Bicentennial Celebration*. Durham: Carolina Academic Press, 1978.

———. *A New Birth of Freedom*. Lanham, Md.: Rowman and Littlefield, 2000.

Jividen, Jason R. *Claiming Lincoln: Progressivism, Equality, and the Battle for Lincoln's Legacy in Presidential Rhetoric*. DeKalb: Northern Illinois University Press, 2011.

Kaplan, Fred. *Lincoln: The Biography of a Writer*. New York: Harper, 2008.

Kendall, Willmoore, and George Carey. *The Basic Symbols of the American Political Tradition*. Washington, D.C.: Catholic University Press, 1995.

Landy, Marc, and Sidney Milkis. *Presidential Greatness*. Lawrence: University Press of Kansas, 2001.

Lawson, Melinda. *Patriotic Fires: Forging a New American Nationalism in the Civil War North*. Lawrence: University Press of Kansas, 2002.

Lehrman, Lewis E. *Lincoln at Peoria: The Turning Point*. New York: Simon and Schuster, 2008.

Lerner, Ralph. "Lincoln's Revolution." In *Revolutions Revisited: Two Faces of the Politics of Enlightenment*. Chapel Hill: University of North Carolina Press, 1994.

Lincoln, Abraham. *The Collected Works of Abraham Lincoln*, ed. Roy P. Basler. New Brunswick, N.J.: Rutgers University Press, 1953.

Long, David E. *The Jewel of Liberty: Abraham Lincoln's Re-election and the End of Slavery*. Mechanicsburg, Pa.: Stackpole, 1994.

Lowenthal, David. *The Mind and Art of Abraham Lincoln, Philosopher Statesman: Texts and Interpretations of Twenty Great Speeches*. Lanham, Md.: Lexington Books, 2012.

McGinty, Brian. *Lincoln and the Court*. Cambridge: Harvard University Press, 2008.

McPherson, James M. *Abraham Lincoln and the Second American Revolution*. New York: Oxford University Press, 1991.

———. *Battle Cry of Freedom: The Civil War Era*. New York: Pallantine, 1988.

———. *The Struggle for Equality: Abolitionists and the Negro in the Civil War and Reconstruction*. 2nd ed. Princeton: Princeton University Press, 1995.

———. *Tried by War: Abraham Lincoln as Commander in Chief*. New York: Penguin Books, 2008.

Miller, William Lee. *Lincoln's Virtues: An Ethical Biography*. New York: Knopf, 2002.

———. *President Lincoln: The Duty of a Statesman*. New York: Knopf, 2008.

Morel, Lucas E. *Lincoln's Sacred Effort*. Lanham, Md.: Lexington Books, 2000.

Murray, John Courtney. *We Hold These Truths: Catholic Reflections on the American Proposition*. Kansas City: Sheed and Ward, 1960.

Neely, Mark E., Jr. *The Fate of Liberty: Abraham Lincoln and Civil Liberties*. New York: Oxford University Press, 1992.

———. *The Last Best Hope of Earth: Abraham Lincoln and the Promise of America*. Cambridge, Mass.: Harvard University Press, 1993.

———. *Lincoln and the Triumph of the Nation: Constitutional Conflict in the American Civil War.* Chapel Hill. University of North Carolina Press, 2011.

Nevins, Allan. *The Emergence of Lincoln.* Vol. 1, *Douglas, Buchanan, and Party Chaos, 1857–1859.* New York: Scribner's, 1950.

———. *The Emergence of Lincoln.* Vol. 2, *Prologue to Civil War, 1859–1861.* New York: Scribner's, 1950.

Nicolay, John G., and John Hay. *Abraham Lincoln: A History.* 10 vols. New York: Century, 1890.

Niebuhr, Reinhold. "The Religion of Abraham Lincoln." In *Lincoln and the Gettysburg Address: Commemorative Papers,* ed. Allan Nevins, 72–87. Urbana: University of Illinois Press, 1964.

Noll, Mark A. "'Both . . . Pray to the Same God': The Singularity of Lincoln's Faith in the Era of the Civil War." *Journal of the Abraham Lincoln Association* 18 (Winter 1997): 1–26.

Oakes, James. *Freedom National: The Destruction of Slavery.* New York: Norton, 2013.

———. *The Radical and the Republican: Frederick Douglass, Abraham Lincoln, and the Triumph of Antislavery Politics.* New York: Norton, 2007.

Oates, Stephen B. *With Malice toward None: The Life of Abraham Lincoln.* New York: Mentor/New American Library, 1978.

Paludan, Phillip Shaw. *The Presidency of Abraham Lincoln.* Lawrence: University Press of Kansas, 1994.

Peterson, Merril D. *Lincoln in American Memory.* New York: Oxford University Press, 1994.

Pinsker, Matthew. Lincoln's *Sanctuary: Abraham Lincoln and the Soldiers' Home.* Oxford: Oxford University Press, 2004.

Potter, David M. *The Impending Crisis: 1848–1861.* Ed. Don E. Fehrenbacher. New York: Harper and Row, 1976.

Randall, J. G. *Lincoln the President.* Vol. 1, *Springfield to Gettysburg.* New York: Dodd, Mead, 1945.

———. *Lincoln the President.* Vol. 2, *Midstream.* New York: Dodd, Mead, 1952.

Randall, J. G., and Richard N. Current. *Lincoln the President.* Vol. 3, *The Last Full Measure.* New York: Dodd, Mead, 1955. Reprint, Urbana: University of Illinois Press, 1991.

Ross, Frederick A. *Slavery Ordained of God.* J. B. Lippincott, 1857. Reprint, Miami: Mnemosyne, 1969.

Sands, Eric S. *American Public Philosophy and the Mystery of Lincolnism.* Columbia: University of Missouri Press, 2009.

Schneider, Thomas E. *Lincoln's Defense of Politics: The Public Man and His Opponents in the Crisis over Slavery.* Columbia: University of Missouri Press, 2006.

Shenk, Joshua Wolf. *Lincoln's Melancholy: How Depression Challenged a President and Fueled His Greatness.* Boston: Houghton Mifflin, 2005.

Simon, John Y., Harold Holzer, and Dawn Vogel eds. *Lincoln Revisited.* New York: Fordham University Press, 2007.

Smith, Steven B. *The Writings of Abraham Lincoln.* New Haven: Yale University Press, 2012.

Steers, Edward. *Blood on the Moon.* Lexington: University Press of Kentucky, 2001.

Steiner, Mark E. *An Honest Calling: The Law Practice of Abraham Lincoln.* DeKalb: Northern Illinois University Press, 2006.

Stone, Geoffrey R. *Perilous Times: Free Speech in Wartime: From the Sedition Act of 1798 to the War on Terrorism.* New York: Norton, 2004.

Strauss, Leo. *What Is Political Philosophy? And Other Studies.* Free Press, 1959. Reprint, Chicago: University of Chicago Press, 1988.

———. "Natural Rights and the Distinction between Facts and Values." Chap. 2 in *Natural Rights and History.* 1953. Reprint, Chicago: University of Chicago Press, 1965.

Striner, Richard. *Father Abraham: Lincoln's Relentless Struggle to End Slavery.* New York: Oxford University Press, 2006.

Strozier, Charles B. *Lincoln's Quest for Union: Public and Private Meanings.* New York: Basic Books, 1982.

Thomas, Benjamin P. *Abraham Lincoln.* New York: Knopf, 1952.

Thomas Aquinas, St.. *Summa Theologica*: Volumes I–IV. Westminster, Md.: Christian Classics, 1981.

Thurow, Glen E. *Abraham Lincoln and American Political Religion.* Albany: State University of New York Press, 1976.

Waugh, John C. *One Man Great Enough: Abraham Lincoln's Road to the Civil War.* Orlando: Harcourt, 2007.

Weaver, Richard. *The Ethics of Rhetoric.* Davis, Calif.: Hermagoras Press, 1985.

White, Jonathan W. *Abraham Lincoln and Treason in the Civil War: The Trials of John Merryman.* Baton Rouge: Louisiana State University, 2013.

White, Ronald C., Jr. *The Eloquent President.* New York: Random House, 2005.

———. *Lincoln's Greatest Speech: The Second Inaugural.* New York: Simon and Schuster, 2002.

Williams, Frank J., *Judging Lincoln.* Carbondale: Southern Illinois University Press, 2002.

Williams, Frank J., William D. Pederson, and Vincent J. Marsala, eds. *Abraham Lincoln: Sources and Style of Leadership.* Westport, Conn.: Greenwood Press, 1994.

Williams, Harry T. *Lincoln and the Radicals.* Madison: University Of Wisconsin Press, 1972.

Wills, Garry. *Lincoln at Gettysburg: The Words That Remade America.* New York: Simon and Schuster, 1992.

Wilson, Douglas L. *Honor's Voice: The Transformation of Abraham Lincoln.* New York: Knopf, 1998.

———. *Lincoln's Sword: The Presidency and the Power of Words.* New York: Knopf, 2006.

Winger, Stewart. *Lincoln, Religion, and Romantic Cultural Politics.* DeKalb: Northern Illinois University Press, 2002.

Wolf, William J. *The Religion of Abraham Lincoln.* New York: Seabury, 1963.

Zarefsky, David. *Lincoln, Douglas and Slavery in the Crucible of Public Debate.* Chicago: University of Chicago Press, 1990.

———. "Lincoln's 1862 Annual Message: A Paradigm of Rhetorical Leadership." *Rhetoric and Public Affairs* 3 (2000): 5–14.

———. "'Public Sentiment Is Everything': Lincoln's View of Political Persuasion." *Journal of the Abraham Lincoln Association* 15 (1994): 23–40.

INDEX

JOSEPH R. FORNIERI is a professor of political science at the Rochester Institute of Technology, where he teaches American politics, political philosophy, and constitutional rights and liberties. He is the author of *Abraham Lincoln's Political Faith*, an acclaimed scholarly work that explores Lincoln's religion and politics, and is the author or a coeditor of three other books on Abraham Lincoln's political thought and statesmanship: *The Language of Liberty: The Political Speeches and Writings of Abraham Lincoln*; *Lincoln's American Dream: Clashing Political Perspectives*, with Kenneth L. Deutsch; and *Lincoln's America*, with Sara Vaughn Gabbard. He is also a coeditor, with Ken Deutsch, of *An Invitation to Political Thought*, a text reader and guide to the classic political thinkers of the Western tradition from Plato to Nietzsche. His latest and forthcoming book is *The Renewal of American Statesmanship*, coedited with Ken Deutsch and Sean Sutton.

Fornieri was the recipient of a Fulbright award, for which he taught American political thought and constitutional rights and liberties in Prague, Czech Republic, in 2008–9. He is the winner of both the Eisenhart Provost's Award for outstanding teaching among the junior faculty in 2002 and the Eisenhart Award for outstanding teaching among the senior faculty in 2011.

He is the director of the Center for Statesmanship, Law, and Liberty at Rochester Institute of Technology, which is dedicated to enhancing the study of statesmanship and political greatness at both the secondary and college levels. On the side, he plays in a blues band with his brother, Peter.